SECURITY ANALYSIS
AND
PORTFOLIO MANAGEMENT

SECURITY ANALYSIS AND PORTFOLIO MANAGEMENT

Dr. Sudhir Gupta

CENTRUM PRESS
NEW DELHI-110002 (INDIA)

CENTRUM PRESS
H.O.: 4360/4, Ansari Road, Daryaganj,
New Delhi-110002 (India)
Tel: 23278000, 23261597, 23255577, 23286875
B.O.: No. 1015, Ist Main Road, BSK IIIrd Stage,
IIIrd Phase, IIIrd Block, Bangalore-560085 (INDIA)
Tel: 080-41723429
Email: centrumpress@gmail.com
Visit us at: www.centrumpress.com

Security Analysis and Portfolio Management

First Edition, 2011

ISBN 978-93-80921-02-0

PRINTED IN INDIA

Printed at Balaji Offset, Delhi.

Contents

Preface

Security analysis and portfolio management discusses the concepts, models and case studies on investment management, security analysis and portfolio management in a practical and reader-friendly manner. The book provides deep insight into the subject matter of investment management-financial markets, investment avenues, functioning of stock market and depository system and valuation of securities and others.

Topics such as fundamental analysis, technical analysis using real-life share prices and index values. The book talks in detail about derivatives, Modern Portfolio Theory, Markowitz Portfolio Theory, Sharpe's Single Index Model, CAPM, APT, Mutual Funds and performance evaluation of managed portfolios.

Author

1

Investments Management

CONCEPT

Investment is the commitment of money or capital to purchase financial instruments or other assets in order to gain profitable returns in form of interest, income, or appreciation of the value of the instrument. It is related to saving or deferring consumption. Investment is involved in many areas of the economy, such as business management and finance no matter for households, firms, or governments. An investment involves the choice by an individual or an organization such as a pension fund, after some analysis or thought, to place or lend money in a vehicle, instrument or asset, such as property, commodity, stock, bond, financial derivatives or the foreign asset denominated in foreign currency, that has certain level of risk and provides the possibility of generating returns over a period of time.

Investment comes with the risk of the loss of the principal sum. The investment that has not been thoroughly analysed can be highly risky with respect to the investment owner because the possibility of losing money is not within the owner's control. The difference between speculation and investment can be subtle. It depends on the investment owner's mind whether the purpose is for lending the resource to someone else for economic purpose or not.

In the case of investment, rather than store the good produced or its money equivalent, the investor chooses to use that good either to create a durable consumer or producer good, or to lend the original saved good to another in exchange for either interest or a share of the profits. In the first case, the individual creates durable consumer goods, hoping the services from the good will make his life better. In the second, the individual becomes an entrepreneur using the resource to produce goods and services for others in the hope of a profitable sale. The third case describes a lender, and the fourth describes an investor in a share of the business. In each case, the consumer obtains a durable asset or investment, and accounts for that asset by recording an equivalent liability. As time passes, and both prices and interest rates change, the value of the asset and liability also change.

An asset is usually purchased, or equivalently a deposit is made in a bank, in hopes of getting a future return or interest from it. The word originates in the Latin "vestis", meaning garment, and refers to the performance of putting things into others' pockets.. The basic meaning of the term being an asset held to have some recurring or capital gains. It is an asset that is expected to give returns without any work on the asset per se. The term "investment" is used differently in economics and in finance. Economists refer to a real investment while financial economists refer to a financial asset, such as money that is put into a bank or the market, which may then be used to buy a real asset.

IN ECONOMICS OR MACRO-ECONOMICS

In all economics or macro-economics, fixed asset investment or formation is the production per unit time of goods which are not consumed but are to be used for future production. Examples include tangibles and intangibles. In measures of national income and output, gross investment is also a component of Gross domestic product, given in the formula $GDP = C + I + G + NX$, where C is consumption, G is government spending, and NX is net exports. Thus investment is everything that remains of production after consumption, government spending, and net exports are subtracted.

Both non-residential investment and residential investment combine to make up I. Net investment deducts depreciation from gross investment. It is the value of the net increase in the capital stock per year. Investment, as production over a period of time is not capital. The time dimension of investment makes it a *flow*. By contrast, capital is a *stock*, that is, an accumulation measurable *at a point* in time.

Investment is often modeled as a function of Income and Interest rates, given by the relation $I = f(Y, r)$. An increase in income encourages higher investment, whereas a higher interest rate may discourage investment as it becomes more costly to borrow money. Even if a firm chooses to use its own funds in an investment, the interest rate represents an opportunity cost of investing those funds rather than lending out that amount of money for interest.

INVESTMENT RELATED TO BUSINESS OF A FIRM—BUSINESS MANAGEMENT

The investment decision is one of the fundamental decisions of business management: Managers determine the investment value of the assets that a business enterprise has within its control or possession. These assets may be physical, intangible or financial. Assets are used to produce streams of revenue that often are associated with particular costs or outflows. All together, the manager must determine whether the net present value of the investment to the enterprise is positive using the marginal cost of capital that is associated with the particular area of business.

In terms of financial assets, these are often marketable securities such as a company stock or bonds. At times the goal of the investment is for producing future cash flows, while at others it may be for purposes of gaining access to more assets by establishing control or influence over the operation of a second company.

IN FINANCE

In finance, investment is the commitment of funds by buying securities or other monetary or paper assets in the money markets or capital markets, or in fairly liquid real assets, such as gold or collectibles. Valuation is the method for assessing whether a potential investment is worth its price.

Returns on investments will follow the risk-return spectrum. Types of financial investments include shares, other equity investment, and bonds. These financial assets are then expected to provide income or positive future cash flows, and may increase or decrease in value giving the investor capital gains or losses. Trades in contingent claims or derivative securities do not necessarily have future positive expected cash flows, and so are not considered assets, or strictly speaking, securities or investments. Nevertheless, since their cash flows are closely related to those of specific securities, they are often studied as or treated as investments.

Investments are often made indirectly through intermediaries, such as banks, mutual funds, pension funds, insurance companies, collective investment plans, and investment clubs. Though their legal and procedural details differ, an intermediary generally makes an investment using money from many individuals, each of whom receives a claim on the intermediary. Within personal finance, money used to purchase shares, put in a collective investment plan or used to buy any asset where there is an element of capital risk is deemed an investment. Saving within personal finance refers to money put aside, normally on a regular basis. This distinction is important, as investment risk can cause a capital loss when an investment is sold, unlike saving(s) where the more limited risk is cash devaluing due to inflation.

In many instances the terms saving and investment are used interchangeably, which confuses this distinction. For example many deposit accounts are labeled as investment accounts by banks for marketing purposes. Whether an asset is a saving(s) or an investment depends on where the money is invested: if it is cash then it is savings, if its value can fluctuate then it is investment.

REAL ESTATE AS THE INSTRUMENT OF INVESTMENT

In real estate, investment money is used to purchase property for the purpose of holding or leasing for income and there is an element of capital risk.

Residential Real Estate

The most common form of real estate investment as it includes property purchased as a primary residence. In many cases the buyer does not have the full purchase price for a property and must engage a lender such as a bank, finance company or private lender. Different countries have their individual normal lending levels, but usually they will fall into the range of 70-90% of the purchase price. Against other types of real estate, residential real estate is the least risky.

Commercial Real Estate

Commercial real estate consists of multifamily apartments, office buildings, retail space, hotels and motels, warehouses, and other commercial properties. Due to the higher risk of commercial real estate, loan-to-value ratios allowed by banks and other lenders are lower and often fall in the range of 50-70%.

INVESTMENT ENVIRONMENT

Let us visualize the world and its economy. There are many countries with their many economies in this environment. The interaction between countries at different stages in their development. The many markets to enable this interaction between the various countries. Each of these markets has its regulator, the trading platform and its system, its agents and the participants. Here it is a question of demand and supply of various commodities, products and services and trading instruments.

And the analysis would encompass the demand-supply match/mismatch. In this global environment, we have India with its economy and its own many markets. Among these markets we have the securities market, with its regulator, the trading platform and its systems, its agents and its many participants. Here again it is a question of demand and supply of various commodities, products and services and trading instruments. And the analysis would encompass the demand-supply match/mismatch. It would be advisable to note at this stage, that due to the liberalization process undertaken by

India over the last 18 years, we are today in an environment where events that take place in other parts of the world have a direct or indirect effect on our economy. This would further effect the specific market and finally would have an effect on the equity market. Let us visualize a scenario of an industrial slowdown in the U.S. Amongst other things, this would have a direct bearing on the demand of steel.

To protect its own domestic steel industry, the U.S. government would temporarily introduce trade barriers on steel imports. This in turn would cause a reduced export of steel from India to the U.S., causing a temporary over supply of steel in the domestic market. The steel manufacturers would have to tackle the higher levels of inventory and its associated costs. In the domestic steel market, even if the demand were constant, the excess supply would cause a reduction in the price realization per marketable ton of steel.

This in turn would directly effect the incomes and profit margins of the steel manufacturers. Such a situation would temporarily cause a drop in the share prices of steel stocks in the equity market. This example is to describe to you how logical the sequence of events is and what the end result would be. However, this sequence does take a long duration of time to unfold, sometimes may even take years.

INVESTMENT AVENUES

There are a large number of investment instruments available today. To make our lives easier we would classify or group them under 4 main types of investment avenues.

We shall name and briefly describe them:

1. *Financial securities*: These investment instruments are freely tradable and negotiable. These would include equity shares, preference shares, convertible debentures, non-convertible debentures, public sector bonds, savings certificates, gilt-edged securities and money market securities.
2. *Non-securitized financial securities*: These investment instruments are not tradable, transferable nor negotiable. And would include bank deposits, post

office deposits, company fixed deposits, provident fund plans, national savings plans and life insurance.

3. *Mutual fund plans*: If an investor does not directly want to invest in the markets, he/she could buy units/ shares in a mutual fund plan. These plans are mainly growth oriented, income oriented or balanced plans.
4. *Real assets*: Real assets are physical investments, which would include real estate, gold and silver, precious stones, rare coins and stamps and art objects.

Before choosing the avenue for investment the investor would probably want to evaluate and compare them. This would also help him in creating a well diversified portfolio, which is both maintainable and manageable.

INVESTMENT ATTRIBUTES

To enable the evaluation and a reasonable comparison of various investment avenues, the investor should study the following attributes:

1. Rate of return
2. Risk
3. Marketability
4. Taxes
5. Convenience

Each of these attributes of investment avenues is briefly described and explained:

1. *Rate of return*: The rate of return on any investment comprises of 2 parts, namely the annual income and the capital gain or loss:

   Rate of return = Annual income + (Ending price – Beginning price)/ Beginning price

   The rate of return on various investment avenues would vary widely.
2. *Risk*: The risk of an investment refers to the variability of the rate of return. To explain further, it is the deviation of the outcome of an investment from its expected value. A further study can be done with the help of variance, standard deviation and beta.
3. *Marketability*: It is desirable that an investment

instrument be marketable, the higher the marketability the better it is for the investor. An investment instrument is considered to be highly marketable when:

- It can be transacted quickly.
- The transaction cost is low.

The price change between 2 transactions is negligible. Shares of large, well-established companies in the equity market are highly marketable. While shares of small and unknown companies have low marketability. To gauge the marketability of other financial instruments like provident fund. Then we would consider other factors like, can we make a substantial withdrawal without much penalty, or can we take a loan against the accumulated balance at an interest rate not much higher than our earning rate of interest on the provident fund account.

4. *Taxes*: Some of our investments would provide us with tax benefits while other would not. This would also be kept in mind when choosing the investment avenue.

   Tax benefits are mainly of 3 types:

   - *Initial tax benefits*: This is the tax gain at the time of making the investment, like life insurance.
   - *Continuing tax benefit*: Is the tax benefit gained on the periodic return from the investment, such as dividends.
   - *Terminal tax benefit*: This is the tax relief the investor gains when he liquidates the investment. For example, a withdrawal from a provident fund account is not taxable.

5. *Convenience*: Here we are talking about the ease with which an investment can be made and managed. The degree of convenience would vary from one investment instrument to the other.

INVESTMENT DECISION-MAKING: APPROACHES

As investors we would have diverse investment strategies

with the primary aim to achieve superior performance, which would also mean a higher rate of return on our investments. All investment strategies can be broadly classified under 4 approaches.

Fundamental approach: In this approach the investor is concerned with the intrinsic value of the investment instrument. The basic rules followed by the fundamental investor. -There is an intrinsic value of a security, which in turn is dependent on the underlying economic factors. This intrinsic value can be ascertained by an in-depth analysis of the fundamental or economic factors related to an economy, industry and company.

At any point in time, many securities have current market prices, which are different from their intrinsic values. However, sometime in the future the current market price would become the same as its intrinsic value. We as fundamental investors can achieve superior results by buying undervalued securities and selling overvalued securities.

Psychological approach: The psychological investor would base his investment decision on the premise that stock prices are guided by emotions and not reason. This would imply that the stock prices are influenced by the prevalent mood of the investors. This mood would swing and oscillate between the two extremes of "greed" and "fear". When "greed" has the lead stock prices tend to achieve dizzy heights. And when "fear" takes over stock prices get depressed to lower than lower levels.

As psychic values seem to be more important than intrinsic values, it is suggested that it would be more profitable to analyse investor behaviour as the market is swept by optimism and pessimism. Which seem to alternate one after the other. This approach is also called "Castle-in-the-air" theory. In this approach the investor uses some tools of technical analysis, with a view to study the internal market data, towards developing trading rules to make profits.

In technical analysis the basic premise is that price movement of stocks have certain persistent and recurring patterns, which can be derived from market trading data.

Technical analysts use many tools like bar charts, point and figure charts, moving average analysis, market breadth analysis amongst others.

Academic approach: Over the years, the academics have studied many aspects of the securities market and have developed advanced methods of analysis. The basic rules are:

The stock markets are efficient and react rationally and fast to the information flow over time. So, the current market price would reflect its intrinsic value at all times. This would mean "Current market price = Intrinsic value".

Stock prices behave in a random fashion and successive price changes are independent of each other. Thus, present price behaviour can not predict future price behaviour.

In the securities market there is a positive and linear relationship between risk and return. That is the expected return from a security has a linear relationship with the systemic or non-diversifiable risk of the market.

Fundamental analysis would help us in establishing standards and benchmarks. Technical analysis would help us gauge the current investor mood and the relative strength of demand and supply. The market is neither well ordered nor speculative.

The market has imperfections, but reacts reasonably well to the flow of information. Although some securities would be mispriced, there is a positive correlation between risk and return.

COMMON ERRORS IN INVESTMENT MANAGEMENT

In any endeavor we undertake, we are sometimes right and make correct decisions and sometimes we are wrong and prone to errors. We are prone to these errors, when we do not have a correct perspective of the environment or lack a correct assessment of the current situation in the environment.

We would have to watch out for these errors to reduce the probability of losses. For instance, it would be very difficult and an error to be in a buy or hold position if the market is in a bearish mode. Similarly, it would be difficult and an error to be in a sell or short position if the market is in a bullish trend. It would be advisable, correct and profitable to trade with the trend and not against it. Still investors of all hues and levels of experience are prone to errors.: Goals beyond rational expectation: Here the investor probably thinks that he owns the company lock, stock and barrel. Or that the market owes him his profits for having exposed himself to the market risks.

Or the investor may have a targeted expected rate of return beyond what the market would be able to give him consistently over time. On the other hand, unrealistic goals could also be a result of unjustified claims made by a company going for a new issue.

Or misplaced expectations due to exceptionally good past performance of the investment instrument or a mutual fund or a portfolio manager. Or promises not kept by tipsters, market operators and fly by night operators.

An investment policy not clearly defined: This would also include an unclear view on risk. Here, the investor would be prone to greed and fear as the market goes up and down, respectively. This vacillation would cause the investor much loss and pain.

Seat of the pant decision making: Investors without even realizing it base their decisions on incomplete information.

Some of the thoughts of the investor would be:

- Come on! I know what is going on in the market, and there isn't any time to do a detailed analysis. I don't want an opportunity loss if I delay.
- All that hard work is strictly for the mediocre. I know I am right.
- He is my guru and can't be wrong.

We must clarify at the beginning whether we are doing an investment exercise or are we indulging in ego satisfaction. If it is investment then do the analysis as the markets and the investment instruments will still be there tomorrow. Another situation could cause the investor a loss of balance.

As the market goes up and continues going up, the investor tends to set aside all thoughts on the various investment risks and follows the investing public. Here, the investor is being greedy, and sooner or later would pay the price for this error of judgment.

Stock switching: In this situation, the investor is selling one stock and at the same time buying another stock. This is interesting, as here the investor expects that the first stock would go down in value, while the second stock would go up. This is unique and is rarely successful.

Two scenarios require our attention:

1. It maybe the right time to sell the first stock, but it may not be the right time to buy the second stock, as that too maybe on its way down.
2. It maybe the right time to buy the second stock, but it may not be the right time to sell the first stock, as it may still have some upside left.

The love for a cheap stock: A cheap stock is a very attractive proposition for any investor, as he is able to buy large quantities of the same. Investors find it easier to buy 1,000 shares of a INR 10.00 stock, and find it difficult to buy 100 shares of a INR 100.00 stock. The total investment amount is the same in both cases.

In certain situations, when a stock price moves down, investors start buying and continue to buy larger quantities of the same stock. The investor here is averaging his price down. But, he does not have a guarantee that in the foreseeable future the price trend of this stock would reverse and go above his average purchase price. Averaging can be dangerous.

Over-diversification: Is a situation, when an investor has a large number of names in his portfolio, maybe 50 or 60 or even more.

It is like owning an index and more. Therefore the investor's portfolio performance would be about the same as the index or marginally above or below it depending on the names in the portfolio.

Secondly, managing and monitoring would become a Herculean task. The investor would get a false sense of safety in numbers. Decision-making would become slow and ineffective. If the market goes down due to a systemic risk factor, all the stocks including the best would move down in price. And the investor would not know what to sell, at what price to sell and when to sell. Ideally, a portfolio should consist of 10-15 well-researched stocks. In any case as individual investors we are not institutions, nor do we have the requisite staffing to effectively monitor and manage a larger number of stocks.

Under-diversification: Is a situation in which an investor has only 1-2 stocks in his portfolio. This maybe due to a situation of over-confidence in the expected performance of these stocks. Or maybe the result of plain complacency.

This is not a good portfolio strategy, as the investor has exposed himself to all market risks to a larger extent due to a lack of diversification. We must always remember that we diversify our portfolio to minimize the systemic or non-diversifiable risks. In any case, this high level of risk exposure is not really necessary if we view ourselves as long term investors.

The lure of known companies: Investors are tempted to buy shares of companies that they know and are familiar with. However, the investor should keep in mind, that his knowing a company is not correlated to the returns he expects to derive from his investments in its stock.

Wrong attitude towards profits and losses: An average investor due to ego and pride does not want to recognize or admit that he may have made a mistake. Let's look at two situations:

An investor buys a stock, and soon thereafter its price goes down. Instead of applying a stop loss and getting out of the stock, the investor holds the stock in expectation of a rebound or trend reversal. However, the price continues moving down with a potential of a further decline. Now, the investor is holding the stock at a 30%-40% loss. Here, the investor wants to postpone the booking of this substantial loss and the acknowledgement of having made a mistake.

When the stock price does move up, the investor is ready and waiting to sell this stock at or marginally above his purchase price, even if the stock is expected to move up into a higher trading range. Here the investor sells to gain the relief of not having incurred a substantial loss and also he does not have to acknowledge his mistake at the start of this investment. Both these situations are loaded towards the reinfo-rcement of losses and not profits.

INVESTMENT AND SPECULATION

There is a very thin and blurred line between investing and speculating. To have a clearer understanding of this, we would differentiate between the two.

There is a tendency for investors to be speculative when the markets are bullish and buoyant. However, for long term and profitable survival in the markets we must try and control this urge to speculate. After all, we are here to learn and apply investment management and not speculation management.

To be part of the speculative herd in a bull market situation has been the waterloo of many participants in the financial markets across the globe. This participant maybe an individual investor, a NBFC, a financial institution, a pension fund, a bank, or a brokerage. Some are responsible corporate citizens while others are not.

INVESTMENT WISDOM: ONE LINERS

Listed are wisdom one liners which would give an investor an insight to what he or she is up against:

- The market is a discounting machine.
- A cynic knows the price of everything and the value of nothing.
- Investment management is 10% inspiration and 90% perspiration.
- To err is human, to hedge divine.
- No stock is good or bad, it is the price that makes it so.
- No price is too high for a bull or too low for a bear.
- Somebody is wrong every time a trade is made.
- Ride the winners and sell the losers.
- You never understand a stock unless you are long or short in it.
- Be long term but watch the ticks.

- Never throw good money after bad.
- To achieve superior performance, you have to differ from the majority.
- Two things cause stocks to move – the expected and the unexpected.
- No tree grows to the sky.
- A pie doesn't grow through its slices.
- Never confuse brilliance with a bull market.
- Successful investment managers have brains, nerves and luck.
- All generalizations are false, including this one.
- The market makes mountains out of molehills.
- Investigate, then invest.
- The memory of people in the stock market is very short.
- Open-mindedness and independent thinking will pay big dividends in the stock market.
- It is only a step from the sublime to the ridiculous.
- It is only a step from common stock investment to common stock speculation.
- The market is a pendulum that swings back and forth through the median line of rationality.
- The only way to beat the market is to discover and exploit other investors' mistakes.
- No investment manager can perform successfully in all kinds of markets. There is no man for all seasons.
- Better is one forethought than two after.
- The greatest of all gifts is the power to estimate things at their true worth.
- Shallow men believe in luck, wise and strong men in cause and effect.

SECURITIES MARKET

The term securities markets enclose a number of markets in which securities can be bought and sold.

These securities markets can be classified into four types of markets:

1. *Primary market*: Corporate entities offer new issues

to the investing public through the issue of equity shares. After the initial issue, the securities are subsequently shifted to the secondary market, where the can be traded.

2. *Secondary market*: Have securities of corporate entities that are already outstanding and owned by investors. These securities can be traded in the secondary market.
3. *Money market*: Enables trading of securities with maturity of one year or less.
4. *Capital market*: Securities with a maturity period of more than one year are traded in the capital market.

The existence of these markets is advantageous to both the issuer of the security and the investor. The "issuers", *i.e.* business entities and government need to raise funds or capital at competitive rates for productive and improvement activities, respectively.

The markets allow the transfer of funds from the surplus to the deficit sectors both efficiently and at low cost. The investors also benefit, as they are able to invest their excess funds or savings through the market in the expectation of a future return on their investments. The investors are also able to trade these securities through the markets.

BROKER

As investors we are not able to deal with the market directly. It would be like entering and trying to find our way through an unending maze. The markets on their part, are too large, to attend to every single investor directly. This would be a Herculean task and a management nightmare for it. So, the markets introduce and authorize the middleman to performance on its behalf. This middleman is also called the "Broker".

To reinforce this point, consider the following:

- We want an insurance policy, we would deal with the insurance company's agent.
- We want to buy a car or motor cycle or scooter, we would deal with the dealer of the automobile manufacturer.

- We want to buy a pair of trousers or shirt or a dress, we would go to the retail store which sells these products. The retail store would be the representatives of Raymond Ltd. or Reliance or Bombay Dyeing.
- We want to buy the shares of a company traded in the NSE or BSE. We would have to deal with the broker of these exchanges.

Agents, dealers, representatives and brokers mean the same thing, and they perform the same function. Which is that of a middleman. They do this function as they would be receiving commissions in return for the services they provide. For instance, whether an investor buys or sells a stock in the stock exchange the middleman or broker would receive a commission either ways. Which is a percentage of the value traded by the investor. For investors it is very important to choose a broker correctly. Also that the broker is able to provide the services that the investor requires.

In this selection of a broker, the investor would be well advised to consider the following:

- Is the brokerage well established and known in the market?
- Is the representative of the brokerage house able to attend to him or is he overloaded with too many accounts?
- Does the brokerage have a research department. How many qualified professionals do they have on their staff?

There are many other questions, which may be asked and answered. The main aim here is whether the broker we are proposing to deal with, meets all our requirements or not.

SOURCES OF INVESTMENT INFORMATION

Ten sources of information about investment banking firms:

1. Inquiries to securities lawyers.
2. Inquiries to accounting firms experienced in underwriting of initial public offers of securities.

3. Interviews and meetings with investment banking firm professionals.
4. Telephone calls or meetings with personnel of firms listed on an investment banking firm's transaction/client list.
5. Telephone calls or meeting with industry peers who have dealt with investment banking firms.
6. Telephone calls or meetings with commercial bankers involved in corporate finance.
7. Inquiries to venture capital firms.
8. Financial trade publications such as Institutional Investor and Corporate Finance, particularly periodic publications with directories of investment banking firms, as well as the Securities Industry Association's Securities Industry Yearbook and Standard and Poor's Security Dealers of North America.
9. A telephone call to the NASD Regulation's Public Disclosure programme at (800) 289-9999 to ascertain whether a particular investment bank or any of its professionals has been the subject of disciplinary action.
10. Brochures and Internet web sites distributed or offered by investment banking firms.

SECURITIES CONTRACTS (REGULATION) ACT, 1956

PRELIMINARY

Short Title, Extent and Commencement

1. (1) This Act may be called the Securities Contracts (Regulation) Act, 1956.
   (2) It extends to the whole of India.
   (3) It shall come into force on such date as the Central Government may, by notification in the Official Gazette appoint.

Definitions

2. In this Act, unless the context otherwise requires,-

(a) "Contract" means a contract for or relating to the purchase or sale of securities;

(aa) "derivative" includes -

A. a security derived from a debt instrument, share, loan whether secured or unsecured, risk instrument or contract for differences or any other form of security;

B. a contract which derives its value from the prices, or index or prices, of underlying securities;

(b) "Government security" means a security created and issued, whether before or after the commencement of this Act, by the Central Government or a State Government for the purpose of raising a public loan and having one of the forms specified in clause (2) of section 2 of the Public Debt Act, 1944 (18 of 1944);

(c) "Member" means a member of a recognised stock exchange;

(d) "Option in securities" means a contract for the purchase or sale of a right to buy or sell, or a right to buy and sell, securities in future, and includes *a teji, a mandi, a teji mandi, a galli,* a put, a call or a put and call in securities;

(e) "Prescribed" means prescribed by rules made under this Act;

(f) "Recognised stock exchange" means a stock exchange which is for the time being recognised by the Central Government under section 4;

(g) "Rules", with reference to the rules relating in general to the constitution and management of a stock exchange, includes, in the case of a stock exchange which is an incorporated association, its memorandum and substances of association;

(ga) "Securities Appellate Tribunal" means a Securities Appellate Tribunal established under sub-section (1) of section 15K of the

Securities and Exchange Board of India Act, 1992.

(h) "Securities" include-

(i) shares, scrips, stocks, bonds, debentures, debenture stock or other marketable securities of a like nature in or of any incorporated company or other body corporate;

(a) Derivative;

(b) Units or any other instrument issued by any collective investment plan to the investors in such plans;

(ii) Government securities;

(a) Such other instruments as may be declared by the Central Government to be securities;

(iii) Rights or interests in securities; (i) Spot delivery contract means a contract which provides for,-

(a) Actual delivery of securities and the payment of a price therefor either on the same day as the date of the contract or on the next day, the actual period taken for the despatch of the securities or the remittance of money therefor through the post being excluded from the computation of the period aforesaid if the parties to the contract do not reside in the same town or locality;

(b) Transfer of the securities by the depository from the account of a beneficial owner to the account of another beneficial owner when such securities are dealt with by a depository;]

(j) "Stock exchange" means any body of individuals, whether incorporated or not, constituted for the purpose of assisting, regulating or controlling the business of buying, selling or dealing in securities.

2A. Words and expressions used herein and not defined in this Act but defined in the Companies Act, 1956 or the Securities and Exchange Board of India Act, 1992 or the Depositories Act, 1996 shall have the same meanings respectively assigned to them in those Acts.

RECOGNISED STOCK EXCHANGES

Application for Recognition of Stock Exchanges

3. (1) Any stock exchange, which is desirous of being recognised for the purposes of this Act may make an application in the prescribed manner to the Central Government.

(2) Every application under sub- section (1) shall contain such particulars as may be prescribed, and shall be accompanied by a copy of the bye-laws of the stock exchange for the regulation and control of contracts and also a copy of the rules relating in general to the constitution of the stock exchange and in particular, to-

a. The governing body of such stock exchange, its constitution and powers of management and the manner in which its business is to be transacted;
b. The powers and duties of the office bearers of the stock exchange;
c. The admission into the stock exchange of various classes of members, the qualifications, for membership, and the exclusion, suspension, expulsion and re-admission of members therefrom or thereinto;
d. The procedure for the registration of partnerships as members of the stock exchange in cases where the rules provide for such membership; and the nomination and appointment of authorised representatives and clerks.

Grant of Recognition to Stock Exchanges

4. (1) If the Central Government is satisfied, after

making such inquiry as may be necessary in this behalf and after obtaining such further information, if any, as it may require:

(a) That the rules and bye-laws of a stock exchange applying for registration are in conformity with such conditions as may be prescribed with a view to ensure fair dealing and to protect investors;

(b) That the stock exchange is willing to comply with any other conditions (including conditions as to the number of members) which the Central Government, after consultation with the governing body of the stock exchange and having regard to the area served by the stock exchange and its standing and the nature of the securities dealt with by it, may impose for the purpose of carrying out the objects of this Act; and

(c) That it would be in the interest of the trade and also in the public interest to grant recognition to the stock exchange; it may grant recognition to the stock exchange subject to the conditions imposed upon it as aforesaid and in such form as may be prescribed.

(2) The conditions which the Central Government may prescribe under clause,

(a) Of sub-section (1) for the grant of recognition to the stock exchanges may include, among other matters, conditions relating to:

(i) The qualifications for membership of stock exchanges;

(ii) The manner in which contracts shall be entered into and enforced as between members;

(iii) The representation of the Central Government on each of the stock exchanges by such number of persons not exceeding three as the Central Government may nominate in this behalf;

(iv) The maintenance of accounts of members and their audit by chartered accountants whenever such audit is required by the Central Government.

(3) Every grant of recognition to a stock exchange under this shall be published in the Gazette of India and also in the Official Gazette of the State in which the principal office as of the stock exchange is situate, and such recognition shall have effect as from the date of its publication in the Gazette of India.

(4) No rules of a recognised stock exchange relating to any of the matters specified in sub- section (2) of section 3 shall be amended except with the approval of the Central Government.

Withdrawal of Recognition

5. If the Central Government is of the opinion that the recognition granted to a stock exchange under the provisions of this Act should, in the interest of the trade or in the public interest, be withdrawn, the Central Government may serve on the governing body of the stock exchange a written notice that the Central Government is considering the withdrawal of the recognition for the reasons stated in the notice and after giving an opportunity to the governing body to be heard in the matter, the Central Government may withdraw, by notification in the Official Gazette, the recognition granted to the stock exchange: Provided that no such withdrawal shall affect the validity of any contract entered into or made before the date of the notification, and the Central Government may, after consultation with the stock exchange, make such provision as it deems fit in the notification of withdrawal or in any subsequent notification similarly published for the due

performance of any contracts outstanding on that date.

Power of Central Government to call for Periodical Returns or Direct Inquiries to be Made

6. (1) Every recognised stock exchange shall furnish to the *[Securities and Exchange Board of India]*such periodical returns relating to its affairs as may be prescribed.

(2) Every recognised stock exchange and every member thereof shall maintain and preserve for such periods not exceeding five years such books of account, and other documents as the Central Government, after consultation with the stock exchange concerned, may prescribe in the interest of the trade or in the public interest, and such books of account, and other documents shall be subject to inspection at all reasonable times by the *[Securities and Exchange Board of India]*.

(3) Without prejudice to the provisions contained in sub- sections (1) and (2), the *[Securities and Exchange Board of India]*, if it is satisfied that it is in the interest of the trade or in the public interest so to do, may, by order in writing,-

a. Call upon a recognised stock exchange or any member thereof to furnish in writing such information or explanation relating to the stock exchange as the *[Securities and Exchange Board of India]* may require;

b. Appoint one or more persons to make an inquiry in the prescribed manner in relation to the affairs of any of the members of the stock exchange in relation to the stock exchange and submit a report of the result of such inquiry to the *[Securities and Exchange Board of India]*.

(4) Where an inquiry in relation to the affairs of a recognised stock exchange or the affairs of any

of its members in relation to the stock exchange has been undertaken under sub-section (3),-

(a) Every director, manager, secretary or other officer of such stock exchange;

(b) Every member of such stock exchange;

(c) If the member of the stock exchange is a firm, every partner, manager, secretary or other officer of the firm; and

(d) Every other person or body of persons who has had dealings in the course of business with any of the persons mentioned in clauses (a), (b) and (c) whether directly or indirectly;

shall be bound to produce before the authority making the inquiry all such books of account, and other documents in his custody or power relating to or having a bearing on the subject-matter of such inquiry and also to furnish the authorities within such time as may be specified with any such statement or information relating thereto as may be required of him.

Annual Reports to be Furnished to Central Government by Stock Exchanges

7. Every recognised stock exchange shall furnish the Central Government with a copy of the annual report, and such annual report shall contain such particulars as may be prescribed.

Power of Recognised Stock Exchange to Make Rules Restricting Voting Rights, etc

7A. (1) A recognised stock exchange may make rules or amend any rules made by it to provide for all or any of the following matters, namely:

(a) The restriction of voting rights to members only in respect of any matter placed before the stock exchange at any meeting;

(b) The regulation of voting rights in respect

of any matter placed before the stock exchange at any meeting so that each member may be entitled to have one vote only, irrespective of his share of the paid-up equity capital of the stock exchange;

(c) The restriction on the right of a member to appoint another person as his proxy to attend and vote at a meeting of the stock exchange; and

(d) Such incidental, consequential and supplementary matters as may be necessary to give effect to any of the matters specified in clauses (a), (b) and (c).

(2) No rules of a recognised stock exchange made or amended in relation to any matter referred to in clauses (a) to (d) of sub-section (1) shall have effect until they have been approved by the Central Government and published by that Government in the Official Gazette and, in approving the rules so made or amended, the Central Government may make such modifications therein as it thinks fit, and on such publication, the rules as provided by the Central Government shall be deemed to have been validly made, notwithstanding anything to the contrary contained in the Companies Act, 1956 (1 of 1956).

Power of Central Government to Direct Rules to be Made or to Make Rules

8. (1) Where, after consultation with the governing bodies of stock exchanges generally or with the governing body of any stock exchange in particular, the Central Government is of the opinion that it is necessary or expedient so to do, it may, by order in writing together with a statement of the reasons therefor, direct recognised stock exchanges generally or any recognised stock exchange in particular, as the case may be, to make any rules or

to amend any rules already made in respect of all or any of the matters specified in sub-section (2) of section 3 within a period of *[two months]*from the date of the order.

(2) If any recognised stock exchange fails or neglects to comply with any order made under sub-section (1) within the period specified therein, the Central Government may make the rules for, or amend the rules made by, the recognised stock exchange, either in the form proposed in the order or with such modifications thereof as may be agreed to between the stock exchange and the Central Government.

(3) Where in pursuance of this section any rules have been made or amended, the rules so made or amended shall be published in the Gazette of India and also in the Official Gazette or Gazettes of the State or States in which the principal office or offices of the recognised stock exchange or exchanges is or are situate, and, on the publication thereof in the Gazette of India, the rules so made or amended shall, notwithstanding anything to the contrary contained in the Companies Act, 1956 (1 of 1956), or in any other law for the time being in force, have effect as it they had been made or amended by the recognised stock exchange or stock exchanges, as the case may be.

Power of Recognised Stock Exchange to Make Bye-Laws

9. (1) Any recognised stock exchange may, subject to the previous approval of the *[Securities and Exchange Board of India]*, make bye-laws for the regulation and control of contracts.

(2) In particular, and without prejudice to the generality of the foregoing power, such bye- laws may provide for:

(a) The opening and closing of markets and the regulation of the hours of trade;

(b) A clearing house for the periodical settlement of contracts and differences thereunder, the delivery of and payment for securities, the passing on of delivery orders and the regulation and maintenance of such clearing house;

(c) The submission to the *[Securities and Exchange Board of India]* by the clearing house as soon as may be after each periodical settlement of all or any of the following particulars as the *[Securities and Exchange Board of India]* may, from time to time require, namely:

   (i) The total number of each category of security carried over from one settlement period to another.

   (ii) The total number of each category of security, contracts in respect of which have been squared up during the course of each settlement period.

   (iii) The total number of each category of security actually delivered at each clearing;

(d) The publication by the clearing house of all or any of the particulars submitted to the *[Securities and Exchange Board of India]* under clause (c) subject to the directions, if any, issued by the *[Securities and Exchange Board of India]* in this behalf;

(e) The regulation or prohibition of blank transfers;

(f) The number and classes of contracts in respect of which settlements shall be made or differences paid through the clearing house;

(g) The regulation, or prohibition of *badlas* or carry-over facilities;

(h) The fixing, altering or postponing of days for settlements;

(i) The determination and declaration of market rates, including the opening, closing, highest and lowest rates for securities;

(j) The terms, conditions and incidents of contracts, including the prescription of margin requirements, if any, and conditions relating thereto, and the forms of contracts in writing;

k) The regulation of the entering into, making, performance, rescission and termination, of contracts, including contracts between members or between a member and his constituent or between a member and a person who is not a member, and the consequences of default or insolvency on the part of a seller or buyer or intermediary, the consequences of a breach or omission by a seller or buyer, and the responsibility of members who are not parties to such contracts;

(l) The regulation of *taravani* business including the placing of limitations thereon;

(m) The listing of securities on the stock exchange, the inclusion of any security for the purpose of dealings and the suspension or withdrawal of any such securities, and the suspension or prohibition of trading in any specified securities;

(n) The method and procedure for the settlement of claims or disputes, including settlement by arbitration;

(o) The levy and recovery of fees, fines and penalties;

(p) The regulation of the course of business between parties to contracts in any capacity;

(q) The fixing of a scale of brokerage and other charges;

(s) The emergencies in trade which may arise,

whether as a result of pool or syndicated operations or cornering or otherwise, and the exercise of powers in such emergencies including the power to fix maximum and minimum prices for securities;

(t) The regulation of dealings by members for their own account;

(u) The separation of the functions of jobbers and brokers;

(v) The limitations on the volume of trade done by any individual member in exceptional circumstances;

(w) The obligation of members to supply such information or explanation and to produce such documents relating to the business as the governing body may require.

(3) The bye-laws made under this section may:

(a) Specify the bye-laws, the contravention of which shall make a contract entered into otherwise than in accordance with the bye-laws void under sub-section (1) of section 14;

(b) Provide that the contravention of any of the bye-laws shall render the member concerned liable to one or more of the following punishments, namely:

(i) Fine,

(ii) Expulsion from membership,

(iii) Suspension from membership for a specified period,

(iv) Any other penalty of a like nature not involving the payment of money.

(4) The *[Securities and Exchange Board of India]*, shall be published in the Gazette of India and also in the Official Gazette of the State in which the principal office of the recognised stock exchange is situate, and shall have effect as from the date of its publication in the Gazette of India:

Provided that if the *[Securities and Exchange Board of India]* is satisfied in any case that in the interest of the trade or in the public interest any bye-laws should be made immediately, it may, by order in writing specifying the reasons therefor.

Power of [*Securities and Exchange Board of India*] to Make or Amend Bye-laws of Recognised Stock Exchanges

10. (1) The *[Securities and Exchange Board of India]* may, either on a request in writing received by it in this behalf from the governing body of a recognised stock exchange or on its own motion, if it is satisfied after consultation with the governing body of the stock exchange that it is necessary or expedient so to do and after recording its reasons for so doing, make bye-laws, for all or any of the matters specified in section 9 or amend any bye-laws made by such stock exchange under that section.

(2) Where in pursuance of this section any bye-laws have been made or amended, the bye-laws so made or amended shall be published in the Gazette of India and also in the Official Gazette of the State in which the principal office of the recognised stock exchange is situate, and on the publication thereof in the Gazette of India, the bye-laws so made or amended shall have effect as if they had been made or amended by the recognised stock exchange concerned.

(3) Notwithstanding anything contained in this section, where the governing body of a recognised stock exchange objects to any bye-laws made or amended under this section by the *[Securities and Exchange Board of India]* on its own motion, it may, within *[two months*] of the publication thereof in the Gazette of India under sub-section (2), apply to the *[Securities and Exchange Board of India*] for revision thereof the *[Securities and Exchange Board*

of India] may, after giving an opportunity to the governing body of the stock exchange to be heard in the matter, revise the bye-laws so made or amended, and where any bye-laws so made or amended are revised as a result of any action taken under this sub- section, the bye-laws so revised shall be published and shall become effective as provided in sub-section (2).

(4) The making or the amendment or revision of any bye-laws under this section shall in all cases be subject to the condition of previous publication:

Provided that if the *[Securities and Exchange Board of India]* is satisfied in any case that in the interest of the trade or in the public interest any bye-laws should be made, amended or revised immediately, it may, by order in writing specifying the reasons therefor, dispense with the condition of previous publication.

Power of Central Government to Supersede Governing Body of a Recognised Stock Exchange

11. (1) Without prejudice to any other powers vested in the Central Government under this Act, where the Central Government is of the opinion that the governing body of any recognised stock exchange should be superseded, then, not withstanding anything contained in any other law for the time being in force, the Central Government may serve on the governing body a written notice that the Central Government is considering the supersession of the governing body for the reasons specified in the notice and after giving an opportunity to the governing body to be heard in the matter, it may, by notification in the Official Gazette declare the governing body of such stock exchange to be superseded, and may appoint any person or persons to exercise and perform all the powers and duties of the governing body, and, and where more persons than one are appointed, may appoint one of such persons to be the

chairman and another to be the vice- chairman thereof.

(2) On the publication of a notification in the Official Gazette under sub-section (1), the following consequences shall ensue, namely:-

(a) The members of the governing body which has been superseded shall, as from the date of the notification of super-session, cease to hold office as such members;

(b) The person or persons appointed under sub-section (1) may exercise and perform all the powers and duties of the governing body which has been superseded;

(c) All such property of the recognised stock exchange as the person or persons appointed under sub-section (1) may, by order in writing, specify in this behalf as being necessary for the purpose of enabling him or them to carry on the business of the stock exchange, shall vest in such person or persons.

(3) Notwithstanding anything to the contrary contained in any law or the rules or bye-laws of the recognised stock exchange the governing body of which is superseded under sub-section (1), the person or persons appointed under that sub-section shall hold office for such period a may be specified in the notification published under that sub-section and, the Central Government may from time to time, by like notification, vary such period.

(4) The Central Government may at any time before the determination of the period of office of any person or persons appointed under this section call upon the recognised stock exchange to reconstitute the governing body in accordance with its rules and on such re- constitution all the property of the recognised stock exchange which has vested in, or was in the possession of, the person or persons

appointed under sub- section (1), shall re-vest, as the case may be, in the governing body so re-constituted: Provided that until a governing body is so re- constituted, the person or persons appointed under sub- section (1), shall continue to exercise and perform their powers and duties.

Power to Suspend Business of Recognised Stock Exchanges

12. If in the opinion of the Central Government an emergency has arisen and for the purpose of meeting the emergency the Central Government considers it expedient so to do, it may, by notification in the Official Gazette, for reasons to be set out therein, direct a recognised stock exchange to suspend such of its business for such period not exceeding seven days and subject to such conditions as may be specified in the notification, and if, in the opinion of the Central Government, the interest of the trade or the public interest requires that the period should be extended may, by like notification extend the said period from time to time.
Provided that where the period of suspension is to be extended beyond the first period, no notification extending the period of suspension shall be issued unless the governing body of the recognised stock exchange has been given an opportunity of being heard in the matter.

CONTRACTS AND OPTIONS IN SECURITIES

Contracts in Notified Areas Illegal in Certain Circumstances

13. If the Central Government is satisfied, having regard to the nature or the volume of transactions in securities in any State or area, that it is necessary so to do, it may, by notification in the Official Gazette, declare this part to apply to such State or area, and thereupon every contract in such State or area which

is entered into after date of the notification otherwise than between members of a recognised stock exchange in such State or area or through or with such member shall be illegal.

Additional Trading Floor

13A. A stock exchange may establish additional trading floor with the prior approval of the Securities and Exchange Board of India in accordance with the terms and conditions stipulated by the said Board. *Explanation*: For the purposes of this part 'additional trading floor' means a trading ring or trading facility offered by a recognised stock exchange outside its area of operation to enable the investors to buy and sell securities through such trading floor under the regulatory framework of the stock exchange.]

Contracts in Notified Areas to be Void in Certain Circumstances

14. (1) Any contract entered into in any State or area specified in the notification under section 13 which is in contravention of any of the bye- laws specified in that behalf under clause (a) of sub-section (3) of section 9 shall be void:

(i) As respects the rights of any member of the recognised stock exchange who has entered into such contract in contraven-tion of any such bye-laws, and also

(ii) As respects the rights of any other person who has knowingly participated in the transaction entailing such contravention.

(2) Nothing in sub-section (1) shall be construed to affect the right of any person other than a member of the recognised stock exchange to enforce any such contract or to recover any sum under or in respect of such contract if such person had no knowledge that the transaction was in

contravention of any of the bye-laws specified in clause (a) of sub-section (3) of section 9.

Members may not Performance as Principals in Certain Circumstances

15. No member of a recognised stock exchange shall in respect of any securities enter into any contract as a principal with any person other than a member of a recognised stock exchange, unless he has secured the consent or authcrity of such person and discloses in the note, memorandum or agreement of sale or purchase that he is acting as a principal: Provided that where the member has secured the consent or authority of such person otherwise than in writing he shall secure written confirmation by such person of such consent or authority within three days from the date of the contract: Provided further that no such written consent or authority of such person shall be necessary for closing out any outstanding contract entered into by such person in accordance with the bye-laws, if the member discloses in the note, memorandum or agreement of sale or purchase in respect of such closing out that he is acting as a principal.

Power to Prohibit Contracts in Certain Cases

16. (1) If the Central Government is of opinion that it is necessary to prevent undesirable speculation in specified securities in any State or area, it may, by notification in the Official Gazette, declare that no person in the State or area specified in the notification shall, save with the permission of the Central Government, enter into any contract for the sale or purchase of any security specified in the notification except to the extent and in the manner, if any, specified therein.

(2) All contracts in contravention of the provisions of sub-section (1) entered into after the date of the notification issued thereunder shall be illegal.

Licensing of Dealers in Securities in Certain Cases

17. (1) Subject to the provision of sub-section (3) and to the other provisions contained in this Act, no person shall carry on or purport to carry on, whether on his own behalf or on behalf of any other person, the business of dealing in securities in any State or area to which section 13 has not been declared to apply and to which the Central Government may, by notification in the Official Gazette declare this part to apply, except under the authority of a licence granted by the [Securities and Exchange Board of India] in this behalf.

(2) No notification under sub- section (1) shall be issued with respect to any State or area unless the Central Government is satisfied, having regard to the manner in which securities are being dealt with in such State or area, that it is desirable or expedient in the interest of the trade or in the public interest that such dealings should be regulated by a system of licensing.

(3) The restrictions imposed by sub-section (1) in relation to dealings in securities shall not apply to the doing of anything by or on behalf of a member of any recognised stock exchange.

Exclusion of Spot Delivery Contracts from Sections 13, 14, 15 and 17

18. (1) Nothing contained in sections 13, 14, 15 and 17 shall apply to spot delivery contracts.

(2) Notwithstanding anything contained in sub-section (1), if the Central Government is of opinion that in the interest of the trade or in the public interest it is expedient to regulate and control the business of dealing in spot delivery contracts also in any State or are (whether section 13 has been declared to apply to that State or area or not), it may, by notification in the Official Gazette, declare that the

provisions of section 17 shall also apply to such State or area in respect of spot delivery contracts generally or in respect of spot delivery contract for the sale or purchase of such securities as may be specified in the notification, and may also specify the manner in which, and the extent to which, the provision of that section shall so apply.

18A. Notwithstanding anything contained in any other law for the time being in force, contracts are -

a. Traded on a recognised stock exchange;
b. Settled on the clearing house of the recognised stock exchange,in accordance with the rules and bye-laws of such stock exchange.

Stock Exchanges Other than Recognised Stock Exchanges Prohibited

19. (1) No person shall, except with the permission of the Central Government, organise or assist in organising or be a member of any stock exchange (other than a recognised stock exchange) for the purpose of assisting in, entering into or performing any contracts in securities.

(2) This section shall come into force in any State or area on such date, as the Central Government may, by notification in the Official Gazette, appoint.

[Prohibition of options in securities

20. Omitted by the Securities Laws (Amendment) Act, 1995, w.e.f. 25-1-1995]

LISTING OF SECURITIES [****]

Conditions for Listing

21. Where securities are listed on the application of any person in any recognised stock exchange, such person shall comply with the conditions of the listing agreement with that stock exchange.] 34

Right of Appeal Against Refusal of Stock Exchanges to List Securities of Public Companies

22. Where a recognised stock exchange acting in

pursuance of any power given to it by its bye- laws, refuses to list the securities of any public company *or collective investment plan,* the company *or plan* shall be entitled to be furnished with reasons for such refusal, any may,-

(a) Within fifteen days from the date on which the reasons for such refusal are furnished to it, or

(b) Where the stock exchange has omitted or failed to dispose of, within the time specified in sub-section (1) of section 73 of the Companies Act, 1956 (1 of 1956) (hereafter in this section referred to as the "specified time"), the application for permission for the shares or debentures to be dealt with on the stock exchange, within fifteen days from the date of expiry of the specified time or within such further period, not exceeding one month, as the Central Government may, on sufficient cause being shown, allow, appeal to the Central Government against such refusal, omission or failure, as the case may be, and there upon the Central Government may, after giving the Stock Exchange an opportunity of being heard,

   (i) Vary or set aside the decision of the stock exchange; or

   (ii) Where the stock exchange has omitted or failed to dispose of the application within the specified time, grant or refuse the permission,and where the Central Government sets aside the decision of the recognised stock exchange or grants the permission, the stock exchange shall performance in conformity with the orders of the Central Government.

Provided that no appeal shall be preferred against refusal, omission or failure, as the case may be, under this section on and after the commencement of the Securities Laws (Second Amendment) Act, 1999.

Right of Appeal to Securities Appellate Tribunal against Refusal of Stock Exchange to List Securities of Public Companies

22A.(1) Where a recognised stock exchange, acting in pursuance of any power given to it by its bye-laws, refuses to list the securities of any public company, the company shall be entitled to be furnished with reasons for such refusal, and may,

a. Within fifteen days from the date on which the reasons for such refusal are furnished to it, or

b. Where the stock exchange has omitted or failed to dispose of, within the time specified in sub-section (1A) of section 73 of the Companies Act, 1956 (hereafter in this section referred to as the "specified time"), the application for permission for the shares or debentures to be dealt with on the stock exchange, within fifteen days from the date of expiry of the specified time or within such further period, not exceeding one month, as the Securities Appellate Tribunal may, on sufficient cause being shown, allow,appeal to the Securities Appellate Tribunal having jurisdiction in the matter against such refusal, omission or failure, as the case may be, and thereupon the Securities Appellate Tribunal may, after giving the stock exchange, an opportunity of being heard,:

   i. Vary or set aside the decision of the stock exchange;

   ii. Where the stock exchange has omitted or failed to dispose of the application within the specified time, grant or refuse the permission, and where the Securities Appellate Tribunal sets aside the decision of the recognised stock exchange or grants the permission, the stock exchange shall performance in conformity with the orders of the Securities Appellate Tribunal.

(2) Every appeal under sub-section (1) shall be in such form and be accompanied by such fee as may be prescribed.

(3) The Securities Appellate Tribunal shall send a copy of every order made by it to the Board and parties to the appeal.

(4) The appeal filed before the Securities Appellate Tribunal under sub-section (1) shall be dealt with by it as expeditiously as possible and endeavour shall be made by it to dispose of the appeal finally within six months from the date of receipt of the appeal.

Procedure and Powers of Securities Appellate Tribunal

(1) The Securities Appellate Tribunal shall not be guided by the principles of natural justice and, subject to the other provisions of this Act and of any rules, the Securities Appellate Tribunal shall have powers to regulate their own procedure including the places at which they shall have their sittings.

(2) The Securities Appellate Tribunal shall have for the purpose of discharging their functions under this Act, the same powers as are vested in a civil court under the Code of Civil Procedure, 1908, while trying a suit, in respect of the following matters, namely:

a. Summoning and enforcing the attendance of any person and examining him on oath;
b. Requiring the discovery and production of documents;
c. Receiving evidence on affidavits;
d. Issuing commissions for the examination of witnesses or documents;
e. Reviewing its decisions;

f. Dismissing an application for default or deciding it ex-parte;
g. Setting aside any order of dismissal of any application for default or any order passed by it ex-parte; and
h. Any other matter which may be prescribed.

Right to Legal Representations

22C. The appellant may either appear in person or authorise one or more chartered accountants or company secretaries or cost accountants or legal practitioners or any of its officers or present his or its case before the Securities Appellate Tribunal.

Explanation: For the purposes of this section,

a. "Chartered accountant" means a chartered accountant as defined in clause (b) of sub-section (1) of section 2 of the Chartered Accountants Act, 1949 and who has obtained a certificate of practice under sub-section (1) of section 6 of that Act;
b. "Company secretary" means a company secretary as defined in clause (c) of sub-section (1) of section 2 of the Company Secretaries Act, 1980 and who has obtained a certificate of practice under sub-section (1) of section 6 of that Act;
c. "Cost accountant" means a cost accountant as defined in clause (b) of sub-section (1) of section 2 of the Cost and Works Accountants Act, 1959 and who has obtained a certificate of practice under sub-section (1) of section 6 of that Act;
d. "Legal practitioner" means an advocate, vakil or an attorney of any High Court, and includes a pleader in practice.

Limitation

22D. The provisions of the Limitation Act, 1963 shall as far as may be apply to an appeal made to a Securities Appellate Tribunal.

Civil Court not to have Jurisdiction

22E. No civil court shall have jurisdiction to entertain any suit or proceeding in respect of any matter which a Securities Appellate Tribunal is empowered by or under this Act to determine and no injunction shall be granted by any court or other authority in respect of any action taken or to be taken in pursuance of any power conferred by or under this Act.

Appeal to High Court

22F. Any person aggrieved by any decision or order of the Securities Appellate Tribunal may file an appeal to the High Court within sixty days from the date of communication of the decision or order of the Securities Appellate Tribunal on any question of fact or law arising out of such order; Provided that the High Court may, if it is satisfied that the appellant was prevented by sufficient cause from filing the appeal within the said period, allow it to be filed within a further period not exceeding sixty days.

PENALTIES AND PROCEDURES

Penalties

23. (1) Any person who

(a) Without reasonable excuse (the burden of proving which shall be on him) fails to comply with any requisition made under sub- section (4) of section 6; or

(b) Enters into any contract in contravention of any of the provisions contained in section 13 or section 16; or (c) contravenes the provisions contained in section 17 or section 19; or

(d) Enters into any contract in derivative in contravention of section 18 A or the rules made under section 30.

(e) Owns or keeps a place other than that of a

recognised stock exchange which is used for the purpose of entering into or performing any contracts in contravention of any of the provisions of this Act and knowingly permits such place to be used for such purposes; or

(f) Manages, controls, or assists in keeping any place other than that of a recognised stock exchange which is used for the purpose of entering into or performing any contracts in contravention of any of the provisions of this Act or at which contracts are recorded or adjusted or rights or liabilities arising out of contracts are adjusted, regulated or enforced in any manner whatsoever; or

(g) Not being a member of a recognised stock exchange or his agent authorised as such under the rules or bye- laws of such stock exchange or not being a dealer in securities licensed under section 17

(h) Not being a member of a recognised stock exchange or his agent authorised as such under the rules or bye- laws of such stock exchange or not being a dealer in securities licensed under section 17, canvasses, advertises or touts in any manner either for himself or on behalf of any other person for any business connected with contracts in contravention of any of the provisions of this Act; or

(i) Joins, gathers or assists in gathering at any place other than the place of business specified in the bye-laws of a recognised stock exchange any person or persons for making bids or offers or for entering into or performing any contracts in contravention of any of the provisions of this Act; shall, on conviction, be punishable with imprisonment for a term which may extend to one year, or with fine, or with both.

(2) Any person who enters into any contract in contravention of the provisions contained in section 15 [or who fails to comply with the provisions of section 21 or with the orders of] the Central Government under section 22 or with the orders of the Securities Appellate Tribunal shall, on conviction, be punishable with fine which may extend to one thousand rupees.

Offences by Companies

24. (1) Where an offence has been committed by a company, every person who, at the time when the offence was committed, was incharge of, and was responsible to, the company for the conduct of the business of the company, as well as the company, shall be deemed to be guilty of the offence, and shall be liable to be proceeded against and punished accordingly: Provided that nothing contained in this sub-section shall render any such person liable to any punishment provided in this Act, if he proves that the offence was committed without his knowledge or that he exercised all due diligence to prevent the commission of such offence.

(2) Notwithstanding anything contained in sub-section (1), where an offence under this Act has been committed by a company and it is proved that the offence has been committed with the consent or connivance of, or is attributable to any gross negligence on the part of any director, manager, secretary or other officer of the company, such director, manager, secretary or other officer of the company, shall also be deemed to be guilty of that offence and shall be liable to be proceeded against and punished accordingly.

Explanation

For the purpose of this section,

(a) "Company" means any body corporate and includes a firm or other association of individuals, and

(b) "Director", in relation to -

(i) A firm, means a partner in the firm;

(ii) Any association of persons or a body of individuals,means any member controlling the affairs thereof.

(iii) The provisions of this section shall be in addition to, and not in derogation of, the provisions of section 22A.

Certain Offences to be Cognizable

25. Notwithstanding anything contained in the [Code of Criminal Procedure, 1898 (5 of 1898)], any offence punishable under sub-section (1) of section 23, shall be deemed to be a cognizable offence within the meaning of that Code.

Jurisdiction to Try Offences Under This Act

26. No court inferior to that of a presidency magistrate or a magistrate of the first class shall take cognizance of or try any offence punishable under this Act.

MISCELLANEOUS

Title to Dividends

27. (1) It shall be lawful for the holder of any security whose name appears on the books of the company issuing the said security to receive and retain any dividend declared by the company in respect thereof for any year, notwithstanding that the said security has already been transferred by him for consideration, unless the transferee who claims the dividend from the transferor has lodged the security and all other documents relating to the transfer which may be required by the company with the

company for being registered in his name within fifteen days of the date on which the dividend became due.

Explanation

The period specified in this section shall be extended:

(i) In case of death of the transferee, by the actual period taken by his legal representative to establish his claim to the dividend;

(ii) In case of loss of the transfer deed by theft or any other cause beyond the control of the transferee, by the actual period taken for the replacement thereof; and

(iii) In case of delay in the lodging of any security and other documents relating to the transfer due to causes connected with the post, by the actual period of the delay.

(2) Nothing contained in sub- section (1) shall affect -

a. The right of a company to pay any dividend which has become due to any person whose name is for the time being registered in the books of the company as the holder of the security in respect of which the dividend has become due;

b. The right of the transferee of any security to enforce against the transferor or any other person his rights, if any, in relation to the transfer in any case where the company has refused to register the transfer of the security in the name of the transferee.

Right to Receive Income From Collective Investment Plan

27A (1) It shall be lawful for the holder of any securities, being units or other instruments issued by collective investment plan, whose name appears on the books of the collective investment plan issuing the said security to receive and retain any income in respect of units or other instruments issued by the collective investment plan declared by the collective investment plan in respect thereof for any year notwithstanding that the said security, being units or other instruments issued by collective investment plan, has already been transferred by him for consideration, unless the transferee who claims the income in respect of units or other instruments issued by collective investment plan from the transfer or has lodged the security and all other documents relating to the transfer which may be required by the collective investment plan with the collective investment plan for being registered in his name within fifteen days of the date on which the income in respect of units or other instruments issued by the collective investment plan became due.

Explanation

The period specified in this section shall be extended:

(i) In case of death of the transferee, by the actual period taken by his legal representative to establish his claim to the income in respect of units or other instrument issued by collective investment plan;

(ii) In case of loss of the transfer deed by theft or any other cause beyond the control of the transferee, by the actual period taken for the replacement thereof; and

(iii) In case of delay in the lodging of any security, being units or other instruments issued by collective investment plan, and other documents relating to the transfer due to causes connected with the post, by the actual period of the delay.

(2) Nothing contained in sub-section (1) shall affect

a. The right of a collective investment plan to pay any income from units or other instruments issued by collective investment plan which has become due to any person whose name is for the time being registered in the books of the collective investment plan as the holder of the security being units or other instruments issued by collective investment plan in respect of which the income in respect of units or other instruments issued by collective plan has become due;

b. The right of transferee of any security, being units or other instruments issued by collective investment plan, to enforce against the transferor or any other person his rights, if any, in relation to the transfer in any case where the company has refused to register the transfer of the security being units or other instruments issued by collective investment plan in the name of the transferee.

Act not to Apply in Certain Cases

28. (1) *The provisions of this Act shall not apply to*:

(a) The Government, the Reserve Bank of India, any local authority or any corporation set up by a special law or any person who has effected any transaction with or through the agency of any such authority as is referred to in this clause;

(b) Any convertible bond or share warrant or any option or right in relation thereto, in so far as it entitles the person in whose favour any of the foregoing has been issued to obtain at his option from the company or other body corporate, issuing the same or from any of its shareholders or duly appointed agents, shares of the company or other body corporate, whether by conversion of the bond or warrant or otherwise, on the basis of the price agreed upon when the same was issued.

(2) Without prejudice to the provisions contained in sub-section (1), if the Central Government is satisfied that in the interests of trade and commerce or the economic development of the country it is necessary or expedient so to do,it may, by notification in the Official Gazette, specify any class of contracts as contracts to which this Act or any provision contained therein shall not apply, and also the conditions, limitations or restrictions, if any, subject to which it shall not so apply.

Protection of Action Taken in Good Faith

29. No suit, prosecution or other legal proceeding whatsoever shall lie in any court against the governing body or any member, office bearer or servant of any recognised stock exchange or against any person or persons appointed under sub-section (1) of section 11 for anything which is in good faith done or intended to be done in pursuance of this Act or of any rules or bye-laws made thereunder.

Power to Delegate

29A. The Central Government may, by order published in the Official Gazette, direct that the powers (except the power under section 30) exercisable by such conditions, if any, as may be specified in the order, be exercisable also by the Securities and Exchange Board of India or the Reserve Bank of India constituted under section 3 of the Reserve Bank of India Act, 1934.

Power to Make Rules

30. (1) The Central Government may, by notification in the Official Gazette, make rules for the purpose of carrying into effect the objects of this Act.

(2) In particular, and without prejudice to the

generality of the foregoing power, such rules may provide for,

(a) The manner in which applications may be made, the particulars which they should contain and the levy of a fee in respect of such applications;

(b) The manner in which any inquiry for the purpose of recognizing any stock exchange may be made, the conditions which may be imposed for the grant of such recognition, including conditions as to the admission of members if the stock exchange concerned is to be the only recognised stock exchange in the area; and the form in which such recognition shall be granted;

(c) The particulars which should be contained in the periodical returns and annual reports to be furnished to the Central Government;

(d) The documents which should be maintained and preserved under section 6 and the periods for which they should be preserved;

(e) The manner in which any inquiry by the governing body of a stock exchange shall be made under section 6;

(f) The manner in which the bye-laws to be made or amended under this Act shall before being so made or amended be published for criticism;

(g) The manner in which applications may be made by dealers in securities for licences under section 17, the fee payable in respect thereof and the period of such licences, the conditions subject to which licences may be granted, including conditions relating to the forms which may be used in making contracts, the documents to be maintained by licensed dealers and the furnishing of periodical information to such authority as may be specified and the revocation of licences for breach of conditions;

(h) *The requirements which shall be complied with*:

(A) By public companies for the purpose of getting their securities listed on any stock exchange;

(B) By collective investment plan for the purpose of getting their units listed on any stock exchange".

(ha) the form in which an appeal may be filed before the Securities Appellate Tribunal under section 22A and the fees payable in respect of such appeal.

(i) Any other matter which is to be or may be prescribed.

(3) Any rules made under this section [***] shall, as soon as may be, after their publication in the Official Gazette, be laid before both Houses of Parliament.

Repeal

31. Repealed by the Repealing and Amending Act, 1960 (58 of 1960), section 2 and Schedule 1.

INVESTOR PROTECTION

The term "investor protection" defines the entity of efforts and activities to observe, safeguard and enforce the rights and claims of a person in his role as an investor. This includes advise and legal action. The assumption of a need of protection is based on the experience that financial investors are usually structurally inferior to providers of financial services and products due to lack of professional knowledge, information and/or experience.

SECURITIES TRADING

Individuals and organizations are always looking for a way to increase revenues. An enticing concept to do this is to invest in trading securities. While all securities investments pose a risk of losing the capital investment, trading securities increases the the chance of profits and losses. There are many factors involved when considering trading securities. To understand this, let's look at each of the components individually.

SECURITIES

Securities are equities or debentures of publicly traded companies that are bought and sold through brokerage firms. They are regulated by the U.S. Securities and Exchange Commission and offer no guarantee of return on investment. Securities, even bonds, fluctuate in value and pose a risk to the principal investment. Securities investments are offered for corporations ranging from large capitalization companies to extremely high risk penny stock ventures.

TRADING

Trading is the purchase or sale of a specific security. It can be either an equity or debenture and is done via a brokerage firm. Individuals can have trades done either through a registered representative or make trades without a broker through an online brokerage trading firm.

Trading can be done either in a cash account or through a margin account. Cash accounts require all transactions to be paid for in full by the settlement date three days after the trade execution. Margin accounts allow the investor to borrow money for the purchase of securities in hopes that they will not go down in price and a margin call for the difference is demanded by the brokerage firm.

TRADING SECURITIES DEFINED

Trading securities is the performance of buying and selling securities with the intention of making a quick profit. Brokerage firms and investment advisers recommend buying securities for the anticipated long-term appreciation of the company. Trading securities involve the same stocks and bonds available to all investors on public exchanges.

The difference is trading securities are timed by investors

to buy low and sell high in short time frames. While all securities can be traded in this fashion, some securities have a natural ebb and flow that can be traded more regularly. For example, retail store chains expect higher fourth-quarter earnings as a result of holiday shopping that may lead investors to time early fourth quarter buying to be sold in the early first quarter.

REWARDS

The profits that can be made in the short term by trading securities is enormous. Investors who can time the market have the ability to reap the highs while re-buying at lows. Unlike long-term investors who ride out the high and lows of investments.

Mutual fund managers make a living by moving capital in and out of securities by timing news, technology and sales reports. Those who are good at this are well worth the fees they charge.

RISKS

Many long-term financial advisers liken trading securities for the average investor to gambling. The investor may be lucky once or twice, but more than likely does not have the resources or time to follow the international market and how it affects domestic securities for well-timed trades. Ultimately, the possibility of high returns is slapped with the reality of extremely fast losses. Additionally, the constant buying and selling, even for successful investors, may have a good portion of profits eaten up by capital gains taxes.

MARGIN TRADING

Margin trading is buying stocks without having the entire money to do it. The exchanges have an institutionalised method of buying stocks without having the capital through the futures market. For example, if you were to buy 2000 shares of Company A, which trades at Rs 300, you will need about Rs 6 lakh. But if you buy a future contract of that company, which comprises 2000 shares, you only need to pay a margin of 15 per cent. So by putting Rs 90,000, you can get an exposure of Rs 6 lakh.

The same operation can also be executed through margin trading. Here, the trader will buy 2,000 shares, which are partly funded by the broker, and the rest by the trader.

SENSEX'S RISE AND FALL: COVERAGE

The percentage of margin funding may range between 50-90 per cent, depending on the broker and his relationship with the client. The broker, in turn, funds his line of credit from a bank, and keeps the shares in his account with any profit/loss going to the client.

Margin Trading vs Futures

Most investors buy the futures, but there are times when margin trading makes mores sense. If a stock is not in the futures list, the client can go for margin funding.

Since futures are generally not available beyond one or two months, if the client has a longer view, then margin trading is better. Also, some brokers offer lower interest rates on margin trading than the prevalent rates in the futures market.

Margin Call

Once the trader buys a future or stocks in the margin account, the client gets the profit/loss since his purchase in his account. In both futures market and margin trading, if the value of the share falls below the purchase price, the broker will make margin calls, asking the client to deposit additional margin.

In a normal market, these margin calls are not a problem as clients can deposit the additional amount easily. When clients are not able to meet the margin requirement, the broker sells the security so that he does not have to bear the risk in case the stock falls further.

This typically become a problem when the markets fall far more than expected and traders are not liquid enough to meet the margin calls. And when a lot of traders can't meet margin calls, the situation snowballs. This is what happened in the past few days when traders, who were over-leveraged could not meet the margin calls, and their securities kept being sold.

CLEARING AND SETTLEMENT PROCEDURES

Recently, Europe has emerged as the place where major issues in the securities market are to be decided. The issue of consolidation of stock exchanges has been fought and, so far, lost in Europe.

The focus of market participants was then brought to bear on settlement, with a call for the amalgamation and consolidation of the central securities depositories —the organisations responsible for the settlement of securities transactions — from the large and expanding population of stock exchanges and 'execution platforms'.

This also failed. Attention then was brought to bear on the clearing houses, with representatives of market users agreeing, in public, that the right European structure for clearing was a single central counterparty serving the transaction stream between Europe's execution venues and the various settlement systems.

This was the 'hour glass' structure, where competition between exchanges for execution and competition between settlement systems would be separated by a single European central counterparty, from which it was expected that industry efficiency and cost reduction would result. This appeared to trigger in a number of market servicing organisations' immediate recognition of the 'value generating' potential of clearing houses, which led to a rapid increase in new central counterparty clearing houses in the European markets.

The accepted emphasis in European securities markets continues to be on consolidation. The prevailing view is that market infrastructure in Europe is too fragmented and therefore expensive to operate as a whole. The immediate solution is to have less of it — fewer stock exchanges, one central counterparty and fewer settlement systems. Yet, with the exception of the Euronext organisation, little serious consolidation has resulted. Alliances are being discussed and some valuable efforts to find common standards and practices between settlement systems have been made by ECSDA, although neither of these initiatives actually removes surplus capacity from the marketplace.

IDENTIFYING THE PROBLEMS

The failure rate of securities transactions in Europe, arguably the most sophisticated trading market, is reported by a leading settlement agent to be 15%. This poor performance has given rise to a number of significant studies into the issues raised which have in turn catalysed a number of separate initiatives.

In no particular order these include:

- *Lamfalussy:* Wise Men Report
- *Giovannini*: Report into EU Clearing and Settlement
- *G–30*: New recommendations in Global Clearing and Settlement
- *European Securities Forum*: User lobby group
- European Central Securities Depositories Association
- *Global Straight-through Processing Association*: GSTPA
- Central Counterparties Association

These initiatives have a variety of remits and backing ranging from governments and central banks through to industry/user groups. Their agenda and objectives also cover a wide range of targets, although they share one principal goal in attempting to bring to pass greater efficiency in post transaction processing — clearing and settlement.

At a distance they would appear to have achieved remarkably little, given the industry and the increasing political pressure that is being brought to bear. The proof of this lies in the continuing fragmentation and variety of processes, independent of both governance and management of the organisations involved.

Indeed, the current G-30 initiative has established a remarkable consensus on the prime causes of the industrial problem from a wide ranging series of interviews with investment banks, investors, custodians, clearing houses, settlement systems, exchanges and brokers. One of the principle causes is claimed to be failure of 'interoperability' which describes the ability of different market services, such as clearing houses and settlement systems, to work in harmony.

The main contributors to the lack of interoperability are the absence of agreed terminology and market practices and the many different ways in which information is presented and recorded from top to bottom in the transaction chain. This, surprisingly, is true within certain national markets as much as in cross-border equities markets. The most significant contributor to this is the lack of standardisation in legal, regulatory and taxation rules and practices between one national market and another. One example of this problem is the wide variety of legal approaches to the concept of 'property'. So if something goes wrong during the process of clearing and settlement, ownership of the asset being transferred may be hard to define. And of course if something has gone wrong, it is highly likely that each counterparty has a vested interest in the outcome and goodwill cannot necessarily be relied upon to resolve the situation.

TRANSACTION CHAIN

Title to traded assets is a pretty basic concept in the process of transaction performance. Frequently, it is not until the laws of property in question have been tested in court that the precise position in current and past transactions can be relied upon. There is a predictable and sequential flow of events and processes that must take place after trading to achieve satisfactory transaction performance. Some are by-passed as the specific market participants are prepared to accept additional risks which other markets are not. But in general the flow can be represented as follows:

Surprisingly, though, 'clearing and settlement' are often used as a single term, rather in the way that sales and marketing are frequently used in blended form — the two terms being brought together to disguise the fact that the individual meanings of the functions are not fully understood or appreciated. In terms of the development of market infrastructure it is increasingly relevant to consider them as separate and distinct processes, since an important body of opinion in the market is keen to see clearing and settlement delivered on a separate basis. In Europe the issue was handed over by the industry to politicians, when the EU competition commissioner, Mario Monti, was asked to review the competitive aspects of clearing, settlement and execution combined in what are termed 'silos'.

Silos describe the grouping of a stock exchange, clearing house and settlement system in one organisation. The alternative to silos are 'service providers', where each process is delivered by separate and distinct organisations, the implication being that this enables more transparent and competitive pricing. In individual geographic markets, it is sometimes hard to understand the argument between silos and service providers where there are effective monopolies, and in Europe cross- border competition in the execution, clearing and settlement of domestically-issued equity and fixed income has yet to joined on any scale.

The nature of the traded asset has a large impact on the functional market infrastructure required to handle transactions efficiently. Similarly, the method by which transactions are executed points to the sophistication of the clearing and settlement processes required. Equities are traded in greater volume than most corporate bonds. For settlement, the transfer of title to shares is made clear through transparent processes delivered by sophisticated organisations, the central securities depositories and increasingly supported by regulatory oversight. Significantly, corporate bonds may be settled through both CSDs and the ICSDs — Euroclear and Clearstream. These two organisations have presided over the smooth operation of the Eurobond market for some thirty years. The Eurobond market has, during this time, offered both the primary and secondary markets global, multi-currency and multinational settlement, with cross-border transactions being the rule rather than the exception.

Whilst domestic market service organisations have been wrestling with cross-border issues, the Eurobond market has smoothly encompassed global bonds which add domestic linkages to CSDs. This adds domestic populations of investors to the Euromarket contingent and is increasingly applied to equities. The reason why, in aiming to provide the best service to their domestic equity markets, CSDs did not surrender their domestic and cross-border process flows to the ICSDs raises a number of sensitive and vital issues.

- *Costs*: Domestic organisations contend that the ICSD tariffs are significantly more expensive than their own.
- *Control*: The ICSDs have traditionally been owned and controlled by the large multinational broker-dealers, rather than market participants more domestically aligned.

This is where the real barriers to consolidation lie. Although high profile cross-border transactions are dominated by a comparatively small number of large broker-dealers, domestic transactions involve a much more diverse population of intermediaries, many of whom are both powerful in their domestic context and are less interested in the needs of cross-border transactions. Consolidation of market infrastructure, therefore, carries different levels of appeal to domestic players whose local power-base may be disproportionately large in comparison to their market share. And within their own domestic markets, many of the European providers compare very favourably with the US on a cost per basis.

However, the Centre for European Policy Studies recently published its own view, following the Lamfalussy report. This outlined that the best way of providing market infrastructure most appropriate to the needs of the European marketplaces lay in allowing the forces of competition to prevail. Also, that allowing the various providers to compete for the transaction flows of national and cross-border markets would result in efficient and cost-competitive services. Is this the climate likely to allow the development of genuine user-driven solutions to the problems? Providers with large monopolistic market positions are not likely to cede their markets without a fight. Domestic markets will take some convincing that their legal, taxing and regulatory frameworks should be disbanded. So under the competition option it seems unlikely that significant changes will happen quickly.

However, solutions to the problems of administering cross-border transaction flows have been around for many, many years. These include depository receipts, nominee accounts, global custody and various trust-based initiatives.

These instruments vary from the well known, such as American and global depository receipts — ADRs and GDRs — to more arcane structures. They all, in some form, rely upon the continuing inability of different geographical markets to achieve common standards and processes and therefore seek to provide a fungible bridge between them. Either they adopt a dominant set of standards, as in the case of ADRs adopting US standards and market processes and CDIs using UK market practices, or they seek to find an acceptable compromise as 'global shares' aim to do.

COMMODITIES

Transactions in commodities involve transfers not only of ownership, but also, frequently, commitments in terms of the movement and physical delivery of the agreed consignment. In addition, successful settlement of a commodity transaction requires the buyer to formally accept the quality and physical terms of the delivery for the transaction. Unlike securities, where transfer of property involves, at worst, the receipt of a bearer certificate, and can be quickly achieved soon after transaction, settlement of commodity transactions can take place a significant time after execution. For example in the electricity market, deliveries against a forward electricity contract are delivered over a year after the transaction was executed. As the experience of Enron has shown, within that period a number of major market problems can arise to render successful delivery uncertain. Yet the electricity markets remain outside the auspices of clearing houses and settlement systems, although scheduling agents perform valuable roles in terms of identifying the route for the transfer of property between seller and buyer.

WARRANTS OF ENTITLEMENT

Physical delivery under a commodity futures contract is not, as is often amusingly claimed, a large wagon arriving at the buyer's front door with several tonnes of grain or metal on board, but rather takes place through the allocation by the clearing house of a bearer document of title -- a warrant of entitlement. This document gives the holder legal claim to a quantity of the physical commodity held by a warehouse within the network of the futures exchange's delivery locations. Invariably, the quality of the commodity will be of an acceptable commercial standard, which could be sold efficiently and immediately in the open market place. All the document holder must do is arrange for collection and pay for storage since the time of transfer of title.

Typically, as these warrants of entitlement are allocated to open buyers in the market, they are immediately handed on, via a sale, to other open buyers, or are actually used as strategic supplies for commercial operations. The point is that these warrants performance on the exchange as'securitised' quantities of the physical commodity, much in the way a banknote was, in the past, securitised gold. The advantages of a warrant are that is it easier to handle for the purposes of satisfying transactions, whilst the variable factors which govern its value are standardised. The warrants are supported by formal dispute resolution machinery and, ultimately, effective redress against the deliverer and/or store-keeper.

So providing the means for warrants to be transferred between counterparties in exchange for good payment removes the majority of the traditional process and quality risks of commodity transactions on futures exchanges. If the warrants were then to be made available in electronic form, via computer records, the performance of commodity transactions would move to new levels of security and efficiency.

CONTRACTS

Within the context of clearing and settlement, contracts include derivatives -- futures and options, but also swaps and contracts for differences. Transactions in contracts are now mainly confined to agreements between counterparties to exchange cash-flows relating to defined and stipulated events. No transfer of title of the underlying asset takes place.

Settlement of contracts therefore amounts to accurate valuation techniques of the counterparties' contracts, an assessment of the balance of payments and a single cash transfer.

REGISTRATION

Share registration is a securities service that is often overlooked. In a registered as opposed to bearer market, providing shares are efficiently deregistered from a seller's name and registered into the buyer's name, and the various entitlements from share ownership flow to investors, little thought is given to the function of the registrar.

However, as pressure builds to smooth the movement of securities across markets and jurisdictions, so more focus may come to bear on how registers of members can help cross-border trading. A company is required by law to hold a list of its registered shareholders. Commonly, this is delegated either to external specialist companies, such as registrars or stock transfer agents, or to the market infrastructure itself. The UK currently occupies a middle ground with a well-developed industry of share registrars but where the legal record of holders of dematerialised shares is in the computers of Crest, the UK CSD.

Transactions in registered shares are literally the transfer of title to those shares from a seller to a buyer. This can be achieved by altering the holding of the seller on the register and increasing the holding of the buyer. Obviously, these can simply be two adjustments to a computer record, irrespective of the impact of those transactions in the marketplace. This computer record then drives all dividend entitlements, eligible voting and participation in new issues and other corporate actions. The computer record can record foreign names and addresses, apply conditions on incoming transfers and can interface with similar computer records held in other countries and jurisdictions. In fact, arrangements can be made so that a particular transfer of title can automatically remove stock from a register in one country and automatically increase the holdings in another. So, in this case, where is the difficulty in moving stock around the world, from one market to another?

DEPOSITORIES

Whether they performance as the settlement system of one country, or the custodian for a settlement system in another, depositories basically maintain records of holders in securities. These records, again, drive the various investor services and entitlements. Often the only difference between these records and those of the registrar is the fact that the registrar has responsibility to the issuing company, whilst the depository owes its duty to investors.

CUSTODY

Custodians hold records of the securities held by their investor customers to ensure that they are correctly represented to the issuing company in terms of their entitlements. Custodian and depository records are often reconciled to the records of the registrar.

RECORD-KEEPING

Within most modern markets a network of records exists which, if taken together, could track electronically every holding of investors, including those in certificate form, every securities transaction and every movement in title across every market.

Even those markets that remain in bearer format can either trace ownership through the participant records of closed systems, such as Euroclear and Clearstream, where the global notes themselves performance as registers as they record daily the respective collective holding of the participants of each settlement system. Outside these organisations, the trend has been for the Euromarket retail investors to hold their investments through custodian banks, and therefore, on record.

THE FUTURE

It should not be beyond the imagination of the markets collectively to spot the opportunity in linking these record-keeping organisations with the objective of developing improved transfer capabilities from one market to another and across borders. This would be accompanied by increased levels of service efficiency experienced by investors, for example in receiving entitlements, and increased efficiency of capital raisings through rights and secondary offerings. This potential was demonstrated most impressively by the British Telecom rights issue in 2001 which was the first electronic rights issue and, at GBP5.9bn, one of the biggest ever.

The linking of registers in this way is fundamental to the recent Global Registered Shares product that has been developed principally for linking European markets with American markets. At the time of writing, GRS programmes have been established for the US listings of Deutsche Bank, UBS, Daimler Chrysler and Celanese. As GRSs compete with ADRs, their elder brethren, they are faced with the challenge of gaining acceptance in the broker marketplace, and also overcoming the critical reaction that new products often meet in securities markets. The howls of fury over the competitive potential of GRSs will be nothing compared to the likely reception from the securities markets over a new potential development that is already on the drawing board. Termed Digital Bearer Securities, the concept draws heavily from the technology behind 'digital cash', where payments can be beamed from one 'electronic wallet' to another, without any intermediation.

The recipient of digital cash receives spendable value from the sender and relies on the technology to avoid fraud, theft or erroneous payment. Digital Bearer Securities use the same approach to the transfer of title — beaming from one 'electronic portfolio' to another. In fact delivery verses payment would be achieved through simultaneous exchange of 'beamed' title to the securities in question, for the agreed consideration in electronic cash. Once the two 'beamed events' have taken place no further communication is necessary between buyer and seller. No confirmation is necessary because, as with more traditional bearer securities such as Eurobonds, title to the securities passes at exchange.

The buyer is henceforth responsible for care and security of his electronic securities, stored neatly in his electronic portfolio, and for future allocation of 'shapes' to investor customers. The transaction remains invisible to the issuing company until either they need to undertake a roll-call of investors, or there is a dividend distribution, AGM or other routine event in the corporate calendar. At this point, investors can either identify themselves to the 'registrar or paying agent' via the web, or directly to the company.

There is much thought yet to be given to bring this concept to full industrial strength, which is being done. But the idea has merit in offering a vastly different approach to the business of trading and settling securities. Whether the development of post-transaction administration can be left to the market to prosecute sufficiently quickly and even-handedly, or whether external influences from regulators, legislators and politicians are required, is not strictly for debate. What is for debate is in which direction this development should go and how far and fast.

2

Fundamental Analysis

ECONOMIC ANALYSIS

Economic analysis is a process whereby strengths and weaknesses of an economy are analysed. Economic analysis is important in order to understand exact condition of an economy. It can cover a number of important economic issues that keep cropping up within a particular economy, which is being analysed.

MACROECONOMICS AND ECONOMIC ANALYSIS

Macroeconomic issues are important aspects of economic analysis process. However, economic analysis can also be done at a microeconomic level. Macroeconomic analysis helps in understanding fundamentals of an economy. Since such a form of analysis operates on a wide scale, it helps one to analyse strengths and weaknesses of particular economies.

Macroeconomic analysis takes into account growth achieved by a particular economy or rather a particular sector of that economy. It tries to find out reasons behind a particular economic phenomena like growth or reversal of economy.

INFLATION AND ECONOMIC ANALYSIS

Many countries of world are plagued by a rising rate of inflation. Economic analysis helps in providing an explanation of why inflation has taken place. It also suggests ways in which rate of inflation could be brought down, so that economic development could continue.

ECONOMIC ANALYSIS AND GOVERNMENTAL POLICIES

Governmental policies and plans, pertaining to economy, have always been an important part of economic analysis. Since policies and plans adopted by a particular government is responsible for shaping an economy, they are always closely scrutinized by various processes of economic analysis.

ECONOMIC ANALYSIS AND COMPARISON OF ECONOMIC POLICIES

It is a good way to analyse an economy by comparing its policies with those followed by other economies. This is all more applicable in case of economies that are of similar types, for example developing economies.

ECONOMIC FORECAST

Economic forecast is primarily a prediction of future condition of an economy. Economy forecast is normally made by economists and other people connected to economic machinery. They make these predictions after a detailed analysis of economic conditions.

IMPORTANCE OF ECONOMIC FORECAST

Economic forecast is an important aspect of present day financial world as it helps people, connected with economic affairs, get a fair idea of how things may be in future. Forecast economy helps people in charge of economic affairs to take decisions that may help avert a bleak future.

ECONOMIC FORECAST 2008

In financial year 2008, entire economic world has faced a major financial catastrophe of sorts. This chain started with United States of America where major financial organizations like Lehman Brothers went out of business as a result of economic slowdown. This in turn has affected those economies that were, in one way or another, business partners of USA. Examples of such countries include Singapore and India.

Economic forecasts made for each and every country in

world have one thing in common - slowdown. It has been forecast that in financial year 2009 and 2010 every nation would face economic slowdown but of varying degrees. These predictions are made on basis of relative economic strength of various countries. Australia and United Kingdom are in better economic condition compared to countries like India and Singapore. These two countries have necessary financial resources in order to deal with financial crises. An interesting fact in this case is that not all countries have been affected at same time and this has placed certain nations in comparatively better economic position. They are able to prepare themselves for inevitable after effects of global financial crisis. It would be important to note that often politicians make economic forecasts. Much of this could be attributed to a fact that these people are closely connected to economy of their country in some capacity or other, and are able to understand an economy as would a specialist do. This places them in a perfect position to make such predictions and, more often than not.

ECONOMIC BASE ANALYSIS

Economic base analysis was developed by Robert Murray Haig in his work on the Regional Plan of New York in 1928. Briefly, activities in an area divide into two categories - basic and non-basic. Basic industries are those exporting from the region; non-basic industries support basic industries. Because of data problems, it is not practical to study industry output and trade flows to and from a region. As an alternative, basic and non-basic concepts are operationalized using employment data. The basic industries of the region are identified by comparing employment in the region to national norms. If the national norm for employment in, e.g. Egyptian woodwind manufacturing is five per cent and the region's employment is eight per cent, then three per cent of the region's woodwind employment is basic. Once basic employment is identified, the outlook for basic employment is investigated sector by sector and projections made sector by sector. In turn, this permits the projection of total employment in the region. Typically the basic/non-basic employment ratio is about 1:1. Extending by manipulation of data and comparisons, conjectures may be made about population and income. This is a rough, serviceable procedure and it continues in use today. It has the advantage of being readily operationalized, fiddled with, and understandable.

The formula for computing location quotients can be written as:

$$LQ = \frac{e_i / e}{E_i / E}$$

Where:

e_i = Local employment in industry i
e = Total local employment
E_i = Reference area employment in industry i
E = Total reference area employment

It is assumed that the base year is identical in all of the variables.

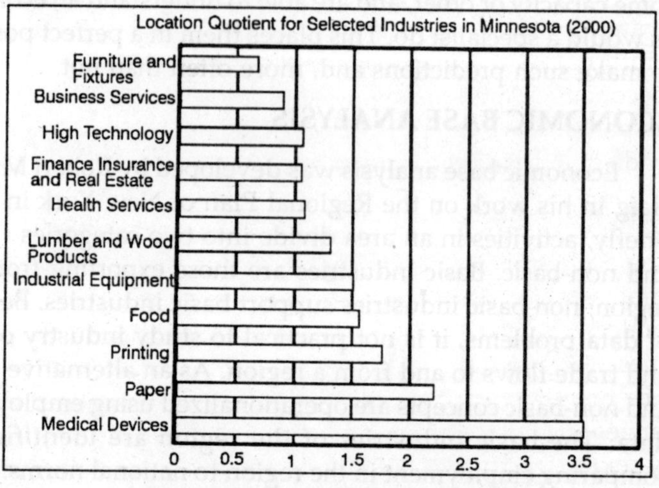

Fig. Location Quotient for Selected Industries in Minnesota

The location quotients uses data from Compare Minnesota: Profiles of Minnesota's Economy and Population, 2002-2003. It uses the term location quotient, a number derived by comparing per cent employment in a place with per cent employment nationwide. Minnesota has about the same percentage of high technology employment as does the nation.

It has more medical devices employment than the national average. Economic base ideas are easy to understand as are measures made of employment. For instance, it's common knowledge that the economy of Seattle, Washington is tied to aircraft manufacturing, Detroit, Michigan to automobiles, and Silicon Valley to high tech manufacturing. When the newspapers discuss the closing of military bases, they will some thing like:"5,000 jobs at the base will be lost. That's going to hit the economy hard because it means a loss of 10,000 jobs in the community."

To forecast, what's mainly done is to compare the region with the nation and national trends. If the economic base of a region is in industries that are declining nationwide, then we have a problem. If our economic base is concentrated in sectors that are growing, then we are in good shape. Methodologically, economic base analysis views the region as if it were a small nation and uses notions of relative and comparative advantage from international trade theory. In a sense the activity is macroeconomics"written small" The analysis usually takes US growth patterns as a given. The fates of regions are determined by trends in the national economy.

Critique of the Economic Base Concept

The economic base concept emerged in the 1920s, when economics focused on different industrial strengths and economic techniques were not as nuanced. The exporting activities were manufacturing and trade activities and they could be readily identified in the data series. One could think of changes in those activities as causing growth or decline. Today, export activities purchase many services, and the comparative advantage of an area may well lie in the services it produces. Peter Drucker imagines a world dominated by trade in ideas and designs. There is little merchandise trade because technology permits small-scale manufacturing. Such a world would change our ideas of what's basic. The concept is that of a trading region. But in practice economic base concepts are often applied to areas that fit the concept. The Minnesota study, cited before, compared the Minnesota to the

US. One can speak of the economic base of Saint Paul, Minneapolis, or Duluth, but to go on and compare such areas using economic base techniques isn't very meaningful.

Forecasting is a precursor to actions, and there is no explicit way to get from the economic base to the kinds of actions most communities are interested in. That is, the economic base study doesn't what to do. Leaders say they want desirable economic activities, such as high tech ones. Indeed, we have seen studies of the transport needs of high tech industries, studies done prior to investments to attract such industries. Again, the economic base study doesn't say what to do. Even if we could make what-to-do linkages, the calculus of"desirable" is not simple.

We suppose that high pay, little environmental insult, upward mobility for workers, and stability or growth are among the attributes desired of new activities. The table gives information on the pay attribute. Clearly, that attribute has to be traded off against other attributes.

Table. Average Weekly Earnings of Production or Non-supervisory Workers on Private Non-farm Payrolls by Major Industry, in Current Dollars

Industry	Average Weekly Earnings
Mining:	774.58
Construction:	721.58
Manufacturing:	629.43
Transportation and public utilities:	670.32
Wholesale trade:	627.13
Retail trade:	296.80
Finance, insurance, and real estate:	611.90
Services:	507.43
Total private:	511.39

SHIFT-SHARE ANALYSIS

Shift/share analysis is a technique sometimes used for retrospectively decomposing changes, usually in employment, in a set of urban areas or regions. Regional scientists widely use the technique to examine the sources of employment growth or decline. We have a study area in which employment and population are growing Total employment in our area is e, and that in the ith activity is ei. We have a larger frame reference area, usually the nation, where total employment is E, and that in the ith activity is Ei.

The shift-share model says that growth in the study area's ith activity employment is a function of:

- The study area's share of national growth.
- The mix change in activities.
- And the shift change of activities towards the study area.

This says that change in employment in the study area's ith activity from time t to time t+n can be measured:

$$e_i^{t+n} - e_i^t = \text{share change} + \text{mix change} + \text{shift change}$$

or,

$$e_i^{t+n} - e_i^t = e_i^t\left[\frac{E^{t+n}}{E^t} - 1\right] + e_i^t\left[\frac{E_i^{t+n}}{E_i^t} - \frac{E^{t+n}}{E^t}\right] + e_i^t\left[\frac{e_i^{t+n}}{e_i^t} - \frac{E_i^{t+n}}{E_i^t}\right]$$

As this brief discussion suggests, shift-share analysis may be viewed as adding explicit considerations to economic base analysis. Economic base analysis asks how an area shares in national growth. Shift-share goes on to look at the changing mix of activities and at whether activities are shifting towards or away from the study area.

INPUT-OUTPUT MODEL

In economics, an input-output model uses a matrix representation of a nation's economy to predict the effect of changes in one industry on others and by consumers, government, and foreign suppliers on the economy. Wassily Leontief is credited with the development of this analysis. Francois Quesnay developed a cruder version of this technique called Tableau économique. Leontief won the Nobel Memorial Prize in Economic Sciences for his development of this model. And, in essence, Léon Walras's work Elements of Pure Economics on general equilibrium theory is both a forerunner and generalization of Leontief's seminal concept.

Leontief's contribution was that he was able to simplify Walras's piece so that it could be implemented empirically. The International Input-Output Association is dedicated to advance knowledge in the field input-output study, which includes"improvements in basic data, theoretical insights and modelling, and applications, both traditional and novel, of input-output techniques." Input-output depicts inter-industry relations of an economy.

It shows how the output of one industry is an input to each other industry. Leontief put forward the display of this information in the form of a matrix. A given input is typically enumerated in the column of an industry and its outputs are enumerated in its corresponding row. This format, therefore, shows how dependent each industry is on all others in the economy both as customer of their outputs and as supplier of their inputs.

Each column of the input-output matrix reports the monetary value of an industry's inputs and each row represents the value of an industry's outputs. Suppose there are three industries. Column 1 reports the value of inputs to Industry 1 from Industries 1, 2, and 3. Columns 2 and 3 do the same for those industries. Row 1 reports the value of outputs from Industry 1 to Industries 1, 2, and 3. Rows 2 and 3 do the same for the other industries.

While most uses of the input-output analysis focuses on the matrix set of interindustry exchanges, the actual focus of the analysis from the perspective of most national statistical agencies is the benchmarking of gross domestic product. Input-output tables therefore are an instrumental part of national accounts.

The core input-output table reports only intermediate goods and services that are exchanged among industries. But an array of row vectors, typically aligned this matrix, record non-industrial inputs by industry like payments for labour; indirect business taxes; dividends, interest, and rents; capital consumption allowances; other property-type income; and purchases from foreign suppliers. At a national level, although excluding the imports, when summed this is called"gross product originating" or"gross domestic product by industry." Another array of column vectors is called"final demand" or"gross product product consumed." This displays columns of spending by households, governments, changes in industry stocks, and industries on investment, as well as net exports. In any case, by employing the results of an economic census which asks for the sales, payrolls, and material/equipment/service input of each establishment, statistical agencies back into estimates of industry-level profits and investments using the input-output matrix as a sort of double-accounting framework.

The mathematics of input-output economics is straightforward, but the data requirements are enormous because the expenditures and revenues of each branch of economic activity has to be represented. As a result, not all countries collect the required data and data quality varies, even though a set of standards for the data's collection has been set out by the United Nations through its System of National Accounts: the replacement for the current 1993 SNA standard is pending. Because the data collection and preparation process for the input-output accounts is necessarily labour and computer intensive, input-output tables are often published long after the year data was collected--typically as much as 5-7 years after. Moreover, the economic"snapshot" the benchmark version of the tables provide of the economy's cross-section are taken only once every few years, at best. Although many developed countries estimate input-output accounts annually and with much greater recency.

Usefulness

In addition to studying the structure of national economies, input-output economics has been used to study regional economies within a nation, and as a tool for national and regional economic planning. Indeed a main use of input-output analysis is for measuring the economic impacts of events as well as public investments or programmes as shown by IMPLAN and RIMS-II. But it is also used to identify economically related industry clusters and also so-called"key" or"target" industries--industries that are most likely to enhance the internal coherence of a specified economy. By linking industrial output to satellite accounts articulating energy use, effluent production, space needs, and so on, input-output analysts have extended the approaches application to a wide variety of uses.

Key Ideas

Leontief's text remains one of the best expositions of input-output analysis. Nonetheless, two books--a rather fundamental one by William Miernyk and another by Ronald E. Miller and Peter D. Blair--probably have greater international currency. The latter is presently being rewritten and re-released, this time by Cambridge University Press.

Consider the production of the ith sector.

We may isolate:

- The quantity of that production that goes to final demand, c_i,
- To total output, x_i, and
- Flows x_{ij} from that industry to other industries. We may write a transactions tableau

Table. Transactions in a Three Sector Economy

Economic Activities	Inputs to Agriculture	Inputs to Manufacturing	Inputs to Transport	Final Demand	Total Output
Agriculture	5	15	2	68	90
Manufacturing	10	20	10	40	80
Transportation	10	15	5	0	30
Labor	25	30	5	0	60

or,

$$x_{11} + x_{12} + x_{13} + c_1 = x_1$$
$$x_{21} + x_{22} + x_{23} + c_2 = x_2$$
$$x_{31} + x_{32} + x_{33} + c_3 = x_3$$
$$x_{41} + x_{42} + x_{43} + c_4 = x_4$$

Note that in the example given we have no input flows from the industries to'Labour'. We know very little about production functions because all we have are numbers representing transactions in a particular instance:

$$\begin{aligned} x_1 &= f(x_{11}, x_{12}, x_{13}, x_{14}) \\ x_2 &= g(x_{21}, x_{22} x_{23} x_{24}) \\ \vdots &= \vdots \end{aligned}$$

The neoclassical production function is an explicit function

$$Q = f(K,L),$$

where Q = Quantity, K = Capital, L = Labour, and the partial derivatives

$$(\partial Q / \partial K = f_k > 0; \partial Q / \partial L = f_L > 0)$$

are the demand schedules for input factors. Leontief, the innovator of input-output analysis, uses a special production function which depends linearly on the total output variables xi. Using Leontief coefficients aij, we may manipulate our transactions information into what is known as an input-output table:

$$\begin{aligned} x_{11} &= a_{11} x_1 \\ x_{12} &= a_{12} x_2 \\ x_{13} &= a_{13} x_3 \\ x_{14} &= a_{14} x_4 \\ \vdots &= \vdots \end{aligned}$$

or,

$$x_{ij} = a_{ij} x_j$$

Now,

$$\begin{aligned} a_{11}x_1 + a_{12}x_2 + a_{13}x_3 + a_{14}x_4 + c_1 &= x_1 \\ \vdots &= \vdots \\ a_{41}x_1 + a_{42}x_2 + a_{43}x_3 + a_{44}x_4 + c_4 &= x_4 \end{aligned}$$

gives,

$$\begin{aligned} x_1 - a_{11}x_1 - a_{12}x_2 - a_{13}x_3 - a_{14}x_4 &= c_1 \\ \vdots &= \vdots \\ x_4 - a_{41}x_1 - a_{42}x_2 - a_{43}x_3 - a_{44}x_4 &= c_4 \end{aligned}$$

Rewriting finally yields,

$$\begin{aligned} (1 - a_{11})x_1 - a_{12}x_2 - a_{13}x_3 - a_{14}x_4 &= c_1 \\ \vdots &= \vdots \\ -a_{41}x_1 - a_{42}x_2 - a_{43}x_3 + (1 - a_{44})x_4 &= c_4 \end{aligned}$$

Introducing matrix notation, we can look how a solution may be obtained.

Let,

$$x=\begin{pmatrix}x_1\\ \vdots\\ x_4\end{pmatrix};c=\begin{pmatrix}c_1\\ \vdots\\ c_4\end{pmatrix};$$

$$I=\begin{pmatrix}1&0&0&0\\0&1&0&0\\0&0&1&0\\0&0&0&1\end{pmatrix};A=\begin{pmatrix}a_{11}&\cdots&a_{14}\\ \vdots&\ddots&\vdots\\ a_{41}&\vdots&a_{42}\end{pmatrix};$$

denote the total output vector, the final demand vector, the unit matrix and the input-output matrix, respectively.

Then:

$$\begin{aligned}Ax+c &= x\\ (I-A)x &= c\\ x &= (I-A)^{-1}c\end{aligned}$$

provided (I – A) is invertible. There are many interesting aspects of the Leontief system, and there is an extensive literature. There is the Hawkins-Simon Condition on producibility. There has been interest in disaggregation to clustered inter-industry flows, and the study of constellations of industries. A great deal of empirical work has been done to identify coefficients, and data have been published for the national economy as well as for regions.

This has been a healthy, exciting area for work by economists because the Leontief system can be extended to a model of general equilibrium; it offers a method of decomposing work done at a macro level. Transportation is implicit in the notion of inter-industry flows. It is explicitly recognized when transportation is identified as an industry - how much is purchased from transportation in order to produce. But this is not very satisfactory because transportation requirements differ, depending on industry locations and capacity constraints on regional production. Also, the receiver of goods generally pays freight cost, and often transportation data are lost because transportation costs are treated as part of the cost of the goods.

Walter Isard and his student, Leon Moses, were quick to see the spatial economy and transportation implications of input-output, and began work in this area in the 1950s developing a concept of interregional input-output. Take a one region versus the world case. We wish to know something about interregional commodity flows, so introduce a column into the table headed"exports" and we introduce an"import" row.

Table. Adding Export And Import Transactions

Economic Activities	1	2	...	...	Z	Exports	Final Demand	Total Outputs
1								
2								
...								
...								
Z								
Imports								

A more satisfactory way to proceed would be to tie regions together at the industry level. That is, we could identify both intra-region inter-industry transactions and inter-region inter-industry transactions. The problem here is that the table grows quickly. Input-output is conceptually simple. Its extension to a model of equilibrium in the national economy is also relatively simple and attractive but requires great skill and high-quality data.

One who wishes to do work with input-output systems must deal skillfully with industry classification, data estimation, and inverting very large, ill-conditioned matrices. Moreover, changes in relative prices are not readily handled by this modeling approach alone. Of course, input-output accounts are part and parcel to a more flexible form of modeling, Computable general equilibrium models. Two additional difficulties are of interest in transportation work. There is the question of substituting one input for another, and there is the question about the stability of coefficients as production increases or decreases. These are intertwined questions. They have to do with the nature of regional production functions.

Forecasting And/or Analysis Using Input-Output

Table. Interregional Transactions

Economic Activities	Ag	North Mfg	...	...	Ag	East Mfg	...	...	Ag	West Mfg	...	...	Exports	Total Outputs
North Mfg														
...														
...														
Ag														
East Mfg														
...														
...														
Ag														
West Mfg														
...														
...														

Table. Input-Output Model for Hypothetical Economy Total Requirements from Regional Industries Per Dollar of Output Delivered to Final Demand

Purchasing Industry	Agriculture	Transport	Manufacturer	Services
Selling Industry				
Agriculture	1.14	0.22	0.13	0.12
Transportation	0.19	1.10	0.16	0.07
Manufacturing	0.16	0.16	1.16	0.06
Services	0.08	0.05	0.08	1.09
Total	1.57	1.53	1.53	1.34

Input-output Analysis Versus Consistency Analysis

Despite the clear ability of the input-output model to depict and analyse the dependence of one industry or sector on another, Leontief and others never managed to introduce the full spectrum of dependency relations in a market economy. In 2003, Mohammad Gani, a pupil of Leontief, introduced Consistency'Foundations of Economic Science' which formally looks exactly like the input-output table but explores the dependency relations in terms of payments and intermediation relations. Consistency analysis explores the consistency of plans of buyers and sellers by decomposing the input-output table into four matrices, each for a different kind of means of payment. It integrates micro and macroeconomics in one model and deals with money in an ideology-free manner.

It deals with the flow of funds via the movement of goods. In a technical sense, input-output analysis can be seen as a special case of consistency analysis without money and without entrepreneurship and transaction cost.

GRINOLD AND KRONER MODEL

The Grinold and Kroner Model is used to calculate expected returns for a stock, stock index or the market as whole. It is a part of a larger framework for making forecasts about market expectations.

The model states that:

Expected Returns= Div1/P0 + i + g – Δ S + Δ (P/E)

Div1 = dividend in next period

P0 = current price

i= expected inflation rate

g= real growth rate in earnings

Δ S= changes in shares outstanding

Δ (P/E)= changes in P/E ratio.

STOCK INVESTMENT DECISION-MAKING

Stock investment is a savings game. For conducting every game you need to know and follow prescribed rules and regulations. Any violation means, you are penalized. The penalty is in proportion to the severity of violations of the rules.

Just as navigation is easy through the calm waters of the sea, apart of the extensive knowledge you possess about investing in shares, the prime condition is that you need to deal with the issues related to buying and selling with a calm mind. Let it be perfectly understood that your emotions have no role to play when you deal with the volatility of the exchange. Even in the normal market, they have no role. When you are not in the proper shape of mind, you make the trade decision at the worst possible moments. Fear and greed combined with emotions is a bad scenario that an investor can create for himself.

Some of the points for consideration before trading in shares are:

- To start with, do not go with the killer instinct. Look out for modest returns.
- Adopt the time-honoured tactic of long term returns. Invest the same amount of money in regular intervals and buy in small lots. Naturally you will buy more shares when the prices are low and fewer when they are high.
- Avail the services of a broker. Before engaging him, meet him face to face at his office. Have a preliminary discussion about your financial objectives. Get a copy of the firm's commission schedule. Determine what type of services you need from the broker. You may need recommendations, research reports and investment advice.
- Once you zero in on engaging a particular broker, give the correct information about your objectives, personal finances, net worth and your previous investment experience. This will enable the broker to take appropriate decisions for you.
- Now you come to the pivotal point. Who will control decision-making for your trades? You need to specifically give in writing that the broker is the authority to take decisions, if that arrangement suits you. Once that authority is vested with the broker, he will take decisions without consulting you. Those decisions will be the best for you under the prevailing conditions. Whether you suffer losses or gain profits in a particular trade is not the concern of the broker. The discretion, therefore, needs o be given after very careful consideration when you are fully convinced about the capability of the broker and past records of success.
- Never invest in a share about which you have no knowledge and avoid guesswork. Know the basic financial terminologies and the fundamentals of investing.

- You do invest for profits, not to lose money. At the same time, you need to know that share investments are always associated with some degree of risks.
- The past performance of a company is no guarantee for future success. Do not make hurried investment decisions on the strength of intensity of the salesperson's appeal. He is doing his business, you please do yours!
- Be wary about the catchy phrases often used in share trading, like" inside information""confidential leak"" an acquisition is in the offing","a dynamic product," etc. Your money can never double in six months as promised by many!
- Try your best to limit the transactions. The more the transactions, the more commission you will pay.
- Do not concentrate on a single product. Let your portfolio take care of different segments of the industry.
- Broadly speaking, there are four types of investment strategies: Fundamental approach, Psychological approach, Academic approach and Eclectic approach. Each approach requires detailed study. Keep your knowledge up-to-date about these strategies and you may have to change your strategies depending upon the conditions and volatility in the market.

You will evolve as a good investor gradually through your experience and theory knowledge. Both are important. Never lose concentration and deviate from the tracks, while investing. Years of hard labour and profit can be nullified with one wrong trade.

FORECASTING TECHNIQUES

Forecasting is the process of making statements about events whose actual outcomes have not yet been observed. A commonplace example might be estimation of the expected value for some variable of interest at some specified future date. Prediction is a similar, but more general term. Both might refer to formal statistical methods employing time series, cross-sectional or longitudinal data, or alternatively to less formal judgemental methods. Usage can differ between areas of application: for example in hydrology, the terms"forecast" and"forecasting" are sometimes reserved for estimates of values at certain specific future times, while the term"prediction" is used for more general estimates, such as the number of times floods will occur over a long period. Risk and uncertainty are central to forecasting and prediction; it is generally considered good practice to indicate the degree of uncertainty attaching to forecasts.

The process of climate change and increasing energy prices has led to the usage of Egain Forecasting of buildings. The method uses Forecasting to reduce the energy needed to heat the building, thus reducing the emission of greenhouse gases. Forecasting is used in the practice of Customer Demand Planning in every day business forecasting for manufacturing companies. The discipline of demand planning, also sometimes referred to as supply chain forecasting, embraces both statistical forecasting and a consensus process.

An important, albeit often ignored aspect of forecasting, is the relationship it holds with planning. Forecasting can be described as predicting what the future will look like, whereas planning predicts what the future should look like. There is no single right forecasting method to use. Selection of a method should be based on your objectives and your conditions. A good place to find a method, is by visiting a selection tree. An example of a selection tress can be found here..

CATEGORIES OF FORECASTING METHODS

Time Series Methods

Time series methods use historical data as the basis of estimating future outcomes:

- Rolling forecast is a projection into the future based on past performances, routinely updated on a regular schedule to incorporate data.
- Moving average
- weighted moving average
- Exponential smoothing
- Extrapolation

- Linear prediction
- Trend estimation
- Growth curve
- Topics

Causal/ Econometric Methods

Some forecasting methods use the assumption that it is possible to identify the underlying factors that might influence the variable that is being forecast. For example, sales of umbrellas might be associated with weather conditions.

If the causes are understood, projections of the influencing variables can be made and used in the forecast:

- Regression analysis using linear regression or non-linear regression
- Autoregressive moving average
- Autoregressive integrated moving average e.g. Box-Jenkins
- Econometrics

Judgmental Methods

Judgmental forecasting methods incorporate intuitive judgements, opinions and subjective probability estimates.

- Composite forecasts
- Surveys
- Delphi method
- Scenario building
- Technology forecasting
- Forecast by analogy

Artificial Intelligence Methods

- Artificial neural networks
- Support vector machines

Other Methods

- Simulation
- Prediction market
- Probabilistic forecasting and Ensemble forecasting
- Reference class forecasting

FORECASTING ACCURACY

The forecast error is the difference between the actual value and the forecast value for the corresponding period.

$$E_t = Y_t - F_t$$

where E is the forecast error at period t, Y is the actual value at period t, and F is the forecast for period t.

Measures of aggregate error:

- Mean Absolute Error (MAE),

$$MAE = \frac{\sum_{t=1}^{N} |E_t|}{N}$$

- Mean Absolute Percentage Error (MAPE),

$$MAPE = \frac{\sum_{t=1}^{N} \left|\frac{E_t}{Y_t}\right|}{N}$$

- Per cent Mean Absolute Deviation (PMAD),

$$MAPE = \frac{\sum_{t=1}^{N} |E_t|}{\sum_{t=1}^{N} |Y_t|}$$

- Mean squared error (MSE),

$$MSE = \frac{\sum_{t=1}^{N} E_t^2}{N}$$

- Root Mean squared error (RMSE),

$$RMSE = \sqrt{\frac{\sum_{t=1}^{N} E_t^2}{N}}$$

- Forecast skill (SS),

$$SS = 1 - \frac{MSE_{forecast}}{MSE_{ref}}$$

Business forecasters and practitioners sometimes use different terminology in the industry. They refer to the PMAD as the MAPE, although they compute this volume weighted MAPE.

APPLICATIONS OF FORECASTING

Forecasting has application in many situations:

- *Supply chain management*: Forecasting can be used in

Supply Chain Management to make sure that the right product is at the right place at the right time. Accurate forecasting will help retailers reduce excess inventory and therefore increase profit margin. Accurate forecasting will also help them meet consumer demand.

- Weather forecasting, Flood forecasting and Meteorology
- Transport planning and Transportation forecasting
- Economic forecasting
- Egain Forecasting
- Technology forecasting
- Earthquake prediction
- Land use forecasting
- Product forecasting
- Player and team performance in sports
- Telecommunications forecasting
- Political Forecasting
- Sales Forecasting

INDUSTRY LIFECYCLE

Like other living creatures, industry also has its circle of life. The industry lifecycle imitates the human lifecycle. The stages of industry lifecycle include fragmentation, shake-out, maturity and decline.

FRAGMENTATION STAGE

Fragmentation is the first stage of the new industry. This is the stage when the new industry develops the business. At this stage, the new industry normally arises when an entrepreneur overcomes the twin problems of innovation and invention, and works out how to bring the new products or services into the market. For example, air travel services of major airlines in Europe were sold to the target market at a high price. Therefore, the majority of airlines' customers in Europe were those people with high incomes who could afford premium prices for faster travel.

In 1985, Ryanair made a huge change in the European

airline industry. Ryanair was the first airline to engage low-cost airlines in Europe. At that time, Ryanair's services were perceived as the innovation of the European airline industry. Ryanair tickets are half the price of British Airways. Some of its sales promotions were as low as £0.01. This made people think that air travel was not just made for the rich, but everybody.

Ryanair overcarne the twin problems of innovation and invention in the airline industry by inventing air travel services that could serve passengers with tight budgets and those who just wanted to reach their destination without breaking their bank savings. Ryanair achieved this goal by eliminating unnecessary services offered by traditional airlines. It does not offer free meals, uses paper-free air tickets, gets rid of mile collecting plan, utilises secondary airports, and offers frequent flights. These techniques help Ryanair save time and costs spent in airline business operation.

SHAKE-OUT

Shake-out is the second stage of the industry lifecycle. It is the stage at which a new industry emerges. During the shake-out stage, competitors start to realise business opportunities in the emerging industry. The value of the industry also quickly rises.

For example, many people die and suffer because of cigarettes every year. Thus, the UK government decided to launch a campaign to encourage people to quit smoking. Nicorette, one of the leading companies is producing several nicotine products to help people quit smoking. Some of its well-known products include Nicorette patches, Nicolette gums and Nicorette lozenges. Smokers began to see an easy way to quit smoking. The new industry started to attract brand recognition and brand awareness among its target market during the shake-out stage. Nicorette's products began to gain popularity among those who wanted to quit smoking or those who wanted to reduce their daily cigarette consumption.

During this period, another company realised the opportunity in this market and decided to enter it by launching nicotine product ranges, including Nic Lite gum and patches. It recently went beyond UK boarder after the UK government introduced non-smoking policy in public places, including pubs and nightclubs. This business threat created a new business opportunity in the industry for Nic Lite to launch a new nicotine-related product called Nic Time.

Nic Time is a whole new way for smokers to"get a cigarette" - an eight-ounce bottle contains a lemon-flavoured drink laced with nicotine, the same amount of nicotine as two cigarettes. Nic Lite was first available at Los Angeles airports for smokers who got uneasy on flights, but now the nicotine soft drinks are available in some convenience stores.

MATURITY

Maturity is the third stage in the industry lifecycle. Maturity is a stage at which the efficiencies of the dominant business model give these organisations competitive advantage over competition. The competition in the industry is rather aggressive because there are many competitors and product substitutes. Price, competition, and cooperation take on a complex form. Some companies may shift some of the production overseas in order to gain competitive advantage.

For example, Toyota is one of the world's leading multinational companies, selling automobiles to customers worldwide. The export and import taxes mean that its cars lose competitiveness to the local competitors, especially in the European automobile industry. As a result, Toyota decided to open a factory in the UK in order to produce cars and sell them to customers in the European market.. The haute couture fashion industry is another good example. There are many western-branded fashion labels that manufacture their products overseas by cooperating with overseas partners, or they could seek foreign suppliers who specialise in particular materials or items. For instance, Nike has factories in China and Thailand as both countries have cheap labour costs and cheap, quality materials, particularly rubber and fabric. However, their overseas partners are not allowed to sell shoes produced for Adidas and Nike. The items have to be shipped back to the US, and then will be exported to countries worldwide, including China and Thailand.

DECLINE

Decline is the final stage of the industry lifecycle. Decline is a stage during which a war of slow destruction between businesses may develop and those with heavy bureaucracies may fail. In addition, the demand in the market may be fully satisfied or suppliers may be running out. In the stage of decline, some companies may leave the industry if there is no demand for the products or services they provide, or they may develop new products or services that meet the demand in the market. In such cases, this will create a new industry. For example, at the beginning of the communication industry, pagers were used as the main communication method among people working in the same organisation, such as doctors and nurses. Then, the cutting edge of the communication industry emerged in the form of the mobile phone. The communication process of pagers could not be accomplished without telephones. To send a message to another pager, the user had to phone the call-centre staff who would type and send the message to another pager.

On the other hand, people who use mobile phones can make a phone-call and send messages to other mobiles without going through call-centre staff. In recent years, the features of mobile phones have been developing rapidly and continually. Now people can use mobiles to send multimedia messages, take pictures, check email, surf the internet, read news and listen to music. As mobile phone feature development has reached saturation, thus the new innovation of mobile phone technology has incorporated the use of computers.

The launch of personal digital assistants is a good example of the decline stage of the mobile phone industry as the features of most mobiles are similar.

PDAs are hand-held computers that were originally designed as a personal organiser but it become much more multi-faceted in recent years. PDAs are known as pocket computers or palmtop computers. They have many uses for both mobile phones and computers such as computer games, global positioning system, video recording, typewriting and wireless wide-area network.

USE OF INDUSTRY LIFECYCLE ANALYSIS

It is important for companies to understand the use of the industry lifecycle because it is a survival tool for businesses to compete in the industry effectively and successfully. The main aspects in terms of strategic issues of the industry lifecycle are described.

Competing over emerging industries:

- The game rules in industry competition can be undetermined and the resources may be constrained. Thus, it is vital for firms to identify market segments that will allow them to secure and sustain a strong position within the industry.
- The product in the industry may not be standardised so it is necessary for companies to obtain resources needed to support new product development and rapid company expansion.
- The entry barriers may be low and the potential competition may be high, thus companies must adapt to shift the mobility barriers.
- Consumers may be uncertain in terms of demand. As a result, determining the time of entry to the industry can help companies to take business opportunities before their rivals.

Competing during the transition to industry maturity:

- When competition in the industry increases, firms can have a sustainable competitive advantage that will provide a basis for competing against other companies.
- The new products and applications are harder to come by, while buyers become more sophisticated and difficult to understand in the maturity stage of the industry lifecycle. Thus, consumer research should be carried out and this could help companies in building up new product lines.
- Slower industry growth constrains capacity growth and

often leads to reduced industry profitability and some consolidation. Therefore, companies can focus greater attention on costs through strategic cost analysis.

- The change in the industry is rather dynamic, and an understanding of the industry lifecycle can help companies to monitor and tackle these changes effectively. Firms can develop organisational structures and systems that can facilitate the transition.
- Some companies may seek business opportunities overseas when the industries reach the maturity stage because during this stage, the demand in the market starts to decline.

COMPETING IN DECLINING INDUSTRIES

The characteristics of declining industries include the following:

- Declining demand for products
- Pruning of product lines
- Shrinking profit margins
- Falling research and development advertisement expenditure
- Declining number of rivals as many are forced to leave the industry

For companies to survive the dynamic environment, it is necessary for them to:

- Measure the intensity of competition
- Assess the causes of decline
- Single out a viable strategy for decline such as leadership, liquidation and harvest.

APPLIED VALUATION TECHNIQUES

Applied Valuation provides students with a working knowledge of the issues involved in the valuation of a business and its equity. Fundamental to any valuation is an understanding of the activities of the business and the reasons for undertaking the valuation. These issues are explored before the various valuation methodologies are outlined and demonstrated. The technical and practical issues involved in valuation are discussed as are the limitations of the various methodologies.

GRAHAM AND DODDS INVESTOR RATIOS

Value investing is an investment paradigm that derives from the ideas on investment and speculation that Ben Graham and David Dodd began teaching at Columbia Business School in 1928 and subsequently developed in their 1934 text Security Analysis. Although value investing has taken many forms since its inception, it generally involves buying securities whose shares appear underpriced by some form(s) of fundamental analysis.

High-profile proponents of value investing, including Berkshire Hathaway chairman Warren Buffett, have argued that the essence of value investing is buying stocks at less than their intrinsic value. The discount of the market price to the intrinsic value is what Benjamin Graham called the"margin of safety".

The intrinsic value is the discounted value of all future distributions. However, the future distributions and the appropriate discount rate can only be assumptions. For the last 25 years, Warren Buffett has taken the value investing concept even further with a focus on"finding an outstanding company at a sensible price" rather than generic companies at a bargain price.

BACKGROUND

Benjamin Graham

Value investing was established by Benjamin Graham and David Dodd, both professors at Columbia Business School and teachers of many famous investors. Graham: The Intelligent Investor, he advocated the important concept of margin of safety - first introduced in Security Analysis with David Dodd - which calls for a cautious approach to investing. In terms of picking stocks, he recommended defensive investment in stocks trading below their tangible book value as a safeguard to adverse future developments often encountered in the stock market.

Further Evolution

However, the concept of value has evolved significantly since the 1970s. Book value is most useful in industries where most assets are tangible.

Intangible assets such as patents, software, brands, or goodwill are difficult to quantify, and may not survive the break-up of a company. When an industry is going through fast technological advancements, the value of its assets is not easily estimated. Sometimes, the production power of an asset can be significantly reduced due to competitive disruptive innovation and therefore its value can suffer permanent impairment.

One good example of decreasing asset value is a personal computer. An example of where book value does not mean much is the service and retail sectors. One modern model of calculating value is the discounted cash flow model (DCF). The value of an asset is the sum of its future cash flows, discounted back to the present.

VALUE INVESTING PERFORMANCE

Performance, Value Strategies

Value investing has proven to be a successful investment strategy. There are several ways to evaluate its success. One way is to examine the performance of simple value strategies, such as buying low PE ratio stocks, low price-to-cash-flow ratio stocks, or low price-to-book ratio stocks.

Numerous academics have published studies investigating the effects of buying value stocks. These studies have consistently found that value stocks outperform growth stocks and the market as a whole.

Performance, Value Investors

Another way to examine the performance of value investing strategies is to examine the investing performance of well-known value investors. Simply examining the performance of the best known value investors would not be instructive, because investors do not become well known unless they are successful.

This introduces a selection bias. A better way to investigate the performance of a group of value investors was suggested by Warren Buffett, in his May 17, 1984 speech that was published as The Superinvestors of Graham-and-Doddsville.

In this speech, Buffett examined the performance of those investors who worked at Graham-Newman Corporation and were thus most influenced by Benjamin Graham. Buffett's is identical to that of the academic research on simple value investing strategies--value investing is, on average, successful in the long run. Warren Buffett,"You couldn't advance in a finance department in this country unless you taught that the world was flat."

WELL-KNOWN VALUE INVESTORS

Benjamin Graham is regarded by many to be the father of value investing. Along with David Dodd, he wrote Security Analysis, first published in 1934. The most lasting contribution of this book to the field of security analysis was to emphasize the quantifiable aspects of security analysis while minimizing the importance of more qualitative factors such as the quality of a company's management.

Graham later wrote The Intelligent Investor, value investing to individual investors. Aside from Buffett, many of Graham's other students, such as William J. Ruane, Irving Kahn and Charles Brandes have gone on to become successful investors in their own right. Graham's most famous student, however, is Warren Buffett, who ran successful investing partnerships before closing them in 1969 to focus on running Berkshire Hathaway. Charlie Munger joined Buffett at Berkshire Hathaway in the 1970s and has since worked as Vice Chairman of the company.

Buffett has credited Munger with encouraging him to focus on long-term sustainable growth rather than on simply the valuation of current cash flows or assets. Columbia Business School has played a significant role in shaping the principles of the Value Investor, with professors and students making their mark on history and on each other. Ben Graham, The Intelligent Investor, was Warren Buffett's bible and he referred to it as"the greatest book on investing ever written." A young Warren Buffett studied under Prof. Ben Graham, took his course and worked for his small investment firm, Graham Newman, from 1954 to 1956.

Twenty years after Ben Graham, Prof. Roger Murray arrived and taught value investing to a young student named Mario Gabelli. About a decade or so later, Prof. Bruce Greenwald arrived and produced his own protégés, including Mr. Paul Sonkin-just as Ben Graham had Mr. Buffett as a protégé, and Roger Murray had Mr. Gabelli.

Mutual Series has a well known reputation of producing top value managers and analysts in this modern era. This tradition stems from two individuals: the late great value mind Max Heine, founder of the well regarded value investment firm Mutual Shares fund in 1949 and his protégé legendary value investor Michael F. Price. Mutual Series was sold to Franklin Templeton in 1996. The disciples of Heine and Price quietly practice value investing at some of the most successful investment firms in the country.

Seth Klarman is a Mutual Series alum and the founder and president of The Baupost Group, a Boston-based private investment partnership, authored Margin of Safety, Risk Averse Investing Strategies for the Thoughtful Investor, which since has become a value investing classic. Now out of print, Margin of Safety has sold on Amazon for $1,200 and eBay for $2,000. Another famous value investor is John Templeton. He first achieved investing success by buying shares of a number of companies in the aftermath of the stock market crash of 1929. Martin J. Whitman is another well-regarded value investor. His approach is called safe-and-cheap, which was hitherto referred to as financial-integrity approach. Martin Whitman focuses on acquiring common shares of companies with extremely strong financial position at a price reflecting meaningful discount to the estimated NAV of the company concerned.

Martin Whitman believes it is ill-advised for investors to pay much attention to the trend of macro-factors not so much because they are not important as because attempts to predict their movement are almost always futile. Joel Greenblatt achieved annual returns at the hedge fund Gotham Capital of over 50% per year for 10 years from 1985 to 1995 before closing the fund and returning his investors' money. He is known for investing in special situations such as spin-offs, mergers, and divestitures. Charles de Vaulx and Jean-Marie Eveillard are well known global value managers. For a time, these two were paired up at the First Eagle Funds, compiling an enviable track record of risk-adjusted outperformance. For example, Morningstar designated them the 2001"International Stock Manager of the Year" and de Vaulx earned second place from Morningstar for 2006. Eveillard is known for his Bloomberg appearances where he insists that securities investors never use margin or leverage.

The point made is that margin should be considered the anathema of value investing, since a negative price move could prematurely force a sale. In contrast, a value investor must be able and willing to be patient for the rest of the market to recognize and correct whatever pricing issue created the momentary value. Eveillard correctly labels the use of margin or leverage as speculation, the opposite of value investing. Christopher H. Browne of Tweedy, Browne was well known for value investing.

Wall Street Journal, Tweedy, Browne was the favourite brokerage firm of Benjamin Graham during his lifetime; also, the Tweedy, Browne Value Fund and Global Value Fund have both beat market averages since their inception in 1993.

CRITICISM

An issue with buying shares in a bear market is that despite appearing undervalued at one time, prices can still drop along with the market. An issue with not buying shares in a bull market is that despite appearing overvalued at one time, prices can still rise along with the market. Another issue is the method of calculating the"intrinsic value". Two investors can analyse the same information and reach different ceases regarding the intrinsic value of the company. There is no systematic or standard way to valuate a stock.

3

Industry Analysis

INDUSTRY

Industry refers to the production of an economic good within an economy. There are four key industrial economic sectors: the primary sector, largely raw material extraction industries such as mining and farming; the secondary sector, involving refining, construction, and manufacturing; the tertiary sector, which deals with services and distribution of manufactured goods; and the quaternary sector, a relatively new type of knowledge industry focusing on technological research, design and development such as computer programming, and biochemistry. A fifth, quinary, sector has been proposed encompassing nonprofit activities. The economy is also broadly separated into public sector and private sector, with industry generally categorized as private. Industries are also any business or manufacturing.

Industry in the sense of manufacturing became a key sector of production and labour in European and North American countries during the Industrial Revolution, which upset previous mercantile and feudal economies through many successive rapid advances in technology, such as the steel and coal production. It is aided by technological advances, and has continued to develop into new types and sectors to this day. Industrial countries then assumed a capitalist economic policy. Railroads and steam-powered ships began speedily establishing links with previously unreachable world markets, enabling private companies to develop to then-unheard of size and wealth. Following the Industrial

Revolution, perhaps a third of the world's economic output is derived from manufacturing industries—more than agriculture's share.

Many developed countries and many developing/semi-developed countries depend significantly on industry. Industries, the countries they reside in, and the economies of those countries are interlinked in a complex web of interdependence.

INDUSTRIAL DEVELOPMENT

The industrial sector play a vital role in the economic development of the National Capital Territory of Delhi. As per 1991 census, about 24.63 per cent of the workers in Delhi were employed in the manufacturing sector while at the national level the percentage was only 10.

The Industries Department estimates indicate that in 1996 more than 1.26 lakh industrial units were functioning in Delhi which provided employment to more than 11 lakh persons. The estimated investment and production in these units was around Rs. 2,524 crore and Rs. 6,310 crore, respectively. The Economic Census of 1998 indicates that Delhi has 1.29 lakh industrial units employing about 14.40 lakh persons. The manufacturing sector in Delhi contributes about 7-8% to the state income.

A door-to-door industrial survey conducted in Delhi in 1988 found that an average unit employs 9 workers while 30% of the units employ 4 workers or less. The survey revealed that textiles products units constitute the largest number, followed by electrical machinery and repair services.

INDUSTRIAL GROWTH

Delhi has gone through a rapid process of urbanization. The Master Plan for Delhi rules out setting up large and heavy industries. There is, however, scope to expand small-scale industries. The availability of infrastructure, wholesale markets, trade and other commercial services have promoted the expansion of small-scale industries in Delhi.

OVERALL GROWTH

There has been tremendous growth in the number of small-scale industries in Delhi since 1951, and it has emerged as one of the biggest centres of small-scale industries in the country:

Year	Numberof Industrial units	Investment (Rs. crore)	Production (Rs. crore)	Employment (Number)
1951	8,160	18.13	35.35	95,137
1961	17,000	60.00	121.00	1,87,034
1971	26,000	190.00	388.00	2,91,585
1981	42,000	700.00	1,700.00	5,68,910
1991	85,050	1,659.00	4,462.00	7,30,951
1996	1,26,218	2,524.00	6,310.00	1,35,962

Chart 9.1

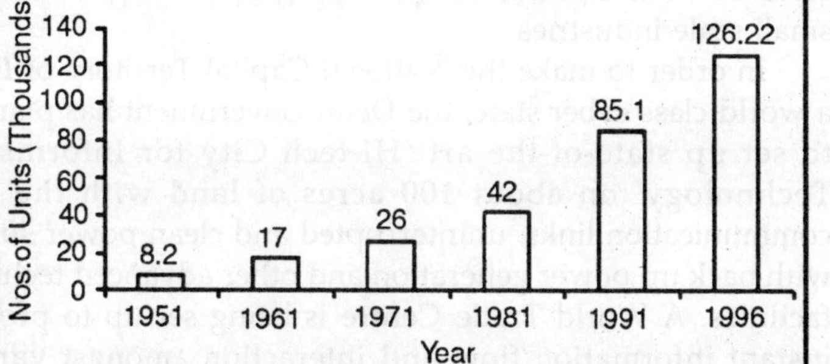

Empolyment in Industrial Sector in Delhi Since 1951

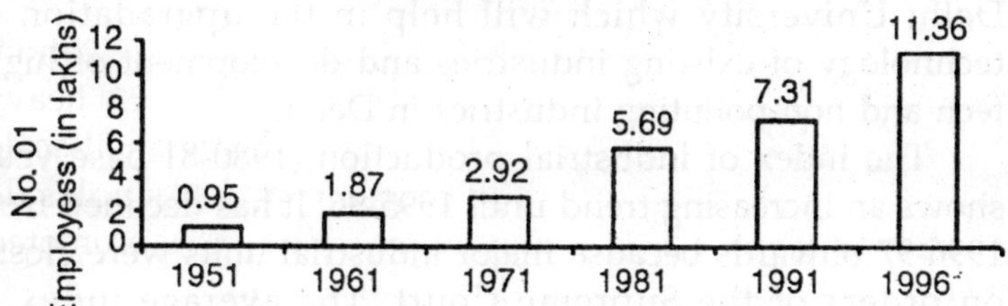

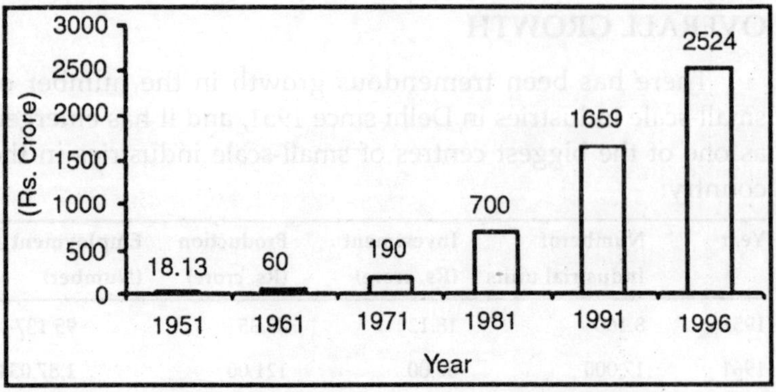

The Industries Department is running a Tool Room and Training Centre with Danish collaboration at Wazirpur Industrial Area with the objective of contributing towards the development of small scale industries through supply of trained man-power and sophisticated tooling. A Hi-Tech Vocational Training Centre has been set up with Italian collaboration at Okhla Industrial Area for providing training on CNC machines and for providing machining facilities to small scale industries.

In order to make the National Capital Territory of Delhi a world class cyber state, the Delhi Government has planned to set up state-of-the art 'Hi-tech City for Information Technology' on about 100 acres of land with the best communication links, uninterrupted and clean power supply with back up power generation and other advanced technical facilities. A World Trade Centre is being set up to provide instant information flow and interaction amongst various players in international trade and commerce. With a view to establish and develop Industry-University-R &D linkages, a "Bio-Technology Park" is being set up in collaboration with Delhi University which will help in the upgradation of technology of existing industries and development of high-tech and non-polluting industries in Delhi.

The index of industrial production (1980-81 base year) shows an increasing trend until 1995-96. It has declined from 1996-97 onwards because major industrial units were closed on orders of the Supreme Court. The average index of industrial production, which was 217.72 in 1994-95, increased to 235.90 in 1995-96 registering a growth of 8.35 per cent. However, it declined to 205.14 in 1996-97 and 196.00 in 1997-98. The index recovered to 205.68 in 1998-99. The Time series containing index of industrial production data with base year 1980-81 in Delhi:

INDEX OF INDUSTRIAL PRODUCTION IN DELHI (Base Year 1980-81)

Year	Index	% over previous year
1980-81	100.00	
1981-82	109.12	+ 9.12
1982-83	119.97	+ 9.94
1983-84	125.53	+ 4.63
1984-85	131.64	+4.87
1985-86	132.89	+ 0.95
1986-87	142.39	+ 7.15
1987-88	154.23	+ 8.31
1988-89	162.43	+5.23
1989-90	173.82	+ 7.01
1990-91	189.03	+ 8.75
1991-92	187.83	(-) 0.63
1992-93	192.57	+ 2.52
1993-94	197.91	+2.77
1994-95	217.72	+ 10.01
1995-96	235.90	+ 8.35
1996-97	205.14	(-) 13.04
1997-98	196.00	(-) 4.46
1998-99	205.68	+ 4.94

Directorate of Economics & Statistics, Government of NCT of Delhi

The average annual index of industrial production for 2000-2001 has been estimated as 103.28 while it was 94.28 during 1999-2000 with base year 1993-94 as 100. This shows 9.55% increase in IIP during current year when compared with the previous year. There is an increasing trend throughout the year as compared to the corresponding months of previous year. During October and November, 2000 general IIP has shown a minor decline of 1.54% and 1.52% respectively as compared with October and November, 1999. Maximum increase of 22.64% and 19.84% may be seen during September and July, 2000 when compared with the corresponding months of 1999.

INDUSTRY LIFE CYCLE

Life cycle models are not just a phenomenon of the life sciences. Industries experience a similar cycle of life. Just as a person is born, grows, matures, and eventually experiences decline and ultimately death, so too do industries. The stages are the same for all industries, yet industries cycle through the stages in various lengths of time. Even within the same industry, various firms may be at different life cycle stages. Strategies of a firm as well as of competitors vary depending on the stage of the life cycle. Some industries even find new uses for declining products, thus extending the life cycle. Others send products abroad in hopes of extending their life.

The growth of an industry's sales over time is used to chart the life cycle. The distinct stages of an industry life cycle are: introduction, growth, maturity, and decline. Sales typically begin slowly at the introduction phase, then take off rapidly during the growth phase. After leveling out at maturity, sales then begin a gradual decline. In contrast, profits generally continue to increase throughout the life cycle, as companies in an industry take advantage of expertise and economies of scale and scope to reduce unit costs over time.

STAGES OF THE LIFE CYCLE

In the introduction stage of the life cycle, an industry is in its infancy. Perhaps a new, unique product offering has been developed and patented, thus beginning a new industry. Some analysts even add an embryonic stage before introduction. At the introduction stage, the firm may be alone in the industry. It may be a small entrepreneurial company or a proven company which used research and development funds and expertise to develop something new. Marketing refers to new product offerings in a new industry as"question marks" because the success of the product and the life of the industry is unproven and unknown.

A firm will use a focus strategy at this stage to stress the uniqueness of the new product or service to a small group of customers. These customers are typically referred to in the marketing literature as the"innovators" and"early adopters." Marketing tactics during this stage are intended to explain the product and its uses to consumers and thus create awareness for the product and the industry. Hitt, Ireland, and Hoskisson, firms establish a niche for dominance within an industry during this phase. For example, they often attempt to establish early perceptions of product quality, technological superiority, or advantageous relationships with vendors within the supply chain to develop a competitive advantage.

Because it costs money to create a new product offering, develop and test prototypes, and market the product from its embryonic stage to introduction, the firm's and the industry's profits are usually negative at this stage. Any profits are typically reinvested into the company to further prepare it for the next life cycle stage. Introduction requires a significant cash outlay to continue to promote and differentiate the offering and expand the production flow from a job shop to possibly a batch flow. Market demand will grow from the introduction, and as the life cycle curve experiences growth at an increasing rate, the industry is said to be entering the growth stage. Firms may also cluster together in close proximity during the early stages of the industry life cycle to have access to key materials or technological expertise, as in the case of the U.S. Silicon Valley computer chip manufacturers.

Growth: Like the introduction stage, the growth stage also requires a significant amount of capital for the firm. The goal of marketing efforts at this stage is to differentiate a firm's offerings from other competitors within the industry. Thus the growth stage requires funds to launch a newly focused marketing campaign as well as funds for continued investment in property, plant, and equipment to facilitate the growth required by the market demands. However, the industry is experiencing more product standardization at this stage, which may encourage economies of scale and facilitate development of a line-flow layout for production efficiency.

Research and development funds will be needed to make changes to the product or services to better reflect customer's needs and suggestions. In this stage, if the firm is successful in the market, growing demand will create sales growth. Earnings and accompanying assets will also grow and profits will be positive for the firms. Marketing often refers to products at the growth stage as"stars." These products have high growth and market share. The key issue in this stage is market rivalry. Because there is industry-wide acceptance of the product, more new entrants join the industry and more intense competition results.

The duration of the growth stage, as all the other stages, depends on the particular industry under study. Some items-like fad clothing, for example-may experience a very short growth stage and move almost immediately into the next stages of maturity and decline. A hot toy this holiday season may be nonexistent or relegated to the back shelves of a deep-discounter the following year. Because many new product introductions fail, the growth stage may be short for some products. However, for other products the growth stage may be longer due to frequent product upgrades and enhancements that forestall movement into maturity. The computer industry today is an example of an industry with a long growth stage due to upgrades in hardware, services, and add-on products and features.

During the growth stage, the life cycle curve is very steep, indicating fast growth. Firms tend to spread out geographically during this stage of the life cycle and continue to disperse during the maturity and decline stages. As an example, the automobile industry in the United States was initially concentrated in the Detroit area and surrounding cities. Today, as the industry has matured, automobile manufacturers are spread throughout the country and internationally.

Maturity: As the industry approaches maturity, the industry life cycle curve becomes noticeably flatter, indicating slowing growth. Some experts have labeled an additional stage, called expansion, between growth and maturity. While sales are expanding and earnings are growing from these "cash cow" products, the rate has slowed from the growth stage. In fact, the rate of sales expansion is typically equal to the growth rate of the economy.

Some competition from late entrants will be apparent, and these new entrants will try to steal market share from existing products. Thus, the marketing effort must remain strong and must stress the unique features of the product or the firm to continue to differentiate a firm's offerings from industry competitors. Firms may compete on quality to separate their product from other lower-cost offerings, or conversely the firm may try a low-cost/low-price strategy to increase the volume of sales and make profits from inventory turnover. A firm at this stage may have excess cash to pay dividends to shareholders. But in mature industries, there are usually fewer firms, and those that survive will be larger and more dominant. While innovations continue they are not as radical as before and may be only a change in color or formulation to stress "new" or "improved" to consumers. Laundry detergents are examples of mature products.

Decline: Declines are almost inevitable in an industry. If product innovation has not kept pace with other competitors, or if new innovations or technological changes have caused the industry to become obsolete, sales suffer and the life cycle experiences a decline. In this phase, sales are decreasing at an accelerating rate, causing the plotted curve to trend downward. Profits may continue to rise, however. There is usually another, larger shake-out in the industry as competitors who did not leave during the maturity stage now exit the industry. Yet some firms will remain to compete in the smaller market. Mergers and consolidations will also be the norm as firms try other strategies to continue to be competitive or grow through acquisition and/or diversification.

PROLONGING THE LIFE CYCLE

Management efficiency can help to prolong the maturity stage of the life cycle. Production improvements, like just-in-time methods and lean manufacturing, can result in extra profits. Technology, automation, and linking suppliers and customers in a tight supply chain are also methods to improve efficiency. New uses of a product can also revitalize an old brand. A prime example is Arm and Hammer baking soda. In 1969, sales were dropping due to the introduction of packaged foods with baking soda as an added ingredient and an overall decline in home baking. New uses for the product as a deodorizer for refrigerators and later as a laundry additive, toothpaste additive, and carpet freshener extended the life cycle of the baking soda industry. Promoting new uses for old brands can increase sales by increasing usage frequency. In some cases, this strategy is cheaper than trying to convert new users in a mature market.

To extend the growth phase and industry profits, firms approaching maturity can pursue expansion into other countries and new markets. Expansion into another geographic region is an effective response to declining demand. The result would be to maintain a positive or at least a constant slope in the product life cycle, past the point where decline would be expected to begin. Because organizations have control over internal factors and can potentially influence external factors, the life cycle does not have to end.

An example is feminine hygiene products. Sales in the United States have reached maturity due to a number of external reasons, like the stable to declining population growth rate and the aging of the baby boomers, who may no longer be consumers for these products. But when makers of these products concentrated on foreign markets which had not previously had access to these product offerings, sales grew and the maturity of the product was prolonged. Often so-called "dog" products can find new life in other parts of the world. However, once world saturation is reached, the eventual maturity and decline of the industry life cycle will result.

LIFE CYCLES ARE EVERYWHER

Just as industries experience life cycles, studies have documented life cycles in many other areas. Countries have life cycles, for example, and we traditionally classify them as ranging from the First World countries to Third World or developing countries, depending on their levels of capital, technological change, infrastructure, or stability. Products also experience life cycles. Even within an industry, various individual companies may be at different life cycle stages depending upon when they entered the industry. The life cycle phenomenon is an important and universally accepted concept to help managers better understand sales growth and change over time.

SWOT ANALYSIS FOR INDUSTRIES

A scan of the internal and external environment is an important part of the strategic planning process. Environmental factors internal to the firm usually can be classified as strengths (S) or weaknesses (W), and those external to the firm can be classified as opportunities (O) or threats (T). Such an analysis of the strategic environment is referred to as a SWOT analysis.

The SWOT analysis provides information that is helpful in matching the firm's resources and capabilities to the competitive environment in which it operates. As such, it is instrumental in strategy formulation and selection. The following diagram shows how a SWOT analysis fits into an environmental scan:

SWOT Analysis Framework:

Environmental Scan	
/	\
Internal Analysis	External Analysis
/ \	/ \
Strengths Weaknesses	Opportunities Threats
|	
SWOT Matrix	

STRENGTHS

A firm's strengths are its resources and capabilities that can be used as a basis for developing a competitive advantage.

Examples of such strengths include:

- Patents
- Strong brand names
- Good reputation among customers
- Cost advantages from proprietary know-how
- Exclusive access to high grade natural resources
- Favourable access to distribution networks

WEAKNESSES

The absence of certain strengths may be viewed as a weakness.

For example, each of the following may be considered weaknesses:

- Lack of patent protection
- A weak brand name
- Poor reputation among customers
- High cost structure
- Lack of access to the best natural resources
- Lack of access to key distribution channels

In some cases, a weakness may be the flip side of a strength. Take the case in which a firm has a large amount of manufacturing capacity.

While this capacity may be considered a strength that competitors do not share, it also may be a considered a weakness if the large investment in manufacturing capacity prevents the firm from reacting quickly to changes in the strategic environment.

OPPORTUNITIES

The external environmental analysis may reveal certain new opportunities for profit and growth.

Some examples of such opportunities include:

- An unfulfilled customer need
- Arrival of new technologies
- Loosening of regulations
- Removal of international trade barriers

THREATS

Changes in the external environmental also may present threats to the firm.

Some examples of such threats include:

- Shifts in consumer tastes away from the firm's products
- Emergence of substitute products
- New regulations
- Increased trade barriers

THE SWOT MATRIX

A firm should not necessarily pursue the more lucrative

opportunities. Rather, it may have a better chance at developing a competitive advantage by identifying a fit between the firm's strengths and upcoming opportunities. In some cases, the firm can overcome a weakness in order to prepare itself to pursue a compelling opportunity. To develop strategies that take into account the SWOT profile, a matrix of these factors can be constructed.

SWOT/TOWS Matrix:

	Strengths	**Weaknesses**
Opportunities	S-O strategies	W-O strategies
Threats	S-T strategies	W-T strategies

- S-O strategies pursue opportunities that are a good fit to the company's strengths.
- W-O strategies overcome weaknesses to pursue opportunities.
- S-T strategies identify ways that the firm can use its strengths to reduce its vulnerability to external threats.
- W-T strategies establish a defensive plan to prevent the firm's weaknesses from making it highly susceptible to external threats.

CORPORATE ANALYSIS

Corporate analysis is a broad term that describes the creation of an in-depth evaluation of a corporate entity. In most situations, the analysis will cover all aspects of the company, including finances, profit margins, organizational structure, and growth opportunities. The idea behind this type of detailed corporate analysis is to gain an understanding of the general corporate health and prospects for future growth of the corporation.

It is not unusual for a corporate analysis to systematically investigate each aspect of the company's operation and seek to develop an opinion of the current efficiency of those aspects. From this perspective, the overall corporate analysis can be viewed as a series of independent yet connected evaluations of each key element of the operation. Thus, it is possible to label subsections of the broad corporate analysis as beings a corporate operations analysis, a corporate risk analysis, or a corporate credit analysis. Together, these individual studies and evaluations come together to create a comprehensive quality analysis of the company.

There are several good reasons for conducting a corporate analysis internally. One of the main reasons is that the process of the analysis can often identify areas of the overall operation that could be enhanced in some manner to increase efficiency and productivity, which leads to the potential for a larger profit margin. The analysis can also sometimes identify policies and procedures connected with one aspect of the operation that would work equally well with some other division or department of the company. The corporate analysis may also yield some inspiration for the modification of key products or the creation of new products as a means of gaining more market share.

Investors and industry analysts can also make constructive use of the independent corporate analysis of a given company. The analysis can yield important information about the current strength of the operation as well as provide valuable clues regarding the direction of the business and the prospects for becoming more profitable or more of an industry leader within a given market sector. From this perspective, a corporate analysis can be viewed as an essential tool that an investor can use to plan both short term and long term investment in the company.

Forward-looking companies conduct a structured corporate analysis on a regular basis. Depending on the structure of the company, the analysis may take place on an annual basis as part of the preparation for presentation to shareholders. In other instances, the corporate analysis may be conducted annually or biannually as a means of evaluating and refining the general operations of the business.

RATIO ANALYSIS

Ratio analysis is one of the techniques of financial analysis to evaluate the financial condition and performance of a business concern. Myers, " Ratio analysis of financial statements is a study of relationship among various financial factors in a business as disclosed by a single set of statements and a study of trend of these factors as shown in a series of statements."

ADVANTAGES AND USES OF RATIO ANALYSIS

There are various groups of people who are interested in analysis of financial position of a company. They use the ratio analysis to workout a particular financial characteristic of the company in which they are interested.

Ratio analysis helps the various groups manner:

- *To workout the profitability*: Accounting ratio help to measure the profitability of the business by calculating the various profitability ratios. It helps the management to know about the earning capacity of the business concern. In this way profitability ratios show the actual performance of the business.
- *To workout the solvency*: With the help of solvency ratios, solvency of the company can be measured. These ratios show the relationship between the liabilities and assets. In case external liabilities are more than that of the assets of the company, it shows the unsound position of the business. In this case the business has to make it possible to repay its loans.
- *Helpful in analysis of financial statement*: Ratio analysis help the outsiders just like creditors, shareholders, debenture-holders, bankers to know about the profitability and ability of the company to pay them interest and dividend etc.
- *Helpful in comparative analysis of the performance*: With the help of ratio analysis a company may have comparative study of its performance to the previous years. In this way company comes to know about its weak point and be able to improve them.
- *To simplify the accounting information*: Accounting ratios are very useful as they briefly summarise the result of detailed and complicated computations.

- *To workout the operating efficiency*: Ratio analysis helps to workout the operating efficiency of the company with the help of various turnover ratios. All turnover ratios are worked out to evaluate the performance of the business in utilising the resources.
- *To workout short-term financial position*: Ratio analysis helps to workout the short-term financial position of the company with the help of liquidity ratios. In case short-term financial position is not healthy efforts are made to improve it.
- *Helpful for forecasting purposes*: Accounting ratios indicate the trend of the business. The trend is useful for estimating future. With the help of previous years' ratios, estimates for future can be made. In this way these ratios provide the basis for preparing budgets and also determine future line of action.

LIMITATIONS OF RATIO ANALYSIS

In spite of many advantages, there are certain limitations of the ratio analysis techniques and they should be kept in mind while using them in interpreting financial statements.

The following are the main limitations of accounting ratios:

- *Limited Comparability*: Different firms apply different accounting policies. Therefore the ratio of one firm can not always be compared with the ratio of other firm. Some firms may value the closing stock on LIFO basis while some other firms may value on FIFO basis. Similarly there may be difference in providing depreciation of fixed assets or certain of provision for doubtful debts etc.
- *False Results*: Accounting ratios are based on data drawn from accounting records. In case that data is correct, then only the ratios will be correct. For example, valuation of stock is based on very high price, the profits of the concern will be inflated and it will indicate a wrong financial position. The data therefore must be absolutely correct.
- *Effect of Price Level Changes*: Price level changes often

make the comparison of figures difficult over a period of time. Changes in price affects the cost of production, sales and also the value of assets. Therefore, it is necessary to make proper adjustment for price-level changes before any comparison.

- *Qualitative factors are ignored*: Ratio analysis is a technique of quantitative analysis and thus, ignores qualitative factors, which may be important in decision making. For example, average collection period may be equal to standard credit period, but some debtors may be in the list of doubtful debts, which is not disclosed by ratio analysis.
- *Effect of window-dressing*: In order to cover up their bad financial position some companies resort to window dressing. They may record the accounting data according to the convenience to show the financial position of the company in a better way.
- *Costly Technique*: Ratio analysis is a costly technique and can be used by big business houses. Small business units are not able to afford it.
- *Misleading Results*: In the absence of absolute data, the result may be misleading. For example, the gross profit of two firms is 25%. Whereas the profit earned by one is just Rs. 5,000 and sales are Rs. 20,000 and profit earned by the other one is Rs. 10,00,000 and sales are Rs. 40,00,000. Even the profitability of the two firms is same but the magnitude of their business is quite different.
- *Absence of standard university accepted terminology*: There are no standard ratios, which are universally accepted for comparison purposes. As such, the significance of ratio analysis technique is reduced.

4

Technical Analysis

FUNDAMENTAL ANALYSIS VS TECHNICAL ANALYSIS

In analysing price action, forex traders make use of two main kinds of analysis. Those who concentrate on price action, and ignore most other factors choose to direct their efforts at perfecting their skills at technical analysis, while traders who prefer to study the economic events that cause the market action mostly focus their efforts in studying fundamental analysis. Many traders combine the information provided by these two types of analysis to generate trading signals.

Others concentrate on one aspect of analysis and exclude the other from their calculations, and it is fair to say that either approach can be valid depending on the circumstances. There are traders such as Martin Schwartz who acquired reputation and wealth by trading on the basis of technical analysis, along with those like Jim Rogers whose success was based on fundamental analysis almost exclusively. But while they would disagree on many subjects, both of these people would probably agree that emotional control and discipline are the most important aspects of a successful trading career, even before analytical prowess.

HOW DIFFERENT ARE FUNDAMENTAL AND TECHNICAL ANALYSIS

We should note here, before going on with our discussion of the various aspects of the two analytical schools, that while the explanations of the fundamental and technical analyst on a phenomenon may differ from each other, the end result, and the trade recommendation can in many cases be the same. To give an example of this, we may examine the classical case of a parabolic price graphic which would make both kinds of analysts cautious, but for different reasons. The technical analyst would look at his charts, notice the extreme values registered on the indicators, and would caution against joining a trend that is in danger of suffering a sharp reversal as the inevitable countertrend movement occurs.

The fundamental analyst would look at the euphoria in news sources and analyst community, consider the declarations of government authorities and important personages, and would probably give the same warning. While the tools and indicators used by these two individuals are different, their actions often coincide with each other. Fundamental and technical analysis are not exactly the same thing, and at least in the longer term, the predictive power of fundamental studies is almost certainly greater. Nonetheless, these two are akin to two different languages describing the same phenomenon, and at least on hindsight, they always show the same direction.

WHAT IS FUNDAMENTAL ANALYSIS

Fundamental analysis is the discipline that tries to make sense of price movements in light of economic data and news flow. In comparison to technical studies, fundamental analysis has a larger selection of indicators. While many traders choose to focus on the news releases and indicators that appear to determine the day-to-day movements in the financial markets, fundamental analysis in fact studies many other aspects of economics including politics, financial law, social attitudes, in addition to the many other aspects of human life.

Fundamental analysis aims to establish a cause and effect relationship between market movements and economic developments. In that sense, it is different from technical analysis which regards the price action as the beginning and end of trading. While technical analysts generally argue that the price action reflects all information available to the market, fundamental analysts seek to identify imbalances and"errors" in the market that may offer profit opportunities. Unlike the technical trader, the fundamental trader is always skeptical of the price action, and seeks alternative explanations to the"wisdom of the market" in evaluating price trends.

While this type of analysis has been proven to be efficient and reliable through the ages, there are a number of issues that we must keep in mind in order to avoid being too optimistic about the predictive powers of our approach. While fundamental analysis can and often does indeed warn us on possible errors in market attitudes to economic realities, there's no indication that the correction will happen anytime soon. Similarly, bubbles and market extremes often cause analysts to rationalize the unhealthy positioning of the market, invalidating the healthy advantage of skepticism inherent in the fundamental approach.

ADVANTAGES OF FUNDAMENTAL ANALYSIS

The greatest benefit derived from study of fundamental analysis is the ability to understand the causes that drive the market action. By understanding market dynamics, we can be confident in maintaining a position as long as the cause that triggered the trade exists.

A thorough grasp of fundamental analysis also ensures that we do not lose our composure in the face of market volatility. Those who employ fundamental studies in gauging the price action are confident that they are on the tracks of the greatest geniuses of forex trading. All those who successfully made millions or billions in this business were users of fundamental analysis; and there is no reason to doubt that if we were to use the same methods we can achieve the similar, if not the same results with them.

WHAT IS TECHNICAL ANALYSIS?

Unlike fundamental analysis, technical analysis is a relatively new discipline that is still being perfected by its practitioners. Still, years of continued use has made it an inseparable part of the traders arsenal: technical studies are probably the only tools used for determining entry or exit points, and in short term trading, technical analysis is probably the only analytical tool that has any predictive power.

Technical analysis is based on three important assumptions about market events. First, technical analysis posits that the prices discount all information available to the public. Secondly, it assumes that price movements are not random, and that technical tools can be used to establish the underlying currents behind the price action. Third, it claims that price trends tend to repeat themselves. In other words, past developments provide some guidance on the direction and magnitude of future price action. In consequence of these three assumptions, technical analysis regards the price action as the conscious activity of a mass of financial actors who performance collectively as if they were one large sentient being with emotions and feelings. In other words, just like the case with a beehive, or an ant layer, the seemingly independent actions of individual traders are targeted towards achieving the most sensible and logical course for prices in general.

Naturally, if collective will of traders is rational and makes meaningful decisions, then the future choices of that body would depend on its past actions. And if such a logical coherence, and a train of reasoning between past and present exists, it would be possible to examine and understand the rules behind that train of reasoning, and consequently to follow it and to profit as a result.

And there lies the basis of technical analysis. Just as we deduce that a person who takes out keys from his pockets is intent on opening the door, we expect that a certain spike or collapse in prices, a period of trending activity, or consolidation must lead to their logical cease in the markets in breakouts, or successive highs or lows, the nature of which is determined by technical analysis.

ADVANTAGES OF TECHNICAL ANALYSIS

Technical analysis is simple and straightforward, with tools available to every one from the seasoned hedge fund manager, to the novice retail trader. In addition, technical tools are easier to interpret than fundamental indicators, the understanding of which usually requires a period of diligent study. Finally, since technical analysis focuses on the price action exclusively, the technical trader has only one needle in his compass: the price, on which any calculation about profits or losses must be based.

Technical studies have been refined and perfected over the years, and by using them we are making use of the heritage of thousands of experienced and knowledgeable traders who have contributed to the effort. By mastering the various aspects of technical trading, we can also minimize the role of guesswork and conjectures in analysing the price action. While technical studies can give conflicting signals about the future, the error, if any, is on the part of the interpreter. By recognizing our flaws, we can better our analytical skills, and with better skills, wealth and success will be just a single blink away.

RESULT

Both types of analysis are useful for examining market action. Your trading style, and attitude to trading will determine which kind of analysis you will find most beneficial. But before making that decision, it is a good idea to study the subject of analysis in slightly greater detail.

MARKET INDICATORS

This substance is designed to introduce the concept of market indicators and explain how to use them in your analysis. As suggested, look how market indicators differ from technical indicators, and why they are just as important for making investment decisions. It covers specific market indicators so you can begin using them to your advantage right away.

Here is a list of some popular market indicators:

- Bullish Per cent Index (BPI)
- Arms Index (TRIN)
- Volatility Index (VIX)
- Advance-Decline Line
- McClellan Oscillator
- McClellan Summation Index
- Stocks above their XX-Day Simple Moving Averages

Like a technical indicator, a market indicator is a series of data points derived from a formula. In this case, however, the formula for market indicators is applied to the price data for multiple securities within the market, instead of just one security. Price data can come from open, high, low or close points for the securities, their volume, or both. This data is entered into the indicator formula and the data point is produced.

Unlike technical indicators, market indicators are not charted above or below the chart. Market indicators are what is being charted, and as such have their own ticker symbols. There are often many symbols that apply the market indicator formula simply to different markets. For example, the $BPSPX and $BPNDX track the Bullish Per cent Index for the S&P 500 and the NASDAQ 100 respectively

TREND

To a trader who uses technical analysis, the trend in price of a financial security is, intuitively, the general direction of its movement. Loosely, if someone who looked at the price chart would generally say the price is going up, the trend is up, and if someone would generally say the price is moving down, the trend is down. In many cases an observer would find it difficult to decide whether the price was generally going up or going down: in this case the trend may be said to be unclear. When price is oscillating back and forth across a range, the trend is often said to be sideways.

COMMON TREND ANALYSIS METHODS

Trend analysis is specific to the time frame of the chart being looked at. A monthly chart might appear to be trending down while a daily chart appears to be trending up. Moreover, even on a specific chart, the direction of the trend can be open to disagreement. A precise definition of the trend may be based on price ranges. If a series of higher highs and higher lows occur on a chart, an up trend is in place, and if a series of lower lows and lower highs occurs, a down trend is occurring.

Other definitions of trend are based on indicators. For

example, the trend may be simplistically defined to be up when a chosen short moving average is higher than a chosen long moving average.

Of course, the choice of which moving averages to use will affect whether an up trend or a down trend is found, and this simplistic approach would associate a trend with many unclear markets.

EXPONENTIAL MOVING AVERAGE

An exponential moving average, sometimes also called an exponentially weighted moving average (EWMA), applies weighting factors which decrease exponentially. The weighting for each older data point decreases exponentially, giving much more importance to recent observations while still not discarding older observations entirely.

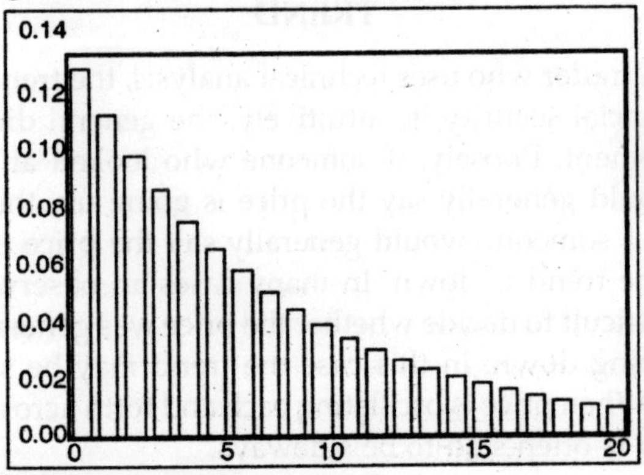

EMA weights N=15

Parametres:

- The degree of weighting decrease is expressed as a constant smoothing factor α, a number between 0 and 1. The smoothing factor may be expressed as a percentage, so a value of 10% is equivalent to $\alpha = 0.1$. A higher α discounts older observations faster. Alternatively, α may be expressed in terms of N time periods, where $\alpha = 2/(N+1)$. For example, N = 19 is equivalent to $\alpha = 0.1$. The half-life of the weights (the interval over which the weights decrease by a factor of two) is approximately N/2.8854.

- The observation at a time period t is designated Yt, and the value of the EMA at any time period t is designated St.

S_1 is undefined. S_2 may be initialized in a number of different ways, most commonly by setting S_2 to Y_1, though other techniques exist, such as setting S_2 to an average of the first 4 or 5 observations. The prominence of the S_2 initialization's effect on the resultant moving average depends on α; smaller α values make the choice of S_2 relatively more important than larger α values, since a higher α discounts older observations faster.

Formula:

The formula for calculating the EMA at time periods t > 2 is,

$$S_t = \alpha \times Y_{t-1} + (1-\alpha) \times S_{t-1}$$

This formulation is just as to Hunter. By repeated application of this formula for different times, we can eventually write St as a weighted sum of the data points Yt, thus:

$$S_t = \alpha \times (Y_{t-1} + (1-\alpha) \times Y_{t-2} + (1-\alpha)^2 \times Y_{t-3} + \cdots + (1-\alpha)^k \times Y_{t-(k+1)}) + (1-\alpha)^{k+1} \times S_{t-(k+1)}$$

for any suitable k = 0, 1, 2... The weight of the general data point Y_{t-i} is $\alpha (1 - \alpha)^{i-1}$.

An alternate approach by Roberts (1959) uses Y_t in lieu of Y_{t-1}:

$$S_{t,\text{alternate}} = \alpha \times Y_t + (1-\alpha) \times S_{t-1}$$

This formula can also be expressed in technical analysis terms as follows, showing how the EMA steps towards the latest data point, but only by a proportion of the difference:

$$EMA_{today} = EMA_{yesterday} + \alpha \times (Price_{today} - EMA_{yesterday})$$

Expanding out $EMA_{yesterday}$ each time results power series, showing how the weighting factor on each data point p_1, p_2, etc, decreases exponentially:

$$EMA = \alpha \times (p_1 + (1-\alpha)p_2 + (1-\alpha)^2 p_3 + (1-\alpha)^3 p_4 + \cdots)$$

This is an infinite sum with decreasing terms. The N periods in an N-day EMA only specify the ? factor. N is not a stopping point for the calculation in the way it is in an SMA or WMA. For sufficiently large N, The first N data points in an EMA represent about 86% of the total weight in the calculation:

$$\frac{\alpha\times(1+(1-\alpha)+(1-\alpha)^2+\cdots+(1-\alpha)^N)}{\alpha\times(1+(1-\alpha)+(1-\alpha)^2+\cdots+(1-\alpha)^\infty)}=1-\left(1-\frac{2}{N+1}\right)^{N+1}$$

i.e. $$\lim_{N\to\infty}\left[1-\left(1-\frac{2}{N+1}\right)^{N+1}\right]$$

simplified, tends to $1-e^{-2}\approx 0.8647$.

The power formula gives a starting value for a particular day, after which the successive days formula shown first can be applied. The question of how far back to go for an initial value depends, in the worst case, on the data.

If there are huge p price values in old data then they'll have an effect on the total even if their weighting is very small. If one assumes prices don't vary too wildly then just the weighting can be considered. The weight omitted by stopping after k terms is,

$$\alpha\times((1-\alpha)^k+(1-\alpha)^{k+1}+(1-\alpha)^{k+2}+\cdots)$$

which is

$$\alpha\times(1-\alpha)^k\times(1+(1-\alpha)+(1-\alpha)^2+\cdots)$$

i.e. a fraction,

$$(1-\alpha)^k$$

out of the total weight.

For example, to have 99.9% of the weight,

$$k=\frac{\log(0.001)}{\log(1-\alpha)}$$

terms should be used. Since $\log(1-\alpha)$ approaches,

$$\frac{-2}{N+1}$$

as N increases, this simplifies to approximately,

$$k=3.45(N+1)$$

for this example (99.9% weight).

Modified Moving Average

This is called modified moving average (MMA), running moving average (RMA), or smoothed moving average.

Definition,

$$MMA_{today} = \frac{(N-1) \times MMA_{yesterday} + price}{N}$$

In short, this is exponential moving average, with $\alpha = 1/N$.

Application to Measuring Computer Performance

Some computer performance metrics, e.g. the average process queue length, or the average CPU utilization, use a form of exponential moving average.

$$S_n = \alpha(t_n - t_{n-1}) \times Y_n + (1 - \alpha(t_n - t_{n-1})) \times S_{n-1}$$

Here α is defined as a function of time between two readings. An example of a coefficient giving bigger weight to the current reading, and smaller weight to the older readings is,

$$\alpha(t_n - t_{n-1}) = 1 - e^{-\frac{t_n - t_{n-1}}{W \times 60}}$$

where time for readings t_n is expressed in seconds, and W is the period of time in minutes over which the reading is said to be averaged. Given the definition of α, the moving average can be expressed as,

$$S_n = \left(1 - e^{-\frac{t_n - t_{n-1}}{W \times 60}}\right) \times Y_n + e^{-\frac{t_n - t_{n-1}}{W \times 60}} \times S_{n-1}$$

For example, a 15-minute average L of a process queue length Q, measured every 5 seconds is computed as,

$$L_n = \left(1 - e^{-\frac{5}{15 \times 60}}\right) \times Q_n + e^{-\frac{5}{15 \times 60}} \times L_{n-1} = (1 - e^{-\frac{1}{180}})$$

$$\times Q_n + e^{-1/180} \times L_{n-1}$$

OSCILLATOR

An oscillator is a technical analysis indicator that varies

over time within a band. Oscillators are used to discover short-term overbought or oversold conditions. Common oscillators are MACD, ROC, RSI, CCI.

MOMENTUM

Momentum and rate of change (ROC) are simple technical analysis indicators showing the difference between today's closing price and the close N days ago. Momentum is the absolute difference:

$$\text{momentum} = \text{close}_{\text{today}} - \text{close}_{\text{N days ago}}$$

Rate of change scales by the old close, so as to represent the increase as a fraction,

$$\text{rate of change} = \frac{\text{close}_{\text{today}} - \text{close}_{\text{N}} \text{ days ago}}{\text{close}_{\text{N}} \text{ days ago}}$$

"Momentum" in general refers to prices continuing to trend. The momentum and ROC indicators show trend by remaining positive while an uptrend is sustained, or negative while a downtrend is sustained.

A crossing up through zero may be used as a signal to buy, or a crossing down through zero as a signal to sell. How high the indicators get shows how strong the trend is. The way momentum shows an absolute change means it shows for instance a $3 rise over 20 days, whereas ROC might show that as 0.25 for a 25% rise over the same period. One can choose between looking at a move in dollar terms, relative point terms, or proportional terms. The zero crossings are the same in each, of course, but the highs or lows showing strength are on the respective different bases.

SMA

Momentum is the change in an N-day simple moving average (SMA) between yesterday and today, with a scale factor N, *i.e.*

$$\frac{\text{momentum}}{\text{N}} = \text{SMA}_{\text{today}} - \text{SAM}_{\text{yesterday}}$$

This is the slope or steepness of the SMA line, like a

derivative. This relationship is not much discussed generally, but it's of interest in understanding the signals from the indicator. When momentum crosses up through zero it corresponds to a trough in the SMA, and when it crosses down through zero it's a peak. How high (or low) momentum gets represents how steeply the SMA is rising. The TRIX indicator is similarly based on changes in a moving average.

PATTERNS- MOVING AVERAGES

Moving averages are one of the oldest and most popular technical analysis tool. Nowadays you get moving averages readily available on most of the websites. To brief you moving average is calculated by adding the closing prices of a stock for most recent 15 days and then dividing by 15 the result what you get is the 15 day moving average.

HOW TO TRADE ON MOVING AVERAGE

Suppose If the stock price is above its 25 day moving average, it means that investor's current expectations are higher than their average expectations over the last 25 days, and that investors are becoming increasingly bullish on this stock and result is that the stock price may go up.

Conversely, if today's price is below then its 25 day moving average, it shows that current expectations are below average expectations over the last 25 days and this may bring stock price lower.

The moving average is used to observe changes in prices. Investors typically buy when a stock price rises above its moving average and sell when the price falls below its moving average.

RSI

A technical momentum indicator that compares the magnitude of recent gains to recent losses in an attempt to determine overbought and oversold conditions of an asset. It is calculated using the following formula:

$$RSI = 100 - \frac{100}{1 + RS}$$

RS = Average of x days' up closes/ Average of x days' down closes The RSI ranges from 0 to 100. An asset is deemed to be overbought once the RSI approaches the 70 level, meaning that it may be getting overvalued and is a good candidate for a pullback. Likewise, if the RSI approaches 30, it is an indication that the asset may be getting oversold and therefore likely to become undervalued.

DOW THEORY

Dow Theory on stock price movements is a form of technical analysis that includes some aspects of sector rotation. The theory was derived from 255 Wall Street Journal editorials written by Charles H. Dow, journalist, founder and first editor of the Wall Street Journal and co-founder of Dow Jones and Company. Following Dow's death, William Peter Hamilton, Robert Rhea and E. George Schaefer organized and collectively represented"Dow Theory," based on Dow's editorials. Dow himself never used the term"Dow Theory," nor presented it as a trading system. The six basic tenets of Dow Theory as summarized by Hamilton, Rhea, and Schaefer.

SIX BASIC TENETS OF DOW THEORY

- The market has thr]ee movements
  - The"main movement", primary movement or major trend may last from less than a year to several years. It can be bullish or bearish.
  - The"medium swing", secondary reaction or intermediate reaction may last from ten days to three months and generally retraces from 33% to 66% of the primary price change since the previous medium swing or start of the main movement.
  - The"short swing" or minor movement varies with opinion from hours to a month or more. The three movements may be simultaneous, for instance, a daily minor movement in a bearish secondary reaction in a bullish primary movement.
- *Market trends have three phases*: Dow Theory asserts

that major market trends are composed of three phases: an accumulation phase, a public participation phase, and a distribution phase. The accumulation phase is a period when investors"in the know" are actively buying stock against the general opinion of the market. During this phase, the stock price does not change much because these investors are in the minority absorbing stock that the market at large is supplying. Eventually, the market catches on to these astute investors and a rapid price change occurs. This occurs when trend followers and other technically oriented investors participate. This phase continues until rampant speculation occurs. At this point, the astute investors begin to distribute their holdings to the market.

- *The stock market discounts all news*: Stock prices quickly incorporate new information as soon as it becomes available. Once news is released, stock prices will change to reflect this new information. On this point, Dow Theory agrees with one of the premises of the efficient market hypothesis.
- *Stock market averages must confirm each other*: In Dow's time, the US was a growing industrial power. The US had population centres but factories were scattered throughout the country. Factories had to ship their goods to market, usually by rail. Dow's first stock averages were an index of industrial companies and rail companies. To Dow, a bull market in industrials could not occur unless the railway average rallied as well, usually first. This logic, if manufacturers' profits are rising, it follows that they are producing more. If they produce more, then they have to ship more goods to consumers. Hence, if an investor is looking for signs of health in manufacturers, he or she should look at the performance of the companies that ship the output of them to market, the railroads. The two averages should be moving in the same direction. When the

performance of the averages diverge, it is a warning that change is in the air.

Both Barron's Magazine and the Wall Street Journal still publish the daily performance of the Dow Jones Transportation Index in chart form. The index contains major railroads, shipping companies, and air freight carriers in the US.

- *Trends are confirmed by volume*: Dow believed that volume confirmed price trends. When prices move on low volume, there could be many different explanations why. An overly aggressive seller could be present for example. But when price movements are accompanied by high volume, Dow believed this represented the"true" market view. If many participants are active in a particular security, and the price moves significantly in one direction, Dow maintained that this was the direction in which the market anticipated continued movement. To him, it was a signal that a trend is developing.
- *Trends exist until definitive signals prove that they have ended*: Dow believed that trends existed despite"market noise". Markets might temporarily move in the direction opposite to the trend, but they will soon resume the prior move. The trend should be given the benefit of the doubt during these reversals. Determining whether a reversal is the start of a new trend or a temporary movement in the current trend is not easy. Dow Theorists often disagree in this determination. Technical analysis tools attempt to clarify this but they can be interpreted differently by different investors.

ANALYSIS

There is little academic support for the profitability of the Dow Theory. Alfred Cowles in a study in Econometrica in 1934 showed that trading based upon the editorial advice would have resulted in earning less than a buy-and-hold strategy using a well diversified portfolio.

Cowles concluded that a buy-and-hold strategy produced 15.5% annualized returns from 1902-1929 while the Dow Theory strategy produced annualized returns of 12%. After numerous studies supported Cowles over the following years, many academics stopped studying Dow Theory believing Cowles's results were conclusive.

In recent years however, Cowles' ceases have been revisited. William Goetzmann, Stephen Brown, and Alok Kumar believe that Cowles' study was incomplete and that Dow Theory produces excess risk-adjusted returns. Specifically, the return of a buy-and-hold strategy was higher than that of a Dow Theory portfolio by 2%, but the riskiness and volatility of the Dow Theory portfolio was lower, so that the Dow Theory portfolio produced higher risk-adjusted returns according to their study.

Nevertheless, adjusting returns for risk is controversial in the context of the Dow Theory. One key problem with any analysis of Dow Theory is that the editorials of Charles Dow did not contain explicitly defined investing"rules" so some assumptions and interpretations are necessary.

Many technical analysts consider Dow Theory's definition of a trend and its insistence on studying price action as the main premises of modern technical analysis.

5

Portfolio Analysis Selection

MODERN PORTFOLIO THEORY

Modern portfolio theory is a theory of investment which tries to maximize return and minimize risk by carefully choosing different assets. Although MPT is widely used in practice in the financial industry and several of its creators won a Nobel prize for the theory, in recent years the basic assumptions of MPT have been widely challenged by fields such as behavioural economics.

MPT is a mathematical formulation of the concept of diversification in investing, with the aim of selecting a collection of investment assets that has collectively lower risk than any individual asset. This is possible, in theory, because different types of assets often change in value in opposite ways. For example, when the prices in the stock market fall, the prices in the bond market often increase, and vice versa. A collection of both types of assets can therefore have lower overall risk than either individually.

More technically, MPT models an asset's return as a normally distributed random variable, defines risk as the standard deviation of return, and models a portfolio as a weighted combination of assets so that the return of a portfolio is the weighted combination of the assets' returns.

By combining different assets whose returns are not correlated, MPT seeks to reduce the total variance of the portfolio. MPT also assumes that investors are rational and markets are efficient. MPT was developed in the 1950s through the early 1970s and was considered an important advance in the mathematical modeling of finance. Since then, much theoretical and practical criticism has been leveled against it. These include the fact that financial returns do not follow a Gaussian distribution and that correlations between asset classes are not fixed but can vary depending on external events. Further, there is growing evidence that investors are not rational and markets are not efficient.

CONCEPT

The fundamental concept behind MPT is that the assets in an investment portfolio cannot be selected individually, each on their own merits. Rather, it is important to consider how each asset changes in price relative to how every other asset in the portfolio changes in price.

Investing is a tradeoff between risk and return. In general, assets with higher returns are riskier. For a given amount of risk, MPT describes how to select a portfolio with the highest possible return. Or, for a given return, MPT explains how to select a portfolio with the lowest possible risk

MPT is therefore a form of diversification. Under certain assumptions and for specific quantitative definitions of risk and return, MPT explains how to find the best possible diversification strategy.

MATHEMATICAL MODEL

In some sense the mathematical derivation *is* MPT, although the basic concepts behind the model have also been very influential. This part develops the "classic" MPT model. There have been many extensions since.

Risk and Return

MPT assumes that investors are risk averse, meaning that given two assets that offer the same expected return, investors will prefer the less risky one. Thus, an investor will take on increased risk only if compensated by higher expected returns. Conversely, an investor who wants higher returns must accept more risk. The exact trade-off will differ by investor based on individual risk aversion characteristics. The implication is that a rational investor will not invest in a portfolio if a second portfolio exists with a more favourable risk-return profile – *i.e.,* if for that level of risk an alternative portfolio exists which has better expected returns.

MPT further assumes that the investor's risk/ reward preference can be described via a quadratic utility function. The effect of this assumption is that only the expected return and the volatility matter to the investor. The investor is indifferent to other characteristics of the distribution of returns, such as its skew or kurtosis.

Note that the theory uses a parametre, volatility, as a proxy for risk, while return is an expectation on the future. This is in line with the efficient market hypothesis and most of the classical findings in finance. There are problems with this.

Under the model:

- Portfolio return is the proportion-weighted combination of the constituent assets' returns.
- Portfolio volatility is a function of the correlation *ñ* of the component assets. The change in volatility is non-linear as the weighting of the component assets changes.

In general:

- *Expected return*:

$$E(R_p) = \sum_i w_i E(R_i)$$

Where R_i is return and w_i is the weighting of component asset *i*.

- *Portfolio variance*:

$$\sigma_p^2 = \sum_i w_i^2 \sigma_i^2 + \sum_i \sum_j w_i w_j \sigma_i \sigma_j p_{ij},$$

where $i \neq j$. Alternatively the expression can be written as:

$$\sigma_p^2 = \sum_i \sum_j w_i w_j \sigma_i \sigma_j p_{ij},$$

where $\rho_{ij} = 1$ for i=j.

- *Portfolio volatility*:

$$\sigma_p = \sqrt{\sigma_p^2}$$

For a two asset portfolio:

- *Portfolio return*:

$$E(R_p) = w_A E(R_A) + (1 - w_A)E(R_B)$$
$$= w_A E(R_A) + w_B E(R_B)$$

- *Portfolio variance*:

$$\sigma_p^2 = w_A^2 \sigma_A^2 + w_B^2 \sigma_B^2 + 2w_A w_B \sigma_A \sigma_B \rho_{AB}$$

For a three asset portfolio:

- *Portfolio return*:

$$w_A E(R_A) + w_B E(R_B) + w_C E(R_C)$$

- *Portfolio variance*:

$$\sigma_p^2 = w^2{}_A \sigma^2{}_A + w^2{}_B \sigma^2{}_B + w^2{}_C \sigma^2{}_C + 2w_A w_B \sigma_A \sigma_B \rho_{AB}$$
$$+2w_A w_C \sigma_A \sigma_C \rho_{AC} + 2w_B w_C \sigma_B \sigma_C \rho_{BC}$$

Diversification

An investor can reduce portfolio risk simply by holding combinations of instruments which are not perfectly positively correlated. In other words, investors can reduce their exposure to individual asset risk by holding a diversified portfolio of assets. Diversification may allow for the same portfolio return with reduced risk. If all the assets of a portfolio have a correlation of +1, *i.e.*, perfect positive correlation, the portfolio volatility will be equal to the weighted sum of the individual asset volatilities. Hence the portfolio variance will be equal to the square of the total weighted sum of the individual asset volatilities. If all the assets have a correlation of 0, *i.e.*, perfectly uncorrelated, the portfolio variance is the sum of the individual asset weights squared times the individual asset variance.

If correlation coefficient is less than zero (r=0), *i.e.*, the assets are inversely correlated, the portfolio variance and hence volatility will be less than if the correlation coefficient is 0.

The Risk-free Asset

The risk-free asset is the asset which pays a risk-free rate.

In practice, short-term Government securities are used as a risk-free asset, because they pay a fixed rate of interest and have exceptionally low default risk. The risk-free asset has zero variance in returns; it is also uncorrelated with any other asset. As a result, when it is combined with any other asset, or portfolio of assets, the change in return and *also in risk* is linear. Because both risk and return change linearly as the risk-free asset is introduced into a portfolio, this combination will plot a straight line in risk-return space.

The line starts at 100% in the risk-free asset and weight of the risky portfolio = 0 and goes through the portfolio in question where risk-free asset holding = 0 and portfolio weight = 1.

Using the formulae for a two asset portfolio:

- Return is the weighted average of the risk free asset, *f*, and the risky portfolio, p, and is therefore linear:

$$\text{Return} = w_f E(R_f) + w_p E(R_p)$$

- Since the asset is risk free, portfolio standard deviation is simply a function of the weight of the risky portfolio in the position. This relationship is linear.

Standard deviation ,

$$= \sqrt{w_f^2\sigma_f^2 + w_p^2\sigma_p^2 + 2w_f w_p \sigma_{fp}}$$

$$= \sqrt{w_f^2 0 + w_p^2\sigma_p^2 + 2w_f w_p .0}$$

$$= \sqrt{w_p^2\sigma_p^2}$$

$$= w_p\sigma_p$$

Capital Allocation Line

The capital allocation line is the line of expected return plotted against risk that connects all portfolios that can be formed using a risky asset and a riskless asset. It can be proven that it is a straight line and that it has the following equation.

$$\text{CAL} : E(r_c) = r_F + \sigma c \frac{E(r_p) - r_F}{\sigma_p}$$

In this formula *P* is the risky portfolio, *F* is the riskless portfolio, and *C* is a combination of portfolios *P* and *F*.

The Efficient Frontier

Every possible asset combination can be plotted in risk-return space, and the collection of all such possible portfolios defines a region in this space. The line along the upper edge of this region is known as the *efficient frontier*. Combinations along this line represent portfolios for which there is lowest risk for a given level of return. Conversely, for a given amount of risk, the portfolio lying on the efficient frontier represents the combination offering the best possible return. Mathematically the Efficient Frontier is the intersection of the *Set of Portfolios with Minimum Variance* and the *Set of Portfolios with Maximum Return*. Formally, the efficient frontier is the set of maximal elements with respect to the partial order of product order on risk and return, the set of portfolios for which one cannot improve *both* risk and return. The efficient frontier with return μ_p on the *y*-axis, and risk σ_p on the *x*-axis. The efficient frontier will be convex – this is because the risk-return characteristics of a portfolio change in a non-linear fashion as its component weightings are changed. The efficient frontier is a parabola when expected return is plotted against variance.

The frontier is unachievable by holding risky assets alone. No portfolios can be constructed corresponding to the points in this region. Points the frontier are suboptimal. A rational investor will hold a portfolio only on the frontier. Matrices are preferred for calculations of the efficient frontier. In matrix form, for a given "risk tolerance" $q \in [0, \infty)$, the efficient front is found by minimizing the following expression:

$$w^T \sum w - q * R^T w$$

where,

- w is a vector of portfolio weights. Each $w_i \geq 0$

$$\sum_i w_i = 1$$

- Σ is the covariance matrix for the assets in the portfolio

- q is a "risk tolerance" factor, where 0 results in the portfolio with minimal risk and ∞ results in the portfolio with maximal return
- R is a vector of expected returns

The front is calculated by repeating the optimization for various $q \geq 0$. Many software packages, including Microsoft Excel, MATLAB, Mathematica and R.

Portfolio Leverage

An investor adds leverage to the portfolio by borrowing the risk-free asset. The addition of the risk-free asset allows for a position in the region the efficient frontier. Thus, by combining a risk-free asset with risky assets, it is possible to construct portfolios whose risk-return profiles are superior to those on the efficient frontier.

- An investor holding a portfolio of risky assets, with a holding in cash, has a positive risk-free weighting. The return and standard deviation will be lower than the portfolio alone, but since the efficient frontier is concave, this combination will sit the efficient frontier – *i.e.,* offering a higher return for the same risk as the point it on the frontier.
- The investor who borrows money to fund his/her purchase of the risky assets has a negative risk-free weighting – *i.e.,* a *leveraged portfolio*. Here the return is geared to the risky portfolio. This combination will again offer a return superior to those on the frontier.

The Market Portfolio

The efficient frontier is a collection of portfolios, each one optimal for a given amount of risk. A quantity known as the Sharpe ratio represents a measure of the amount of additional return a portfolio provides compared to the risk it carries.

The portfolio on the efficient frontier with the highest Sharpe Ratio is known as the market portfolio, or sometimes the super-efficient portfolio. This portfolio has the property that any combination of it and the risk-free asset will produce a return that is the efficient frontier-offering a larger return for a given amount of risk than a portfolio of risky assets on the frontier would.

Capital Market Line

When the market portfolio is combined with the risk-free asset, the result is the Capital Market Line. All points along the CML have superior risk-return profiles to any portfolio on the efficient frontier. Just the special case of the market portfolio with zero cash weighting is on the efficient frontier. Additions of cash or leverage with the risk-free asset in combination with the market portfolio are on the Capital Market Line. All of these portfolios represent the highest possible Sharpe ratio. The CML with return ?p on the y-axis, and risk σ_p on the x-axis.

One can prove that the CML is the optimal CAL and that its equation is:

$$\text{CML}: E(r_C) = r_F + \sigma_C \frac{E(r_M) - r_F}{\sigma_M}.$$

ASSET PRICING USING MPT

A rational investor would not invest in an asset which does not improve the risk-return characteristics of his existing portfolio. Since a rational investor would hold the market portfolio, the asset in question will be added to the market portfolio. MPT derives the required return for a correctly priced asset in this context.

Systematic Risk and Specific Risk

Specific risk is the risk associated with individual assets - within a portfolio these risks can be reduced through diversification. Specific risk is also called diversifiable, unique, unsystematic, or idiosyncratic risk. Systematic risk refers to the risk common to all securities - except for selling short, systematic risk cannot be diversified away. Within the market portfolio, asset specific risk will be diversified away to the extent possible. Systematic risk is therefore equated with the risk of the market portfolio. Since a security will be purchased only if it improves the risk/ return characteristics of the market portfolio, the risk of a security will be the risk it adds to the market portfolio. In this context, the volatility of the asset, and its correlation with the market portfolio, is historically observed and is therefore a given. The price paid for any particular asset should also be determined based on its relationship with the market portfolio.

Systematic risks within one market can be managed through a strategy of using both long and short positions within one portfolio, creating a"market neutral" portfolio.

Security Characteristic Line

The security characteristic line represents the relationship between the market excess return and the excess return of a given asset *i* at a given time *t*. In general, it is reasonable to assume that the SCL is a straight line and can be emphasized as a statistical equation:

$$\text{SCL}: R_{i,t} - R_f = \alpha_i + \beta_i (R_{M,t} - R_f) + \epsilon_{i,t}$$

where α_i is called the asset's alpha and β_i the asset's beta coefficient.

Capital Asset Pricing Model

The asset return depends on the amount for the asset today. The price paid must ensure that the market portfolio's risk/ return characteristics improve when the asset is added to it. The CAPM is a model which derives the theoretical required return for an asset in a market, given the risk-free rate available to investors and the risk of the market as a whole.

The CAPM is usually expressed:

$$E(R_i) = R_f + \beta_i (E(R_m) - R_f)$$

- β, Beta, is the measure of asset sensitivity to a movement in the overall market; Beta is usually found via regression on historical data. Betas exceeding one signify more than average "riskiness"; betas below one indicate lower than average.
- $(E(R_m) - R_f)$ is the market premium, the historically

observed excess return of the market over the risk-free rate.

Once the expected return, $E(r_i)$, is calculated using CAPM, the future cash flows of the asset can be discounted to their present value using this rate to establish the correct price for the asset. A more risky stock will have a higher beta and will be discounted at a higher rate; less sensitive stocks will have lower betas and be discounted at a lower rate. In theory, an asset is correctly priced when its observed price is the same as its value calculated using the CAPM derived discount rate.

If the observed price is higher than the valuation, then the asset is overvalued; it is undervalued for a too low price:

- The incremental impact on risk and return when an additional risky asset, a, is added to the market portfolio, m, follows from the formulae for a two asset portfolio. These results are used to derive the asset appropriate discount rate.

  Risk =

  $$\left(w_m^2\sigma_m^2 + \left[w_a^2\sigma_a^2 + 2w_m w_a \rho_{am}\sigma_a\sigma_m\right]\right)$$

  Hence, risk added to portfolio =

  $$\left[w_a^2\sigma_a^2 + 2w_m w_a \rho_{am}\sigma_a\sigma_m\right]$$

  but since the weight of the asset will be relatively low, $w_a^2 \approx 0$

  i.e. additional risk

  $$= \left[2w_m w_a \rho_{am}\sigma_a\sigma_m\right]$$

  Return =

  $$(w_m E(R_m) + [w_a E(R_a)])$$

  Hence additional return $= [w_a E(R_a)]$
- If an asset, a, is correctly priced, the improvement in risk to return achieved by adding it to the market portfolio, m, will at least match the gains of spending that money on an increased stake in the market portfolio. The assumption is that the investor will purchase the asset with funds borrowed at the risk-free rate, R_f; this is rational if $E(R_a) > R_f$.

Thus:

$$[w_a(E(R_a)-R_f)]/[2w_m w_a \rho_{am}\sigma_a\sigma_m]$$
$$=[w_a(E(R_m)-R_f]/[2w_m w_a \sigma_m\sigma_m]$$

i.e.: $[E(R_a)]=R_f+[E(R_m)-R_f]*[\rho_{am}\sigma_a\sigma_m]/[\sigma_m\sigma_m]$

i.e.: $[E(R_a)]=R_f+[E(R_m)-R_f]*[\sigma_{am}]/[\sigma_{mm}]$

$[\sigma_{am}]/[\sigma_{mm}]$ is the "beta", β — the covariance between the asset and the market compared to the variance of the market, *i.e.* the sensitivity of the asset price to movement in the market portfolio.

CRITICISM

Despite its theoretical importance, some people question whether MPT is an ideal investing strategy, because its model of financial markets does not match the real world in many ways.

Assumptions

The mathematical framework of MPT makes many assumptions about investors and markets. Some are explicit in the equations, such as the use of Normal distributions to model returns. Others are implicit, such as the neglect of taxes and transaction fees.

None of these assumptions are entirely true, and each of them compromises MPT to some degree:

- Asset returns are normally distributed random variables. In fact, it is frequently observed that returns in equity and other markets are not normally distributed. Large swings occur in the market far more frequently than the normal distribution assumption would predict.
- Correlations between assets are fixed and constant forever. Correlations depend on systemic relationships between the underlying assets, and change when these relationships change. Examples include one country declaring war on another, or a general market crash. During times of financial crisis all assets tend to become positively correlated, because they all move together.

In other words, MPT breaks down precisely when investors are most in need of protection from risk.

- All investors aim to maximize economic utility. This is a key assumption of the efficient market hypothesis, upon which MPT relies.
- All investors are rational and risk-averse. This is another assumption of the efficient market hypothesis, but we now know from behavioural economics that market participants are not rational. It does not allow for"herd behaviour" or investors who will accept lower returns for higher risk. Casino gamblers clearly pay for risk, and it is possible that some stock traders will pay for risk as well.
- All investors have access to the same information at the same time. This also comes from the efficient market hypothesis. In fact, real markets contain information asymmetry, insider trading, and those who are simply better informed than others.
- Investors have an accurate conception of possible returns, *i.e.*, the probability beliefs of investors match the true distribution of returns. A different possibility is that investors' expectations are biased, causing market prices to be informationally inefficient. This possibility is studied in the field of behavioural finance, which uses psychological assumptions to provide alternatives to the CAPM such as the overconfidence-based asset pricing model of Kent Daniel, David Hirshleifer, and Avanidhar Subrahmanyam.
- There are no taxes or transaction costs. Real financial products are subject both to taxes and transaction costs and taking these into account will alter the composition of the optimum portfolio. These assumptions can be relaxed with more complicated versions of the model.
- All investors are price takers, *i.e.*, their actions do not influence prices. In reality, sufficiently large sales or purchases of individual assets can shift market prices

for that asset and others An investor may not even be able to assemble the theoretically optimal portfolio if the market moves too much while they are buying the required securities.

- Any investor can lend and borrow an unlimited amount at the risk free rate of interest. In reality, every investor has a credit limit.
- All securities can be divided into parcels of any size. In reality, fractional shares usually cannot be bought or sold, and some assets have minimum orders sizes.

More complex versions of MPT can take into account a more sophisticated model of the world but all mathematical models of finance still rely on many unrealistic premises.

MPT Does not Really Model the Market

The risk, return, and correlation measures used by MPT are expected values, which means that they are mathematical statements about the future In practice investors must substitute predictions based on historical measurements of asset return and volatility for these values in the equations. Very often such predictions are wrong, as captured in the classic disclaimer"past performance is not necessarily indicative of future results."

More fundamentally, investors are stuck with estimating key parametres from past market data because MPT attempts to model risk in terms of the likelihood of losses, but says nothing about why those losses might occur. The risk measurements used are probabilistic in nature, not structural. This is a major difference as compared to many engineering approaches to risk management.

Options theory and MPT have at least one important conceptual difference from the probabilistic risk assessment done by nuclear power [plants]. A PRA is what economists would call a *structural model*. The components of a system and their relationships are modeled in Monte Carlo simulations. If valve X fails, it causes a loss of back pressure on pump Y, causing a drop in flow to vessel Z, and so on.

But in the Black-Scholes equation and MPT, there is no

attempt to explain an underlying structure to price changes. Various outcomes are simply given probabilities. And, unlike the PRA, if there is no history of a particular system-level event like a liquidity crisis, there is no way to compute the odds of it. If nuclear engineers ran risk management this way, they would never be able to compute the odds of a meltdown at a particular plant until several similar events occurred in the same reactor design.

Essentially, the mathematics of MPT view the markets as a collection of dice. By examining past market data we can develop hypotheses about how the dice are weighted, but this isn't helpful if the markets are actually dependent upon a much bigger and more complicated chaotic system — the world. For this reason, accurate structural models of real financial markets are unlikely to be forthcoming because they would essentially be structural models of the entire world. Nonetheless there is growing awareness of the concept of systemic risk in financial markets, which should lead to more sophisticated market models.

Variance is not a Good Measure of Risk

Mathematical risk measurements are also useful only to the degree that they reflect investors' true concerns — there is no point minimizing a variable that nobody cares about in practice. MPT uses the mathematical concept of variance to quantify risk, and this might be justified under the assumption of elliptically distributed returns such as normally distributed returns, but for general return distributions other risk measures might better reflect investor's true preferences.

In particular, variance is a symmetric measure that counts abnormally high returns as just as risky as abnormally low returns. In reality, investors are only concerned about losses, which shows that our intuitive concept of risk is fundamentally asymmetric in nature.

"Optimal" doesn't Necessarily Mean "Most Profitable"

MPT does not account for the social, environmental,

strategic, or personal dimensions of investment decisions. It only attempts to maximize returns, without regard to other consequences. In a narrow sense, its complete reliance on asset prices makes it vulnerable to all the standard market failures such as those arising from information asymmetry, externalities, and public goods. It also rewards corporate fraud and dishonest accounting. More broadly, a firm may have strategic or social goals that shape its investment decisions, and an individual investor might have personal goals. In either case, information other than historical returns is relevant.

EXTENSIONS

Since MPT's introduction in 1952, many attempts have been made to improve the model, especially by using more realistic assumptions. Post-modern portfolio theory extends MPT by adopting non-normally distributed, asymmetric measures of risk. This helps with some of these problems, but not others.

OTHER APPLICATIONS

Applications to Project Portfolios and other"Non-Financial" Assets

Some experts apply MPT to portfolios of projects and other assets besides financial instruments.

When MPT is applied outside of traditional financial portfolios, some differences between the different types of portfolios must be considered:

- The assets in financial portfolios are continuously divisible while portfolios of projects like new software development are"lumpy". For example, while we can compute that the optimal portfolio position for 3 stocks is 44%, 35%, 21%, the optimal position for an IT portfolio may not allow us to simply change the amount spent on a project. IT projects might be all or nothing or, at least, have logical units that cannot be separated. A portfolio optimization method would have to take the discrete nature of some IT projects into account.

- The assets of financial portfolios are liquid can be assessed or re-assessed at any point in time while opportunities for new projects may be limited and may appear in limited windows of time and projects that have already been initiated cannot be abandoned without the loss of the sunk costs.

Neither of these necessarily eliminate the possibility of using MPT and such portfolios. They simply indicate the need to run the optimization with an additional set of mathematically-expressed constraints that would not normally apply to financial portfolios. Furthermore, some of the simplest elements of Modern Portfolio Theory are applicable to virtually any kind of portfolio.

The concept of capturing the risk tolerance of an investor by documenting how much risk is acceptable for a given return could be and is applied to a variety of decision analysis problems. MPT, however, uses historical variance as a measure of risk and portfolios of assets like IT projects don't usually have an"historical variance" for a new piece of software.

In this case, the MPT investment boundary can be expressed in more general terms like"chance of an ROI less than cost of capital" or"chance of losing more than half of the investment".

When risk is put in terms of uncertainty about forecasts and possible losses then the concept is transferable to various types of investment.

Application to other Disciplines

In the 1970s, concepts from Modern Portfolio Theory found their way into the field of regional science. In a series of seminal works, Michael Conroy modeled the labour force in the economy using portfolio-theoretic methods to examine growth and variability in the labour force. This was followed by a long literature on the relationship between economic growth and volatility.

More recently, modern portfolio theory has been used to model the self-concept in social psychology. When the self attributes comprising the self-concept constitute a well-diversified portfolio, then psychological outcomes at the level of the individual such as mood and self-esteem should be more stable than when the self-concept is undiversified.

This prediction has been confirmed in studies involving human subjects. Recently, modern portfolio theory has been applied to modelling the uncertainty and correlation between documents in information retrieval. Given a query, the aim is to maximize the overall relevance of a ranked list of documents and at the same time minimize the overall uncertainty of the ranked list

COMPARISON WITH ARBITRAGE PRICING THEORY

The SML and CAPM are often contrasted with the arbitrage pricing theory, which holds that the expected return of a financial asset can be modeled as a linear function of various macro-economic factors, where sensitivity to changes in each factor is represented by a factor specific beta coefficient. The APT is less restrictive in its assumptions: it allows for an explanatory model of asset returns, and assumes that each investor will hold a unique portfolio with its own particular array of betas, as opposed to the identical"market portfolio". Unlike the CAPM, the APT, however, does not itself reveal the identity of its priced factors - the number and nature of these factors is likely to change over time and between economies.

PORTFOLIO CONSTRUCTION

Robust portfolio construction, in line with SRI fund mandate. Application of strong risk control measures. The investment process ends with the construction of the SRI portfolio, which may vary depending on differing client risk/ return requirements. At this stage, we consider position size, the market capitalisation breakdown, sector and theme weightings and geographical positioning to effectively manage risk.

Parametres applied during portfolio construction:

- Relevant benchmark
- Target range in terms of total stock holdings

- Tracking error
- Market cap weightings
- Sector/geographical weightings relative to benchmark

The responsibility for decisions to purchase or sell stocks rest exclusively with the fund managers. They aim to be fully invested at all times, with cash being held usually for liquidity purposes. In constructing the portfolio, the fund managers are able to draw on the resources of the Henderson Portfolio Risk and Performance Measurement team, to assess the likely impact of portfolio re-organisation, in terms of risk and return to ensure that individual positions reflect the fund manager's level of conviction in each company investment.

UNDERSTANDING PORTFOLIO CONSTRUCTION METHODOLOGY

The methodology used by fund managers to construct their portfolios will very much depend on the type of fund that they are managing, as well as the style of management that they use. Although there are many general funds, such as segregated pension funds, that invest globally, there is a continuing trend towards specialization in particular funds, such as segregated pension funds, that invest globally, there is a continuing trend towards specialization in particular markets, and each market will have its own principal considerations. Equity management involves an element of asset allocation, either to countries managed by the European, Far Eastern Latin America or Emerging Markets desks, or to industries within single countries, especially within the UK. Having said this internationalization of many companies in recent years has resulted in fund managers looking at industry grouping irrespective of the country in which the corporate is based. Since firms derive an increasing proportion of their earnings from countries outside their domicile, it is becoming less and les relevant analyses them on the basis of economic prospects for that country, More relevant are the issues facing each industry.

Glaxo welcome have traditionally derived the greatest proportion (over 40%) of their earnings from overseas. Others, such as Vodafone, are rapidly increasing the percentages earned outside the UK. The number of different influences on a portfolio is quite diverse. This Creates the need For a broad range of different analyses so that the fund manager can look at his portfolio broken down in different ways, particularly useful are analyses of portfolio giving the weights allocated to each category, especially where these weights are compared to the constituents of the index used as part or all of the fund's bench mark.

Other Analyses: Equities are sensitive to a number of different factors affecting their market prices in the short, medium or long term. This means that the fund manager needs to look at his portfolio, and the securities held in them, from a number of different perspectives and involves assimilating the huge quantities of data available to fund managers, sourced from external brokers as well as their own firm's analysts. The Key is the interpretation of the data: what does the news imply for a security or overall industry grouping? Portfolio level analysis includes the following.

Fund Break down By:

- *Company Size*: In an economic upswing smaller companies may grow faster than larger firms, whilst in a recession investors may prefer larger, more resilient companies
- *Economics theme*: E.g. Sensitive to oil prices, interest rates, factors affecting other economics in to products are sold. Over all portfolio factors such as the fund's beta can also provide useful risk information. As with most types of fund level analysis, the comparison of the funds against the bench mark is the most useful. Other security level analysis include the price to earning ratio growth which is a dynamic measure of a trend of changing value.
- If it is important to the fund manager that he receives dividends, then he might look at the 'dividend cover ', which is the ration of earnings per share over dividends per share. Again, the trend of this over time will be useful information.

Industry Case Studies:

- Each industries sector will be affected differently by macro economics news as well as by industry specific factors, such as well as by industry specific factors, such as technological innovation. The Following is a very high level review of three industrial sectors, included in attempts to bring out the fact that industries need to be individually analysed by fund managers.

Telecom Industry:

- The Telecommunications industry is a relatively new sector and is still experiencing a high rate of growth as its market continues to develop. Let us look at the share prices for two participants, Vodafone and British Telecom, for the period from January 1st 1980 to 1sr January 2001, displayed as relative to the FT All share.
- While BT's Relative growth over this period is impressive it is some what eclipsed by the performance of Vodafone at 2,500% growth. How ever, the threats to the industry and consequent risks to market value are serve. In recent months several factors have had a detrimental effect on the sectors; these include the high level of market competition.
- In addition, on – going research and development costs and huge third generation data license fees have given rise to a huge requirement and consequent competition for funding. From 1st January 2000 to 1st January 2001, the industry has struggled.
- Thus this sub – theme can be very important factors: both firms performed well initially, on the back of the general Telecoms Boom, but BSkyB are now in the ascendancy further to their ' first mover' advantage in brining their digital products to market. This analysis also emphasizes the importance of all aspects of a business.

Consumer Goods:

- The consumer goods sectors are strongly affected by

macroeconomic factors, as well as changes in tastes which will affect the sales revenue and profits of individual firms. One of the key assets for consumer goods firms is the strength of their brand. A good examples of this can be seen their company valuation wax and wane on the basis of inter alias, the strength of their brand.

- Macroeconomics factors having a significant impact on consumer goods firms include the following. Rises in the Expected costs of production, particularly labour, which represents a very high proportion of the cost of goods, will have a detrimental effect on this sector. Demand factors, which might include the savings ration, will affect firms 'pricing power 'ie their ability to determine retail prices. Similarly the strengthening of the exchange rate between the firm's currency of domicile and that of its major export market will reduce the competitiveness of goods and tend to reduce sales revenue, profits and consequently equity earnings.

Oil:

- The oil industry is a relatively old, well established industry. The oligopolistic market structure is unlikely to change significantly in the foreseeable future. Other features of the market include the setting of the underlying commodity price by the organization of petroleum exporting countries which is dominated by Saudi Arabia. The market has a very effective political and public pressure.
- In general, stocks are likely to move inline with each other, since they will be affected by the same factors roughly equally, one of the principal factors obviously being the prevailing commodity market barrel price of oil.

CONCEPT OF RISK

Humans have always sought to achieve security and reduce uncertainty.

Risk lies at all levels of human and business activity:

- Big irony-technology has reduced loss frequencies but loss severities have increased leading to greater risk.
- Risk is universal. Individuals, business and government must all cope with it by design or default.
- Risk is often confused with uncertainty. While risk involves an element of uncertainty, a situation is uncertain if decision maker does not have enough information to assign probabilities to possible outcomes.
- Risk and uncertainty are related in that uncertainty leads to risk. When an event has outcomes lacking in predictability it is uncertain.

DEFINITIONS OF RISK

No universal definition exists. Sometimes the meaning of word "risk" varies depending on context e.g. it is commonly used in insurance to refer to insured items like cars, buildings etc.

Risk has also been defined as:

- A combination of hazards measured by probability.
- A condition in which losses are possible.
- Uncertainty of loss.

Statisticians and economists associate risk with variability. From this we define risk to mean the variation of actual outcomes from expected outcomes e.g. in an investment decision-Expected outcome = profit; actual outcome=loss hence risk.

CLASSIFICATION OF RISK

Risks can be classified into several categories depending on context e.g:

- Inherent Business risks
- Incidental risks
- Pure and speculative risks
- Particular and fundamental risks
- Insurable and uninsurable risks
- Event risks. risks organization. Can be company-specific risks

Inherent risks-all activities impacting negatively on operating profit of an or that affect the economy at large.

Unsystematic risks include sales variability, low profitability etc. Incidental Risks arise naturally from a company's business activities but do not form part of its core business e.g. interest rate risk, liquidity risk, investment risk, credit risk, currency risk etc. Also known as financial risks. Such risks generally not insurable.

Use hedging techniques:

- Event risks also known as pure risks arise from natural phenomena mainly and human error. They are one way risks *i.e.* loss/no loss situations e.g. fire, theft, liability, flood etc. Event risks are insurable.
- Event risks can further be divided into particular and fundamental risks. Fundamental risks are impersonal in origin and affect society at large e.g. war, drought etc. Particular risks are personal in origin and affect individuals or small groups e.g. fire, theft, vehicle accidents etc. Distinction between fundamental and particular risks is not rigid e.g. some fundamental risks like earthquake and floods are insurable.
- Pure and speculative risks. This classification looks at risks in terms of their outcomes. Pure risks produce either a loss or no loss. Speculative risks produce a loss, no loss or a gain hence they have an upside and a downside.
- Diversifiable and non-diversifiable risks. A risk is diversifiable if it can be reduced by pooling or risk agreements sharing. A non-diversifiable risk cannot be reduced through pooling e.g. the risk of economic depression. Risk pooling does not eliminate the downside totally because a catastrophe can still affect many exposure units at the same time e.g. a hurricane.

INSURABLE/UNINSURABLE RISKS

Generally pure and particular risks are insurable while fundamental and speculative ones are not.

A risk is insurable if:

- It is measurable in financial terms.

- The possibility of loss is fortuitous and not inevitable.
- A sufficiently large number of homogenous risks can be pooled to enable the law of large numbers to operate.
- The person who insures has insurable interest in the subject matter to be insured.
- The contract of insurance must not be illegal or against public policy.

PERIL AND HAZARD

- Peril is a cause/source of loss e.g. fire, theft, accidents, explosions etc. Existence of perils gives rise to risk.
- Hazards are those factors relating to the environment in which losses may arise. A house built near a big river known to burst its banks often is exposed to the peril of flood and the hazard is the proximity of the house to the river which makes the peril of flood more likely to occur.
- Hazards can be physical or moral. Physical hazards relate to the physical environment e.g. keeping flammable liquids in a building.
- Moral hazard relates to attitudes and behaviour of people especially the propensity of individuals to alter their behaviour because they are insured.

  There are 2 types of moral hazard:

  1. *Ex ante moral hazard*: Relates to the effect insurance can have on the insured's incentive to prevent losses e.g. does a person who has motor insurance drive less carefully than a person without insurance?
  2. *Ex post moral hazard*: This relates to the effect insurance can have on the insured's incentive to mitigate the extent of a loss that has already occurred e.g. does the existence of insurance remove the incentive on the part of the insured to take more bold steps to put out a fire than would otherwise be the case if the person had no insurance?

What then is the effect of moral hazard on insurance markets?

- Suppose X has R10 000 and owns a R60 000 car. The probability of X having an accident depends on careful he drives. When X drives fast probability of an accident is 50%. When he drives slowly probability of an accident goes down to 20%. X estimates that he incurs additional expenses of R5 000 by driving slowly in additional travel time needed to complete his job. If the insurance company assumes that X will drive carefully the pure premium they will charge will be (0.2 × R60 000) = R12 000. If the insurer however assumes X will drive fast the pure premium will be R30 000 *i.e.* (0.5 × R60 000).
- The question then is which premium should the insurer charge? To answer this question we have to look at X's incentives for being careful. With full insurance he will be indemnified if his car is damaged. If he buys insurance at R12 000 what incentive does he have to spend an additional R5 000 driving slowly (carefully)? The benefit of taking care accrues to the insurer not to him. Knowing the X has no incentive to drive carefully, insurer would probably charge him R30 000 not R12 000.

INSURER RESPONSES TO MORAL HAZARD

What actions can insurers take to manage moral hazard? Reason for existence of moral hazard is that insurance transfers benefits of being careful from insured to the insurer while insured retains additional cost of being careful.

To improve this insurers use:

- *Deductibles*: These try to transfer some of the cost of losses back to the insured.
- *Retrospective rating*: Under this method the premium is adjusted at the end of the insurance period to reflect insured's actual loss experience.
- *Experience rating*: The premium varies with the insured's loss experience from previous time periods.

Both methods reward insured for taking care and producing fewer losses.

ADVERSE SELECTION

Key assumption is that buyers and sellers have complete information. In practice this is not the case. Information asymmetry can affect insurance markets because it leads to adverse selection.

Adverse selection arises from:

- Buyers of insurance having superior information about the risk than the insurer.
- The insurer being unable to distinguish between individual risk types.

Adverse selection is managed by compelling disclosure of information. Despite the question can be posed as to why insurance companies are willing and able to accept risks faced by other organizations which in some cases may be financially better off?

Several reasons may be cited:

- Insurers hold large amounts of capital as required by regulation.
- They benefit from the law of large numbers. The law of large numbers basically states that the larger the number of exposure units in the pool the more accurate loss predictions tend to be. In other words the larger the portfolio of homogenous risks held, the smaller the standard deviation tends to be provided the exposure units in question are independently exposed to loss. The standard deviation here is used as a measure of risk.
- Insdurers also benefit from the support they get from reinsurers.
- They are more psychologically prepared to handle risk since it is their business to do so.
- They have wide statistical information networks on risks. This enables them to quantify risk better than those that come to insure.

LIMITATIONS OF INSURANCE

- Unavailability of cover for uninsurable risks.

- Contracts are not tailor-made to the specific needs of individual clients.
- Insurance contracts tend to be classical with much emphasis placed on terms, conditions, exceptions etc. This makes insurance complex for the layman to understand.
- Limited capacity of insurers often leaves clients inadequately covered.
- Premiums are often dictated by other factors that may have no direct bearing on the insured.

MARKET FAILURE IN INSURANCE

In a perfectly competitive market government intervention will only be desirable where:

- Actual or potential market failures exist.
- The market failures could lead to inefficiency or inequity.
- Government action can ameliorate the inefficiency or inequity.

Thus if at least one of the 3 conditions is not met government intervention is not warranted. What are the causes of market failure in insurance?

- Specialized risks that cannot be pooled.
- Adverse selection arising from information asymmetries.
- Public goods-where risk reduction initiatives by X confers benefits on Y then there is no incentive for X to manage the risk in question.
- Inadequate compensation. A market for risk takers can only thrive if the returns for taking the risk justify the investment.
- Market power

FORMS OF MARKET FAILURE IN INSURANCE MARKETS

- *Market power i.e.:* The ability of one or few sellers/ buyers to influence the price of a product/service. Under the competitive model buyers are supposed to be price takers who cannot influence the price.

- *Externalities*: An externality exists when production or consumption has direct uncompensated effects on others. The effects can either be positive or negative. A negative externality would exist where X murders Y to collect the proceeds of an insurance policy.
- *Free rider problems*: Goods available to people at no cost e.g. police protection suffer from free rider problems. In insurance if a trade association lobbies for favourable legislation non-members would also benefit hence a free rider problem.
- *Imperfect information*: Information asymmetries cause market failure.

To deal with these problems insurance markets are subject to regulation.

Problem with regulation is that often:

- It goes beyond what is necessary to cure market failure.
- It leads to undesired consequencies.
- It may deprive consumers of the benefits of competition.
- It may burden the market with additional costs. Regulation itself is not cost-free.

DECISION MAKING UNDER CONDITIONS OF RISK AND UNCERTAINTY

We defined risk as the variation of actual outcomes from expected outcomes. Venturing into a new market can be Presence termed risky because the actual profit/loss is uncertain.

Uncertainty is doubt that arises from inability to predict future outcomes. of risk and uncertainty complicates decision-making. Consider X who has R10 000. He asks a friend what to do with the money. X is advised to either put the money under his mattress or invest it in a one year certificate of deposit guaranteed to earn 7% a year in interest. The decision X faces is simple and assuming he is rational he will invest the money and earn a pay-off of R700 at end of year.

Tossing If we introduce an element of risk and uncertainty

X's decision process becomes more complicated. Suppose we offer X a 3rd option-to invest the R10 000 in a unit trust where the pay-off at end of year depends on a coin. If the coin comes up heads, X will earn 30% on his investment. However if the coin comes up tails, X will earn a negative return of 15%.

The 3 possibilities can therefore be summarized as follows:

- *Option 1*: Do nothing-pay-off =R10 000
- *Option 2*: Invest in certificate of deposit-pay-off=R10 700
- *Option 3*: Invest in a unit trust-pay-off can either be R13 000 or R8 500

To help X make a decision a statistical concept called the Expected Monetary Value can be introduced.

EV = SpiXi

Where *pi* is the probability of a particular outcome *Xi*. The expected value is the value that would prevail on average if many draws were made from a random distribution. Thus the expected value for X would be:

EV3=0.5 × R13 000+0.5 × R8 500=R10 750

The expected values for options 1 and 2 are R10 000 and R10 700 respectively. Given this scenario X would probably choose option 3.

PROBABILITY AND RISK

There are various types of probability that can be used in the measurement of risk.

These are:

- Objective or *a priori* probabilities.
- Subjective probabilities.
- Relative frequencies and empirical probabilities.

A *priori* probabilities are those that are known in advance e.g. when a coin is tossed the probability of it landing either heads or tails is 50%. Subjective probabilities are based on the decision maker's judgment and estimation. Subjective probabilities are used where the decision maker has insufficient information to determine the probability in any other more reliable manner. Experience has shown that people tend to underestimate well-known events and overestimate rare events. This is because the more a risk occurs the more the information we have about it. Empirical probabilities are based on observation and experimentation. This is the most common method in practice. Thus one cannot use a *priori* probabilities to determine the likelihood of death. Probability of death can be more accurately estimated from past events.

PROBABILITY DISTRIBUTIONS

Are useful for evaluating risk:

- The binomial distribution deals with two parametres e.g. loss or no loss. The binomial distribution has two parametres describing the total number of events and the probability that the event will take place. Thus we can use the binomial distribution to determine the probability distribution of the number of accidents which can take place in a fleet of *N* vehicles that are independently exposed to loss.
- The normal distribution is also a two-parametre distribution. It uses the mean and the standard deviation. The normal distribution is bell-shaped and under certain circumstances other distributions like the binomial distribution can be approximated by the normal distribution.
- The Poisson distribution is a single parametre distribution. It approximates the binomial distribution where the number of exposure units *(N)* is very large each facing a very small chance of a loss *(p)*

EXPECTED UTILITY HYPOTHESIS

Utility is loosely defined as an index of satisfaction derived from economic goods. A utility function maps a particular wealth level to a corresponding level of satisfaction.

People are generally risk-averse and a risk-averse utility function is based on the following two assumptions:

- Increasing wealth leads to increasing levels of satisfaction.
- The marginal utility of wealth decreases as wealth increases.

Suppose X picks R100. By the 1st assumption he will feel better because his wealth has increased. If a few minutes later X picks another R100 his satisfaction increases again but by the 2nd assumption it does not increase as much as it did when he picked the 1st R100. The 2nd assumption is known as the law of diminishing marginal utility.

Utility helps us understand why people make decisions that are different from what the expected monetary value may suggest. Consider a person who has a lottery ticket which pays R20 000 if head appears. This means the expected value he faces is R10 000. If the person is offered R8 000 to give up the ticket the general consensus is that the person would accept rather play the game and risk getting nothing if tail appears. The question is why would a person accept less when he has a realistic chance of getting more? The answer is that people do not value money in a linear fashion hence the marginal utility diminishes as wealth increases.

MANAGING RISK

Managing risk in a business context is a process involving the following integrated steps:

- Risk identification
- Risk evaluation
- Risk control
- Risk financing
- Monitoring and control.

Each of the steps affects the one that comes after it e.g. if the identification techniques are inefficient wrong decisions are likely to be taken regarding risk evaluation, control and financing. It must also be noted that insurance is a function within the broader risk financing component of the risk management process.

RISK IDENTIFICATION

Is perhaps the most crucial step in the entire process. Risk identification must start by identifying the sources of risk.

Risk emanates from the following sources:

- The physical environment

- The social environment
- The political environment
- The legal environment
- The operational environment
- The economic environment.

Two approaches are used to identify risks namely the macro approach and the micro approach. Each of these approaches uses a variety of techniques to identify risk e.g. the macro techniques include insurance reviews, financial statement analysis while the micro techniques encompass HAZOP studies, fault tree analysis, and many others. Risk identification is critical as it determines the effectiveness with which risks facing the organization will be tackled.

RISK EVALUATION

This part of the risk management process enables risks to be ranked in terms of their importance to the organization. Information regarding estimates of possible financial consequences and estimates of the likelihood of the risk producing losses are provided under this step of the risk management process. Ranking is important as it influences the allocation of resources within the firm for managing and controlling risks. Techniques such as the maximum possible loss and the estimated maximum loss are often used to evaluate risk.

RISK CONTROL

Includes techniques, tools and strategies that seek to avoid, prevent, reduce or otherwise control the frequency and/or magnitude of loss.

Risk control measures include:

- Risk avoidance-if risk emanates from man's interaction with the environment then abandoning a venture also avoids the attendant risks.
- Loss prevention-seeks to reduce the number of losses or to eliminate them completely. Loss prevention measures seek to alter/modify the hazard, alter/modify the environment in which the hazard exists

and/or intervene in the processes whereby hazard and environment interact.

- Loss reduction-aim to reduce the potential severity of a loss should it occur e.g. sprinkler systems. Loss reduction measures are post-loss measures hence they are a tacit admission on the part of the risk manager that some losses will still occur despite the organization's best efforts.

RISK FINANCING

Risk financing methods fall into two classes: Retention and Transfer. Retention involves the organization using its own resources to finance risks. Retention can be planned or unplanned. Risk can be financed through insurance transfer. Insurance transfers focus on the economic feasibility of the transfer *i.e.* if the cost of transfer exceeds the cost of expected losses then transfer would not be economically feasible.

An insurance transaction involves 4 elements:

1. A contractual agreement;
2. A premium payment or promise to pay by the insured;
3. A benefit payment conditioned on circumstances usually of fortuitous loss; and
4. Presence of a pool of resources held by the insurer to pay claims.

CONSIDERATIONS AFFECTING CHOICE BETWEEN RETENTION AND TRANSFER

The key question here is: What factors should be taken into account by an organization when deciding whether to transfer or retain a risk? A cost/benefit analysis is needed taking into account factors internal and external to the organization.

Some of the key factors influencing the decision are:

- *Legal, economic and public policy limitations*: Because transfer invariably involves use of contracts, these are open to interpretation which leave the firm exposed because it interpreted the contract differently from what courts of law may rule e.g. stacking of limits in the US.

- *Degree of control*: The degree of control that a firm has on the risks it faces has a strong influence on the attractiveness of retention programmes. The larger the degree of control the more attractive retention becomes benefits relative to insurance. From a public policy view, society when the burden of losses falls on the party best equipped to control loss-producing events.
- *Insurance loading fees*: Insurance loadings are the amount by which premium exceeds the expected value of loss reimbursements. These loadings could be to cover administrative expenses, acquisition costs, profit margins etc. Holding other factors constant, the higher the loadings, the more attractive retention becomes.
- *Value of services provided by insurers*: Insurers provide other services whose cost is bundled in the premium charged loss adjustment, loss control and risk management advice.
- *Opportunity costs*: Purchase of insurance usually involves payment of premium upfront. Under this condition issue of retention versus transfer should take into account investment income that could be earned between payment of the premium and payment of the claim. This issue is very relevant in long-tail business like liability insurance.
- *Tax considerations*: In general insurance companies tend to receive favourable tax treatment relative to consumers of insurance. As a result an insurer's cost of financing a risk often is lower than the cost of the insured firm financing the risk itself. Favourable tax treatment comes from the ability of insurers to deduct from current taxable income provisions for future claim payments.
- *Availability of cover in the market*: If there is no cover in the transfer market then retention becomes the only option.

NON-INSURANCE TRANSFERS

Some risks of a financial nature that cannot be insured can be financed through hedging. Hedging involves actions where a possible gain is balanced against a possible loss.

Four types of contracts can be used to hedge risk:

- Forwards
- Futures
- Options
- Swaps

A forward contract specifies trading terms for a transaction to take place at a future time. Forwards are personal contracts customised to needs of one party and are thus not easily transferable. They are written on commodities, financial assets like stocks and bonds as well as currency exchanges. Futures are like forwards but they differ in that futures are traded on exchanges, they contain standard terms and are not customised to individual needs. Futures are more widely used than forwards.

An option is a contract that gives its holder the right to buy/sell assets at a specified price on or before a specified date. Options give the holder protection against unfavourable price movements but allow for the benefit of a price increase.

A swap is the exchange of one security for another and they are popular with traders in interest rates and currency rates. When a manufacturer contracts to sell a fixed product at a fixed price in foreign currency it faces currency risk between the currency where the product is sold and that of where the product is manufactured.

Consider a US manufacturer who agrees to deliver 1 000 tractors to a South African distributor in 6 months at a price of R165 000 per tractor. The current exchange rate between there US$ and the Rand lets assume is R5.5 per US$. This means the Rand selling price of each tractor translates to US$30 000 in current terms (*i.e.* R165 000/5.5). The total amount of the transaction in US$ is $30m or R165m. If manufacturing and shipping costs are $28 000 per tractor, the manufacturer hopes to make a profit of $2 000 per tractor. However the actual profit of the manufacturer depends on the exchange rate between the Rand and the US dollar at the time of performance which is 6 months from now.

The position of the manufacturer is as follows:

- Appreciation of the Rand relative to the US Dollar the manufacturer's profit in US dollars increases.
- If the Rand depreciates relative to the dollar the profit to the manufacturer decreases.The question then is how can the manufacturer manage this risk?
- One way could be for the manufacturer to borrow R165m from a dealer in currencies promising to replace the borrowed funds using proceeds from the sale of tractors. The manufacturer would buy the R165m for US$30m based on the current exchange rate thus locking his eventual profit on the transaction.
- A more common method would be for the manufacturer to use a futures contract. In this context a futures contract would be a promise to deliver a specified amount of a foreign currency at the end of a given time frame. If the manufacturer does not want to bear the currency risk arising from his promise to deliver the tractors, he can offset the risk by directing a dealer in foreign currency to sell a futures contract obligating the manufacturer to deliver R165m in 6 months. At the time payment is received for the tractors, the manufacturer buys back the futures contract. Any gain or loss on the tractor sale caused by currency fluctuation is offset by a corresponding loss or gain on the futures contract.

Use of a futures contract avoids the inconvenience of dealing with large amounts of foreign currencies themselves. Suppose the value of the manufacturer's profit on the tractor sale declines. Due to the decline R165 000 per tractor now converts to US$27 500 a drop of US$500 from the original US$28 000. However this loss would be offset by a gain on the futures transaction. When the value of the Rand drops to 6.0 value of the futures contract also drops meaning the manufacturer will repurchase the contract at less than what he received when he sold it hence a gain on the futures transaction offsets the loss on the tractor sales. Conversely, a gain in the value of the Rand to say 5.0 to the dollar translates into an increased profit on the tractor sales but would be offset by a loss that would be made on the futures contract.

Example of a Swap

Consider 2 firms one in the UK and another in the US. The 2 firms can borrow funds in their own country or that of the other. The US firm wants to finance a project in the UK for which it needs the pound sterling. Similarly the British firm needs to finance a project in US dollars. We assume that each firm can borrow domestically at a lower rate of interest than it can borrow in a foreign market.

Suppose the lenders offer the following rates of interest:

- In the UK a British firm can borrow at 9.0% while a US borrower is charged 11.0%
- In the US a British borrower would be charged 12.0% while a US firm would be charged 10.0%. Clearly each firm has the advantage of borrowing at home. Question is: How can each firm exploit this?
- UK firm borrows 100 pounds at 9% and immediately loans it to the US firm. US firm would have borrowed pounds at 11% so it will be happy to pay 9%.
- In turn US firm borrows US$155 the current equivalent of 100 pounds at 10% and immediately loans it to the UK firm.

After the loan, period which could be 5yrs the firms simply return each other's principals. The net result is that each firm got foreign financing at better rates than it could using its own credit.

MEASURING RISK AND RETURNS

Most investors do not hold stocks in isolation. Instead, they choose to hold a portfolio of several stocks. When this is the case, a portion of an individual stock's risk can be eliminated, *i.e.*, diversified away. This principle is presented on the Diversification page. First, the computation of the expected return, variance, and standard deviation of a portfolio must be emphasized.

Table. Probability Distribution for the returns on stocks A and B.

State	Probability	Return onStock A	Return onStock B
1	20%	5%	50%
2	30%	10%	30%
3	30%	15%	10%
3	20%	20%	–10%

From the Expected Return and Measures of Risk pages we know that the expected return on Stock A is 12.5%, the expected return on Stock B is 20%, the variance on Stock A is.00263, the variance on Stock B is.04200, the standard deviation on Stock S is 5.12%, and the standard deviation on Stock B is 20.49%.

PORTFOLIO EXPECTED RETURN

The Expected Return on a Portfolio is computed as the weighted average of the expected returns on the stocks which comprise the portfolio. The weights reflect the proportion of the portfolio invested in the stocks.

This can be expressed as follows:

$$E[R_p] = \sum_{i=1}^{N} w_i E[R_i]$$

where

- $E[R_p]$ = the expected return on the portfolio,
- N = the number of stocks in the portfolio,
- w_i = the proportion of the portfolio invested in stock i, and
- $E[R_i]$ = the expected return on stock i.

For a portfolio consisting of two assets, the equation can be expressed as,

$$E[R_p] = w_1 E[R_1] + (1 - w_1) E[R_2]$$

Expected Return on a Portfolio of Stocks A and B

Note: E[RA] = 12.5% and E[RB] = 20%

Portfolio consisting of 50% Stock A and 50% Stock B:

$$E[R_p] = .50(12.5\%) + (1 - .50)(20\%) = 16.25\%$$

Portfolio consisting of 75% Stock A and 25% Stock B:

$$E[R_p] = .50(12.5\%) + (1 - .50)(20\%) = 16.25\%$$

PORTFOLIO VARIANCE AND STANDARD DEVIATION

The variance/standard deviation of a portfolio reflects not only the variance/standard deviation of the stocks that make up the portfolio but also how the returns on the stocks which comprise the portfolio vary together. Two measures of how the returns on a pair of stocks vary together are the covariance and the correlation coefficient. *The Covariance between the returns on two stocks can be calculated using the following equation*:

$$Cov(R_1, R_2) = \sigma_{12} = \sum_{i=1}^{N} p_i (R_{1i} - E[R_1])(R_{2i} - E[R_2])$$

where,

- σ_{12} = the covariance between the returns on stocks 1 and 2,
- N = the number of states,
- p_i = the probability of state i,
- R_{1i} = the return on stock 1 in state i,
- $E[R_1]$ = the expected return on stock 1,
- R_{2i} = the return on stock 2 in state i, and
- $E[R_2]$ = the expected return on stock 2.

The Correlation Coefficient between the returns on two stocks can be calculated using the following equation:

$$Corr(R_1, R_2) = \rho_{12} = \frac{\sigma_{12}}{\sigma_1 \sigma_2} = \frac{Cov(R_1, R_2)}{SD(R_1)SD(R_2)}$$

where,

- ρ_{12} = the correlation coefficient between the returns on stocks 1 and 2,
- σ_{12} = the covariance between the returns on stocks 1 and 2,
- $\sigma 1$ = the standard deviation on stock 1, and

- $\sigma 2$ = the standard deviation on stock 2.

Covariance and Correlation Coefficent between the Returns on Stocks A and B:

$$\sigma_{AB} = .2(.05 - .125)(.5 - .2) + .3(.1 - .125)(.3 - 2)$$
$$+ .2(.15 - .125)(.1 - .2) + .2(.2 - .125)(-.1 - .0 - 2)$$
$$\sigma_{AB} = -.0105$$
$$\rho_{AB} = \frac{-.0105}{(.0512)(.2049)} = -1$$

Using either the correlation coefficient or the covariance, the Variance on a Two-Asset Portfolio can be calculated as follows:

$$\sigma_p^2 = (w_1)^2 \sigma_1^2 + (1 - w_1)^2 \sigma_2^2 + 2w_1(1 - w_1)\rho_{12}\sigma_1\sigma_2$$
$$= (w_1)^2 \sigma_1^2 + (1 - w_1)^2 \sigma_2^2 + 2w_1(1 - w_1)\sigma_{12}$$

The standard deviation on the porfolio equals the positive square root of the the variance. Variance and Standard Deviation on a Portfolio of Stocks A and B,

Portfolio consisting of 50% Stock A and 50% Stock B:

$$\sigma_p^2 = (.5)^2 (.0512)^2 + (1 - .5)^2 (.2049)^2 + 2(.5)$$
$$(1 - .5)(-1)(.0512)(.2049) = .00591$$
$$\sigma_p = \sqrt{.00591} = .0768 = 7.68\%$$

Portfolio consisting of 75% Stock A and 25% Stock B:

$$\sigma_p^2 = (.75)^2 (.0512)^2 + (1 - .75)^2 (.2049)^2 + 2(.75)$$
$$(1 - .75)(-1)(.0512)(.2049) = .00016$$
$$\sigma_p = \sqrt{.00016} = .0128 = 1.28\%$$

Notice that the portfolio formed by investing 75% in Stock A and 25% in Stock B has a lower variance and standard deviation than either Stocks A or B and the portfolio has a higher expected return than Stock A. This is the essence of Diversification, by forming portfolios some of the risk inherent in the individual stocks can be eliminated.

BUSINESS RISK

A business risk is a circumstance or factor that may have

a negative impact on the operation or profitability of a given company. Sometimes referred to as company risk, a business risk can be the result of internal conditions, as well as some external factors that may be evident in the wider business community. When it comes to outside factors that can create an element of business risk, one of the most predominant risks is that of a change in demand for the goods and services produced by the company.

If the change is a positive one, and the demand for the offerings of the company increase, the amount of risk is decreased a great deal. However, if consumer demand for the offerings decreases, either due to loss of business to competitors or a change in general economic conditions, the amount of risk involved to investors will increase significantly. When a company's risk factor is considered to be increased due to outside factors that are beyond the control of the company to correct, chances of attracting new investors is severely limited.

Internal factors may also result in the development of significant business risk for the investor. Often, these are factors that can be identified and corrected. If flagging sales can be attributed to an ineffectual marketing effort or a sales force that is not performing up to expectations, making changes in the marketing approach or restructuring the sales effort will often result in minimizing the perception of business risk on the part of potential investors. The same is true if a company's manufacturing facilities are not operating at optimum efficiency. Revamping the operational structure of the plants and facilities will decrease the element of business risk and result in higher profits at the same level of production and sales, which will in turn make the company more attractive to potential investors.

In general, any investor will consider the relationship of a company's securities and the business risk associated with the company before choosing to invest in the future of the corporation. While there is an element of business risk associated with any corporate operation, proper management will result in creating a balance between assets and securities that will keep the degree of business risk attractive to individuals and entities that consider investing funds into the operation.

FINANCIAL RISK

Risk has been know to man ever since he first faced adversity. It is an integral part of the evolution of man. Risk has been encountered primarily in his physical environment, later on in his social environment. With time, risk has evolved alongwith man.

The main risk Neolithic man faced was an attack by a wild animal. This was mitigated with the discovery of fire. Note: Mitigated not eliminated. Risk can rarely, if ever, be completely eliminated. This mitigation has now take the form hedging sales of currencies in the future using forward contracts or options. It is risk, but it has changed with man and his society. Risk is essentially, the probability that the outcome maybe damaging or result in a loss. With risk, the outcomes of an event are thrown open to uncertainty. Tossing a dice, is at a basic level a risky endeavor, that has uncertain outcomes. A risky outcome with a level of uncertainty involved.

STANDARD TYPES OF RISK

- *Pure Risk*: The situation in which a gain will not occur. The best possible outcome is that of no loss occurring.

  E.g.: A pilot flying an airplane will be happy with not crashing the airplane. He has not gained anything, but avoiding the catastrophe is the best possible outcome..
- *Speculative Risk*: A risk in which either a gain or a loss may occur.

  E.g.: You commit to sell a bag of wheat 3 months into the future at $10. Three months down if the price of wheat is $5 you make a profit of $5; if it is $15, you incur a loss of $5 by not being able to sell it at the market price. You speculated on the price of wheat 3 months into the future.

DIVERSIFIABLE V/S NON-DIVERSIFIABLE

Essentially diversifiable risk is that which can be mitigated through a process of pooling risks. Vice versa for non-diversifiable. *E.g.*: This is best exemplified through the theory of portfolio diversification. Buying one stock exposes you to 2 types of risk. Risk of the market and risk of the firm specific stock. Increasing the number of stocks in your portfolio would be a form of pooling that mitigates non-systematic risk of the whole portfolio. But the portfolio is implicitly exposed to the systematic risk of the market.

Risk averse individuals tend to be willing to pay the expected value of the loss rather than face the risk of the loss. This can be explained by the fact that the value of the loss, if incurred, is greater than the amount sacrificed by the individual to cover that loss. *E.g.*: If your house has a 20% chance of catching a fire and being destroyed. The loss you would incur on this would be $20,000. This the absolute amount you would lose given the house caught fire. The expected value of this is (.2)*($20,000) + (.8)*(0) = $4,000*. So the risk averse person would be willing to pay $4,000 to avoid a loss of $20,000 with a 20% probability.

The amount a risk averse person is willing to pay depends on the degree of risk aversion. This also depends on the amount of initial wealth that is at risk. Due to the declining marginal utility of wealth (each additional unit of wealth is less useful, as the level of wealth increase), a larger loss has a greater impact than a smaller loss. The effect of a larger loss is to set back the initial level of wealth, inverting the marginal utility of wealth. Though, the fact that a larger loss sets you back is something very obvious, and would not need an explanation.

In a financial context risk can be mitigated in two ways. One, by hedging using the correlations of stocks (CAPM), secondly using derivatives. Investors normally use both, though their applications are different. In a portfolio, the demand for any financial asset rests on the correlation between all the assets in the portfolio. In a portfolio, if two assets are negatively correlated then they have naturally hedged themselves against each other. Financial models are used to evaluate returns on portfolios. The CAPM is the most popular model.

CAPM or the Capital Asset Pricing model is the most frequently used financial model to enable portfolio diversification. If returns on risky assets have less than perfect correlation, *i.e.*, they do not naturally hedge against each other, risk averse individuals diversify risk in their holding of assets. A well diversified portfolio would have less fluctuation than returns on individually held financial assets.

So how does this work? Assume that you have a portfolio of financial assets. Each stock as explained in the types of risk, has two elements of risk. These are systematic and non-systematic risks. The non- systematic risk of individual securities can be mitigated through a well-diversified portfolio. Theoretically it can be completely negated by holding a diversified portfolio that is identical to the market. This normally does not happened since. This would be a very very large portfolio.

People would make money only based on the entire market moving up or down.. Most people who do hold real portfolios would like to make money regardless of the market movements. Given that non-systematic risk is virtually nullified by a large portfolio, the only risk that remains is the systematic risk. Thus, the only type of risk for which and investor would earn a return would be the systematic risk. This systematic risk is measured as Beta. Beta (β) calculates the volatility/exposure of a security's return to the entire market (CAPM) portfolio.

Mathematically this is how it is understood. A security'a' has its $\beta_a = \sigma_{am}/\sigma^2_m$. βa is the beta of the security'a', σ_{am} is the covariance between the return on security'a' and the CAPM portfolio and σ^2_m is the variance of the return on this CAPM (market) portfolio. The covariance σ_{am} can also be expressed as a function of the correlation coefficient (ρ_{am}) and the standard deviations of the individual security and the market portfolio. $\sigma_{am} = \rho_{am}\sigma_a\sigma_m$. Thus the beta is $\beta_a = \rho_{am}\sigma_a/\sigma_m$.

Exposure of financial assets is a vast topic and very

detailed to get into. This is intended to provide a brief overview.

A simple illustration of risk in financial terms is as follows. You are issue a loan to another person. The risk you are exposed to is that of the interest rates on loans rising after you issued the loan. This means that the amount of money you lent could have been invested to earn a higher return. The issued person is conversely exposed to the risk of interest rates dropping after he borrows from you. In the case of a company that issues debt this changes slightly. Companies would prefer issuing debt when interest rates are low and vice versa for the debtholders.

Financial assets are unique, as they do not necessarily convey rights to specific tangible assets to the holder. Financial assets can entitle the holder to a certain income or the right to buy another asset at a pre-specified price in the future. For instance common stock is a financial asset. The holders of common stock are the owners of the corporation; but they do not exercise direct control over the physical assets of the corporation. Their ownership role is restricted to that of a principle with the management and the board of directors as their agents. Hence, often firms have employees as shareholder, so that their interests are aligned with that of the non-employee shareholders.

A financial asset has one or more of the three following characteristics:

- Ownership rights of a corporation or asset.
- Single or Multiple series of payments.
- Right to buy or sell another asset, subject to certain changes in price, interest rates, volatility, time horizons.

TYPES OF FINANCIAL ASSETS

- *Stock*: In the form of a single share, this certifies an individuals ownership of a certain percentage of the corporation. Individuals rarely own 1 or 2 shares of a corporation. More often than not they own, a block of shares. This can range from 100 to 100,000. These ownership rights are valid as long as the corporation does not become insolvent or not pay any contractual obligations. The return on common stock comes in the form of dividends that are paid out of the net income after all the obligations to other creditors and debtholders are made. The board of directors/ management is not compelled to declare dividends out of the residual net income. This money can be re-invested by the firm, if the deem that there are better investment opportunities. To mitigate the conflict of interest between shareholders and management/directors, companies more often than not insist on employee compensation plan based partially on stock based compensation. In this case the management/directors are more certain to make more prudent investment decisions.

- *Debt*: This is basically a series of promised payment to be made by the borrower to the lender. Often the debt obligation is called a bond. A 3-year $100 bond with a 5% coupon rate would provide 6 semi-annual payments of $2.5 and $100 after 3 years. Debt can have these additional features.
- *Call feature*: This allows the issuer to recall the bond before its maturity date. Early retirement of the bond would require the payment of premium over the bonds value by the issuer.
- *Secured debt*: Debt that has another asset pledged as collateral. In which case the debtholder can claim the asset pledged as a collateral in case of a default by the issuer.
- *Subordinated debt*: Also known as junior debt. The basic implication of this is that in case of default, the subordinated debtholders have a secondary claim on the firms assets, as opposed to senior debtholders.

Note: Junior/Subordinated debtholders are still senior to shareholders in terms of laying claim to a firms assets.

The present value of a stream of bond payments of a 4 year annual bond is with interest payments of I1-I4 is:

$$\text{PV ofbond} = \frac{I1 + I2 + I3 + I4}{(1+I)^1 \ (1+I)^2 \ (1+I)^3 \ (1+I)^4}$$

Assessing the risk of debt is done mainly through the duration of the bond. Duration measure the time-weighted average till payments are received from bonds.

The duration (D) is therefore:

$$\frac{1}{P} \frac{(1 \times I1) \ + (2 \times I2) + (3 \times I3) + (4 \times I4)}{(1+I)^1 \ (1+I)^2 \ 1+I)^3 \ (1+I)^4}$$

Duration conveys that the longer the stream of cash flow payments, the more susceptible the bond is to a change in the interest rates.

This concept of duration is comparable to the systematic risk portion of a security:

- *Future and Forward Contracts*: Futures and forwards are financial derivatives. They are referred to as such since their value is derived from an underlying asset. Options are another type of derivative. Derivatives allow the investor to protect himself against the risk of a price variation while at the same time not owning the asset. An Arab Sheikh, disturbed by world events can choose to enter into a future or forward contract with a Dutch oil development company, by promising to deliver a million barrels of crude oil at 3 months into the future @$21/barrel. He is the writer/seller of the contract.
- Futures also enables a company to possess assets, without physically storing them. In the example, the Dutch company owns $21 million of oil in assets. While the exchange will take place later, the contract has guaranteed them these assets in the future. It is a form of artificially storing the asset for this period. The price is determined at the time of the transaction but the actual payment is not made at that time. The futures contract has a daily"marking to market" where the exchange posts gains and losses on the contract to either parties' account. Futures are traded in standardized sizes and on organized exchanges.

Forwards on the other hand are private agreements that are not traded on exchanges and unlike futures they are not marked to market.

- *Options*: An option provides the holder with a right to buy or sell an asset at an exercise price. A put option is the right to sell and a call is the right to buy the financial asset. The holder has the right, but not the obligation, to buy or sell the asset at a specific expiration date or by a specified expiration date. If the option is not exercised by a specific date, then it expires without value. Options are available on financial assets such as common stock, foreign currencies and even on futures themselves. Options are conceptually the hardest financial assets to understand but they do provide the best insurance at a small premium. But options have a greater upside potential and no downside risk.

6

Options and Futures

INTRODUCTION

A derivative is an agreement or contract that is not based on a real, or true, exchange, *i.e.*: There is nothing tangible like money, or a product, that is being exchanged. For example, a person goes to the grocery store, exchanges a currency for a commodity. The exchange is complete, both parties have something tangible. If the purchaser had called the store and asked for the apple to be held for one hour while the purchaser drives to the store, and the seller agrees, then a derivative has been created. The agreement is derived from a proposed exchange.

In financial terms, a derivative is a financial instrument - or more simply, an agreement between two people or two parties - that has a value determined by the price of something else. It is a financial contract with a value linked to the expected future price movements of the asset it is linked to - such as a share or a currency. There are many kinds of derivatives, with the most notable being swaps, futures, and options. However, since a derivative can be placed on any sort of security, the scope of all derivatives possible is near endless. Thus, the real definition of a derivative is an agreement between two parties that is contingent on a future outcome of the underlying.

A common misconception is to refer to derivatives as assets. This is erroneous, since a derivative is incapable of having value of its own. However, some more commonplace derivatives, such as swaps, futures, and options, which have a theoretical face value that can be calculated using formulas, such as Black-Scholes, are frequently traded on open markets before their expiration date as if they were assets.

Derivatives are usually broadly categorized by the:

- Relationship between the underlying and the derivative
- Type of underlying
- Market in which they trade
- Pay-off profile

Another arbitrary distinction is between:

- Vanilla derivatives and
- Exotic derivatives

There is no definitive rule for distinguishing one from the other, so the distinction is mostly a matter of custom.

Derivatives are used by investors to:

- Provide leverage or gearing, such that a small movement in the underlying value can cause a large difference in the value of the derivative
- Speculate and to make a profit if the value of the underlying asset moves the way they expect
- Hedge or mitigate risk in the underlying, by entering into a derivative contract whose value moves in the opposite direction to their underlying position and cancels part or all of it out
- Obtain exposure to underlying where it is not possible to trade in the underlying
- Create optionability where the value of the derivative is linked to a specific condition or event

USES

Hedging

Hedging is a technique that attempts to reduce risk. In this respect, derivatives can be considered a form of insurance.

Derivatives allow risk about the price of the underlying asset to be transferred from one party to another. For example, a wheat farmer and a miller could sign a futures contract to exchange a specified amount of cash for a specified amount of wheat in the future. Both parties have reduced a future risk:

for the wheat farmer, the uncertainty of the price, and for the miller, the availability of wheat. However, there is still the risk that no wheat will be available because of events unspecified by the contract, like the weather, or that one party will renege on the contract. Although a third party, called a clearing house, insures a futures contract, not all derivatives are insured against counter-party risk.

From another perspective, the farmer and the miller both reduce a risk and acquire a risk when they sign the futures contract: The farmer reduces the risk that the price of wheat will fall below the price specified in the contract and acquires the risk that the price of wheat will rise above the price specified in the contract. The miller, on the other hand, acquires the risk that the price of wheat will fall below the price specified in the contract and reduces the risk that the price of wheat will rise above the price specified in the contract. In this sense, one party is the insurer for one type of risk, and the counter-party is the insurer for another type of risk.

Hedging also occurs when an individual or institution buys an asset and sells it using a futures contract. The individual or institution has access to the asset for a specified amount of time, and then can sell it in the future at a specified price just as to the futures contract. Of course, this allows the individual or institution the benefit of holding the asset while reducing the risk that the future selling price will deviate unexpectedly from the market's current assessment of the future value of the asset.

Derivatives serve a legitimate business purpose. For example, a corporation borrows a large sum of money at a specific interest rate. The rate of interest on the loan resets every six months. The corporation is concerned that the rate of interest may be much higher in six months. The corporation could buy a forward rate agreement. A forward rate agreement is a contract to pay a fixed rate of interest six months after purchases on a notional sum of money. If the interest rate after six months is above the contract rate, the seller pays the difference to the corporation, or FRA buyer. If the rate is lower, the corporation would pay the difference to the seller. The purchase of the FRA would serve to reduce the uncertainty concerning the rate increase and stabilize earnings.

Speculation and Arbitrage

Derivatives can be used to acquire risk, rather than to insure or hedge against risk. Thus, some individuals and institutions will enter into a derivative contract to speculate on the value of the underlying asset, betting that the party seeking insurance will be wrong about the future value of the underlying asset. Speculators will want to be able to buy an asset in the future at a low price just as to a derivative contract when the future market price is high, or to sell an asset in the future at a high price just as to a derivative contract when the future market price is low.

Individuals and institutions may also look for arbitrage opportunities, as when the current buying price of an asset falls below the price specified in a futures contract to sell the asset. Speculative trading in derivatives gained a great deal of notoriety in 1995 when Nick Leeson, a trader at Barings Bank, made poor and unauthorized investments in futures contracts. Through a combination of poor judgment, lack of oversight by the bank's management and by regulators, and unfortunate events like the Kobe earthquake, Leeson incurred a $1.3 billion loss that bankrupted the centuries-old institution.

TYPES OF DERIVATIVES

OTC and Exchange-Traded

In broad terms, there are two distinct groups of derivative contracts, which are distinguished by the way they are traded in the market:

- Over-the-counter (OTC) derivatives are contracts that are traded directly between two parties, without going through an exchange or other intermediary. Products such as swaps, forward rate agreements, and exotic options are almost always traded in this way. The OTC derivative market is the largest market for derivatives, and is largely unregulated with respect to disclosure of information between the parties, since the OTC market is made up of banks and other highly sophisticated parties, such as hedge funds. Reporting of OTC amounts are difficult because trades can occur in private, without activity being visible on any exchange. The Bank for International Settlements, the total outstanding notional amount is $684 trillion. Of this total notional amount, 67% are interest rate contracts, 8% are credit default swaps (CDS), 9% are foreign exchange contracts, 2% are commodity contracts, 1% are equity contracts, and 12% are other. Because OTC derivatives are not traded on an exchange, there is no central counter-party. Therefore, they are subject to counter-party risk, like an ordinary contract, since each counter-party relies on the other to perform.

- Exchange-traded derivative contracts (ETD) are those derivatives instruments that are traded via specialized derivatives exchanges or other exchanges. A derivatives exchange is a market where individuals trade standardized contracts that have been defined by the exchange. A derivatives exchange acts as an intermediary to all related transactions, and takes Initial margin from both sides of the trade to performance as a guarantee. The world's largest derivatives exchanges are the Korea Exchange, Eurex, and CME Group. BIS, the combined turnover in the world's derivatives exchanges totaled USD 344 trillion during Q4 2005. Some types of derivative instruments also may trade on traditional exchanges. For instance, hybrid instruments such as convertible bonds and/or convertible preferred may be listed on stock or bond exchanges. Also, warrants may be listed on equity exchanges. Performance Rights, Cash xPRTs and various other instruments that essentially consist of a complex set of options bundled into a simple package are routinely listed on equity exchanges. Like other derivatives, these publicly traded derivatives provide investors access to risk/reward and volatility characteristics that, while related to an underlying commodity, nonetheless are distinctive.

Common Derivative Contract Types

There are three major classes of derivatives:

1. Futures/Forwards are contracts to buy or sell an asset on or before a future date at a price specified today. A futures contract differs from a forward contract in that the futures contract is a standardized contract written by a clearing house that operates an exchange where the contract can be bought and sold, whereas a forward contract is a non-standardized contract written by the parties themselves.
2. Options are contracts that give the owner the right, but not the obligation, to buy or sell an asset. The price at which the sale takes place is known as the strike price, and is specified at the time the parties enter into the option. The option contract also specifies a maturity date. In the case of a European option, the owner has the right to require the sale to take place on the maturity date; in the case of an American option, the owner can require the sale to take place at any time up to the maturity date. If the owner of the contract exercises this right, the counter-party has the obligation to carry out the transaction.
3. Swaps are contracts to exchange cash on or before a specified future date based on the underlying value of currencies/exchange rates, bonds/interest rates, commodities, stocks or other assets.

More complex derivatives can be created by combining the elements of these basic types. For example, the holder of a swaption has the right, but not the obligation, to enter into a swap on or before a specified future date.

Examples

The overall derivatives market has five major classes of underlying asset:

- Interest rate derivatives
- Foreign exchange derivatives
- Credit derivatives
- Equity derivatives
- Commodity derivatives

Some common examples of these derivatives are:

Table. Contract Types

Underlying	Exchange-traded futures	Exchange-traded options	OTC swap	OTC forward	OTC option
Equity	DJIA Index future Single-stock future	Option on DJIA Index future Single-share option	Equity swap	Back-to-back Repurchase agreement	Stock option Warrant Turbo warrant
Interest rate	Eurodollar future Euribor future	Option on Eurodollar future Option on Euribor future	Interest rate swap	Forward rate agreement	Interest rate cap and floor Swaption Basis swap Bond option
Credit	Bond future	Option on Bond future	Credit default swap Total return swap	Repurchase agreement	Credit default option
Foreign exchange	Currency future	Option on currency future	Currency swap	Currency forward	Currency option
Commodity	WTI crude oil futures	Weather derivatives	Commodity swap	Iron ore forward contract	Gold option

Other examples of underlying exchangeables are:

- Property derivatives
- Economic derivatives that pay off just as to economic reports as measured and reported by national statistical agencies
- Freight derivatives
- Inflation derivatives
- Weather derivatives
- Insurance derivatives
- Emissions derivatives

VALUATION

Market and Arbitrage-free Prices

Two common measures of value are:

1. Market price, *i.e.* the price at which traders are willing to buy or sell the contract

2. Arbitrage-free price, meaning that no risk-free profits can be made by trading in these contracts.

Determining the Market Price

For exchange-traded derivatives, market price is usually transparent. Complications can arise with OTC or floor-traded contracts though, as trading is handled manually, making it difficult to automatically broadcast prices. In particular with OTC contracts, there is no central exchange to collate and disseminate prices.

Determining the Arbitrage-free Price

The arbitrage-free price for a derivatives contract is complex, and there are many different variables to consider. Arbitrage-free pricing is a central topic of financial mathematics. The stochastic process of the price of the underlying asset is often crucial.

A key equation for the theoretical valuation of options is the Black-Scholes formula, which is based on the assumption that the cash flows from a European stock option can be replicated by a continuous buying and selling strategy using only the stock. A simplified version of this valuation technique is the binomial options model.

CRITICISMS

Derivatives are often subject to the following criticisms:

Possible Large Losses

The use of derivatives can result in large losses because of the use of leverage, or borrowing. Derivatives allow investors to earn large returns from small movements in the underlying asset's price. However, investors could lose large amounts if the price of the underlying moves against them significantly.

There have been several instances of massive losses in derivative markets, such as:

- The need to recapitalize insurer American International Group (AIG) with $85 billion of debt provided by the US federal government. An AIG subsidiary had lost more than $18 billion over the preceding three quarters on Credit Default Swaps (CDS) it had written. It was reported that the recapitalization was necessary because further losses were foreseeable over the next few quarters.

- The loss of $7.2 Billion by Société Générale in January 2008 through mis-use of futures contracts.
- The loss of US$6.4 billion in the failed fund Amaranth Advisors, which was long natural gas in September 2006 when the price plummeted.
- The loss of US$4.6 billion in the failed fund Long-Term Capital Management in 1998.
- The bankruptcy of Orange County, CA in 1994, the largest municipal bankruptcy in U.S. history. On December 6, 1994 from which it emerged in June 1995. The county lost about $1.6 billion through derivatives trading. Orange County was neither bankrupt nor insolvent at the time; however, because of the strategy the county employed, it was unable to generate the cash flows needed to maintain services. Orange County is a good example of what happens when derivatives are used incorrectly and positions liquidated in an unplanned manner; had they not liquidated, they would not have lost any money as their positions rebounded. Potentially problematic use of interest-rate derivatives by US municipalities has continued in recent years.

Members of President Clinton's Working Group on Financial Markets: Larry Summers, Alan Greenspan, Arthur Levitt, and Robert Rubin, have been criticized for torpedoing an effort to regulate the derivatives' markets, and thereby helping to bring down the financial markets in Fall 2008.

President George W. Bush has also been criticized because he was President for 8 years preceding the 2008 meltdown and did nothing to regulate derivative trading. Bush has stated that deregulation was one of the core tenets of his political philosophy.

Counter-party Risk

Some derivatives expose investors to counter-party risk. For example, suppose a person wanting a fixed interest rate loan for his business, but finding that banks only offer variable rates, swaps payments with another business who wants a variable rate, synthetically creating a fixed rate for the person. However if the second business goes bankrupt, it can't pay its variable rate and so the first business will lose its fixed rate and will be paying a variable rate again. If interest rates have increased, it is possible that the first business may be adversely affected, because it may not be prepared to pay the higher variable rate. Different types of derivatives have different levels of counter-party risk. For example, standardized stock options by law require the party at risk to have a certain amount deposited with the exchange, showing that they can pay for any losses; banks that help businesses swap variable for fixed rates on loans may do credit checks on both parties. However, in private agreements between two companies, for example, there may not be benchmarks for performing due diligence and risk analysis.

Large Notional Value

Derivatives typically have a large notional value. As such, there is the danger that their use could result in losses that the investor would be unable to compensate for. The possibility that this could lead to a chain reaction ensuing in an economic crisis, has been pointed out by famed investor Warren Buffett in Berkshire Hathaway's 2002 annual report. Buffett called them'financial weapons of mass destruction.' The problem with derivatives is that they control an increasingly larger notional amount of assets and this may lead to distortions in the real capital and equities markets. Investors begin to look at the derivatives markets to make a decision to buy or sell securities and so what was originally meant to be a market to transfer risk now becomes a leading indicator.

Leverage of an Economy's Debt

Derivatives massively leverage the debt in an economy, making it ever more difficult for the underlying real economy to service its debt obligations, thereby curtailing real economic activity, which can cause a recession or even depression. In the view of Marriner S. Eccles, U.S. Federal Reserve Chairman from November, 1934 to February, 1948, too high a level of debt was one of the primary causes of the 1920s-30s Great Depression.

BENEFITS

The use of derivatives also has its benefits:

- Derivatives facilitate the buying and selling of risk, and many people consider this to have a positive impact on the economic system. Although someone loses money while someone else gains money with a derivative, under normal circumstances, trading in derivatives should not adversely affect the economic system because it is not zero sum in utility.
- Former Federal Reserve Board chairman Alan Greenspan, in 2003, that he believed that the use of derivatives has softened the impact of the economic downturn at the beginning of the 21st century.

DEFINITIONS

- *Bilateral netting*: A legally enforceable arrangement between a bank and a counter-party that creates a single legal obligation covering all included individual contracts. This means that a bank's obligation, in the event of the default or insolvency of one of the parties, would be the net sum of all positive and negative fair values of contracts included in the bilateral netting arrangement.
- *Credit derivative*: A contract that transfers credit risk from a protection buyer to a credit protection seller. Credit derivative products can take many forms, such as credit default swaps, credit linked notes and total return swaps.
- *Derivative*: A financial contract whose value is derived from the performance of assets, interest rates, currency exchange rates, or indexes. Derivative

transactions include a wide assortment of financial contracts including structured debt obligations and deposits, swaps, futures, options, caps, floors, collars, forwards and various combinations thereof.

- *Exchange-traded derivative contracts*: Standardized derivative contracts that are transacted on an organized futures exchange.
- *Gross negative fair value*: The sum of the fair values of contracts where the bank owes money to its counter-parties, without taking into account netting. This represents the maximum losses the bank's counter-parties would incur if the bank defaults and there is no netting of contracts, and no bank collateral was held by the counter-parties.
- *Gross positive fair value*: The sum total of the fair values of contracts where the bank is owed money by its counter-parties, without taking into account netting. This represents the maximum losses a bank could incur if all its counter-parties default and there is no netting of contracts, and the bank holds no counter-party collateral.
- *High-risk mortgage securities*: Securities where the price or expected average life is highly sensitive to interest rate changes, as determined by the FFIEC policy statement on high-risk mortgage securities.
- *Notional amount*: The nominal or face amount that is used to calculate payments made on swaps and other risk management products. This amount generally does not change hands and is thus referred to as notional.
- *Over-the-counter derivative contracts*: Privately negotiated derivative contracts that are transacted off organized futures exchanges.
- *Structured notes*: Non-mortgage-backed debt securities, whose cash flow characteristics depend on one or more indices and/ or have embedded forwards or options.
- *Total risk-based capital*: The sum of tier 1 plus tier 2

capital. Tier 1 capital consists of common shareholders equity, perpetual preferred shareholders equity with non-cumulative dividends, retained earnings, and minority interests in the equity accounts of consolidated subsidiaries. Tier 2 capital consists of subordinated debt, intermediate-term preferred stock, cumulative and long-term preferred stock, and a portion of a bank's allowance for loan and lease losses.

OPTIONS MARKET

The exchange where most of the buying and selling of options contracts take place is called the options market. The most common way of trading options is through standardized options contracts. These are listed in various futures and options exchanges. The listing of the contracts and their respective prices is done using ticker symbols.

These exchanges publish the options prices continuously and create live options markets for options trading. Thus, the exchange offers the trading parties a platform to discover prices and execute transactions. These exchanges assume the role of intermediaries for buyers and sellers.

THE ROLE OF AN OPTION MARKET

These exchanges ensure that the contract terms are backed by the credit of the exchange. They also safeguard the anonymity of the counterparties and enforce market regulations to ensure that the trades remain fair and transparent. During fast trading conditions, these exchanges ensure the maintenance of orderly markets.

OPTIONS MARKET AND OVER THE COUNTER OPTIONS

In addition to exchange traded options, there are options that are not traded on any stock exchange. Such options are known as over-the-counter options. The OTC options contracts are agreed upon between two independent parties. Usually, one party is a well-capitalized institution. Avoiding the exchanges enables traders of OTC options to tailor the terms of the trade. These transactions are not usually advertised in the market. They also face little regulatory requirements. Still, it is obligatory for the over-the-counter counterparties to establish credit lines and conform to clearing and settlement procedures.

BASIC TRADES OF AN OPTIONS MARKET

- *Long call*: When a trader believes that the price of a stock would appreciate, he/she can acquire the right to buy an option rather than just opting to purchase the stock. If the price of the stock moves above the exercise price by more than the premium, the trader earns a profit.
- *Long put*: In case the trader believes that the price of the share will decrease, he/she can buy the right to sell.
- *Short call*: A trader expecting a share price to decline can sell a call. The trader will then be obligated to sell the stock to the call buyer.
- *Short put*: A trader expecting a share price to appreciate can sell a put. This will give the trader an obligation to buy the stock from the put buyer.

OPTIONS STRATEGIES

Options strategies are plans implemented by an options trader to maximize profits and minimize risks. An option strategy involves combining options positions on an underlying asset, typically a stock.

While trading in options, an investor can either acquire the right to buy the underlying asset or sell it on or before a specific date at a predetermined price. The value of a call option varies in accordance with the value of the underlying stock, while that of the put option is inversely proportional to the value of the underlying stock.

TYPES OF OPTIONS STRATEGIES

An investor can employ several options strategies based

on the expected price movement in the underlying stock, market sentiment and his/her risk appetite. One of the most common strategies, called straddle, is to acquire both call and put options.

Through this options strategy, a trader can increase the value of his/her holdings significantly irrespective of the direction of the stock price movement. With this options strategy, an investor can lose money only if the underlying stock retains its value over a period of time or its price deviates only marginally.

Some of the other options strategies are:

- *Bullish Strategies*: These strategies are employed when a trader expects the price of the underlying stock to move up. The extent of the price increase and the timeframe in which this might occur are assessed to optimize the trading strategy. A simple call buying strategy can be used in such cases.
- *Bearish Strategies*: They are employed when the trader anticipates a downward movement in the underlying stock price. An investor can opt to acquire a simple put option to capitalize on the price trends in such cases.
- *Neutral Strategies*: They are adopted when traders are unsure of the direction of the price movement of the underlying stock. These are also known as non-directional strategies, since profits are not dependent on the direction of the price of the underlying stock. Thus, a neutral strategy depends on the expected volatility of the stock price. Some examples of neutral strategies are guts, butterfly, strangle and risk reversal. Options, in these cases, could be either long or short, but tend to differ with varying strike prices.

OPTION VALUATION

Because the values of option contracts depend on a number of different variables in addition to the value of the underlying asset, they are complex to value. There are many pricing models in use, although all essentially incorporate the concepts of rational pricing, Moneyness, Option time value and Put-call parity.

Amongst the most common models are:

- Black-Scholes and the Black model
- Binomial options pricing model
- Monte Carlo option model
- Finite difference methods for option pricing

Other approaches include:

- Barone-Adesi and Whaley American option approximation
- Variance Gamma Model
- Heath-Jarrow-Morton framework
- Heston model

BINOMIAL OPTIONS PRICING MODEL

In finance, the binomial options pricing model provides a generalizable numerical method for the valuation of options. The binomial model was first proposed by Cox, Ross and Rubinstein. Essentially, the model uses a"discrete-time" model of the varying price over time of the underlying financial instrument.

Use of the Model

The Binomial options pricing model approach is widely used as it is able to handle a variety of conditions for which other models cannot easily be applied. This is largely because the BOPM is based on the description of an underlying instrument over a period of time rather than a single point. As a consequence, it is used to value American options that are exercisable at any time in a given interval as well as Bermudan options that are exercisable at specific instances of time. Being relatively simple, the model is readily implementable in computer software.

Although computationally slower than the Black-Scholes formula, it is more accurate, particularly for longer-dated options options on securities with dividend payments. For these reasons, various versions of the binomial model are widely used by practitioners in the options markets.

For options with several sources of uncertainty and for options with complicated features, lattice methods are less practical due to several difficulties, and Monte Carlo option models are commonly used instead. Monte Carlo simulation is computationally time-consuming, however.

Methodology

The binomial pricing model traces the evolution of the option's key underlying variables in discrete-time. This is done by means of a binomial lattice, for a number of time steps between the valuation and expiration dates. Each node in the lattice, represents a possible price of the underlying at a given point in time.

Valuation is performed iteratively, starting at each of the final nodes and then working backwards through the tree towards the first node. The value computed at each stage is the value of the option at that point in time.

Option valuation using this method is, as described, a three-step process:

1. Price tree generation,
2. Calculation of option value at each final node,
3. Sequential calculation of the option value at each preceding node.

STEP 1: Create the Binomial Price Tree

The tree of prices is produced by working forward from valuation date to expiration.

At each step, it is assumed that the underlying instrument will move up or down by a specific factor (u or d) per step of the tree (where, by definition, $u \geq 1$ and $0 < d \leq 1$). So, if S is the current price, then in the next period the price will either be $S_{up} = S.u$ or $S_{down} = S.d$.

The up and down factors are calculated using the underlying volatility, σ and the time duration of a step, t, measured in years. From the condition that the variance of the log of the price is $\sigma^2 t$, we have:

$$u = e^{\sigma\sqrt{t}}$$

$$d = e^{-\sigma\sqrt{t}} = \frac{1}{u}.$$

The original Cox, Ross, and Rubinstein (CRR) method; there are other techniques for generating the lattice, such as"the equal probabilities" tree.

The CRR method ensures that the tree is recombinant, i.e. if the underlying asset moves up and then down (u,d), the price will be the same as if it had moved down and then up (d,u) - here the two paths merge or recombine. This property reduces the number of tree nodes, and thus accelerates the computation of the option price. This property also allows that the value of the underlying asset at each node can be calculated directly via formula, and does not require that the tree be built first.

The node-value will be:

$$S_n = S_0 \times u^{N_u - N_d}$$

where:

Nu: Number of up ticks

Nd: Number of down ticks

STEP 2: Find Option Value at Each Final Node

At each final node of the tree - i.e. at expiration of the option - the option value is simply its intrinsic, or exercise, value.

Max [(S – K), 0], for a call option

Max [(K – S), 0], for a put option:

Where: K is the Strike price and S is the spot price of the underlying asset

STEP 3: Find Option Value at Earlier Nodes

Once the step is complete, the option value is then found for each node, starting at the penultimate time step, and working back to the first node of the tree where the calculated result is the value of the option.

In overview: the"binomial value" is found at each node, using the risk neutrality assumption. If exercise is permitted at the node, then the model takes the greater of binomial and exercise value at the node.

The steps are as follows:

- Under the risk neutrality assumption, today's fair price of a derivative is equal to the expected value of its future payoff discounted by the risk free rate. Therefore, expected value is calculated using the option values from the later two nodes weighted by their respective probabilities --"probability" p of an up move in the underlying, and"probability" (1-p) of a down move. The expected value is then discounted at r, the risk free rate corresponding to the life of the option.

  The following formula to compute the expectation value is applied at each node:

  Binomial Value=

  $$[\, p \times \text{Option up} + (1-p) \times \text{Option down}] \times \exp(-r \times \Delta t),$$

  or

  $$C_t - \Delta_{t,i} = e^{-r\Delta t}(pC_{t,i+1} + (1-p)C_{ti-1})$$

  where

  $C_{t,i}$ is the option's value for the ith node at time t,

  $$p = \frac{e^{(r-q)\Delta t} - d}{u - d}$$

  is chosen such that the related Binomial distribution simulates the geometric Brownian motion of the underlying stock with parametres r and s, q is the dividend yield of the underlying corresponding to the life of the option. It follows that in a risk-neutral world futures price should have an expected growth rate of zero and therefore we can consider q = r for futures.
- This result is the"Binomial Value". It represents the fair price of the derivative at a particular point in time given the evolution in the price of the underlying to that point. It is the value of the option if it were to be held - as opposed to exercised at that point.
- Depending on the style of the option, evaluate the possibility of early exercise at each node: if

- The option can be exercised, and
- The exercise value exceeds the Binomial Value, then
- The value at the node is the exercise value.
  a. For a European option, there is no option of early exercise, and the binomial value applies at all nodes.
  b. For an American option, since the option may either be held or exercised prior to expiry, the value at each node is: Max.
  c. For a Bermudan option, the value at nodes where early exercise is allowed is: Max; at nodes where early exercise is not allowed, only the binomial value applies.

In calculating the value at the next time step calculated - i.e. one step closer to valuation - the model must use the value selected here, for"Option up" /"Option down" as appropriate, in the formula at the node.

Discrete Dividends

In practice, the use of continuous dividend yield, q, in the formula can lead to significant mis-pricing of the option near an ex-dividend date. Instead, it is common to model dividends as discrete payments on the anticipated future ex-dividend dates.

To model discrete dividend payments in the binomial model, apply the following rule:

- At each time step, i, calculate,

  $$\sum PV(D_k),$$

  for all k < i where PV(Dk) is the present value of the k-th dividend. Subtract this value from the value of the security price S at each node (i, j).

BLACK MODEL

The Black model is a variant of the Black-Scholes option pricing model. Its primary applications are for pricing bond options, interest rate caps/floors, and swaptions. Black's model can be generalized into a class of models known as log-normal forward models, also referred to as LIBOR market model.

The Black Formula

The Black formula is similar to the Black-Scholes formula for valuing stock options except that the spot price of the underlying is replaced by the forward price F. The Black formula for a European call option on an underlying strike at K, expiring T years in the future is

$$c = e^{-rT}[FN(d1) - KN(d_2)]$$

The put price is

$$p = e^{-rT}[KN(-d_2) - FN(-d_1)]$$

where

$$d_1 = \frac{\ln(F/K) + (\sigma^2/2)T}{\sigma\sqrt{T}}$$

$$d_2 = \frac{\ln(F/K) + (\sigma^2/2)T}{\sigma\sqrt{T}} = d_1 - \sigma\sqrt{T},$$

where r is the risk-free discount rate, continuously compounded.

Derivation and Assumptions

The derivation of the pricing formulas in the model follows that of the Black-Scholes model almost exactly. The assumption that the spot price follows a log-normal process is replaced by the assumption that the forward price at maturity of the option is log-normally distributed. From there the derivation is identical and so the final formula is the same except that the spot price is replaced by the forward - the forward price represents the undiscounted expected future value.

BLACK-SCHOLES

The Black-Scholes model is a mathematical description of financial markets and derivative investment instruments. The model develops partial differential equations whose solution, the Black-Scholes formula, is widely used in the pricing of European-style options.

The model was first articulated by Fischer Black and Myron Scholes,"The Pricing of Options and Corporate Liabilities." The foundation for their research relied on work developed by scholars such as Jack L. Treynor, Paul Samuelson, A. James Boness, Sheen T. Kassouf, and Edward O. Thorp. The fundamental insight of Black-Scholes is that the option is implicitly priced if the stock is traded. Robert C. Merton was the first to publish a paper expanding the mathematical understanding of the options pricing model and coined the term Black-Scholes options pricing model. The uniqueness and originality of the model developed by Black, Scholes, and Merton is disputed today, because as early as 1908, the Italian mathematician Vinzenz Bronzin developed a largely identical model.

Model Assumptions

The Black-Scholes model of the market for a particular equity makes the following explicit assumptions:

- It is possible to borrow and lend cash at a known constant risk-free interest rate. This restriction has been removed in later extensions of the model.
- The price follows a Geometric Brownian motion with constant drift and volatility. It follows from this that the return is a Log-normal distribution. This often implies the validity of the efficient-market hypothesis.
- There are no transaction costs or taxes.
- The stock does not pay a dividend.
- All securities are perfectly divisible.
- There are no restrictions on short selling.
- There is no arbitrage opportunity
- Options use the European exercise terms, which dictate that options may only be exercised on the day of expiration.

From these conditions in the market for an equity, the authors show that"it is possible to create a hedged position, consisting of a long position in the stock and a short position in [calls on the same stock], whose value will not depend on the price of the stock." Several of these assumptions of the original model have been removed in subsequent extensions of the model. Modern versions account for changing interest rates transaction costs and taxes, and dividend payout.

Black-Scholes Tormula

The Black Scholes formula calculates the price of European put and call options. It can be obtained by solving the Black-Scholes partial differential equation.

The value of a call option in terms of the Black-Scholes parametres is:

$$C(S,t) = SN(d_1) - Ke^{-r(T-t)}N(d_2)$$

$$d_1 = \frac{\ln(\frac{S}{k}) + (r + \frac{\sigma^2}{2})(T-1)}{\sigma\sqrt{T-t}}$$

$$d_2 = d_1 - \sigma\sqrt{T-t}.$$

The price of a put option is:

$$P(S,t) = Ke^{-r(T-t)} - S + (SN(d_1) - Ke^{-r(T-t)}N(d_2)) =$$

$$Ke^{-r(T-t)} - S + C(S,t).$$

For both:

- N(o) is the cumulative distribution function of the standard normal distribution
- $T - t$ is the time to maturity
- S is the spot price of the underlying asset
- K is the strike price
- r is the risk free rate
- σ is the volatility in the log-returns of the underlying

Interpretation

$N(d_1)$ and $N(d_2)$ are the probabilities of the option expiring in-the-money under the equivalent exponential martingale probability measure (numéraire = stock) and the equivalent martingale probability measure (numéraire = risk free asset), respectively.

The equivalent martingale probability measure is also called the risk-neutral probability measure. Note that both of these are probabilities in a measure theoretic sense, and neither of these is the true probability of expiring in-the-money under the real probability measure. In order to calculate the probability under the real ("physical") probability measure, additional information is required-the drift term in the physical measure, or equivalently, the market price of risk.

Derivation

We now show how to get from the general Black-Scholes PDE to a specific valuation for an option. Consider as an example the Black-Scholes price of a call option, for which the PDE above has boundary conditions

$$C(0,t) = 0 \text{ for all } t$$

$$C(S,t) \to S \text{ as } S \to \infty$$

$$C(S,t) = \max(S-K,0).$$

The last condition gives the value of the option at the time that the option matures. The solution of the PDE gives the value of the option at any earlier time $E[\max(S-K,0)]$. In order to solve the PDE we transform the equation into a diffusion equation which may be solved using standard methods.

To this end we introduce the change-of-variable transformation,

$$T = T - 1$$

$$u = Ce^{TT}$$

$$x = \ln(S/K) + (r - \frac{\sigma^2}{2})T$$

Then the Black-Scholes PDE becomes a diffusion equation

$$\frac{\partial u}{\partial_T} = \frac{\sigma^2}{2}\frac{\partial^2 u}{\partial x^2}.$$

The terminal condition $C(S,T) = \max(S-K,0)$ now becomes an initial condition,

$$u(x,0) = u_0(x) \equiv K \max(e^x - 1, 0).$$

Using the standard method for solving a diffusion equation we have,

$$u(x,T) = \frac{1}{\sigma\sqrt{2\pi T}}\int_{-\infty}^{\infty} u_o(y) e^{-(x-y)^2/(2\sigma^2 T)} dy.$$

After some algebra we obtain,

$$u(x,T) = Ke^{x+\sigma^2 T/2}N(d_1) - KN(d_2)$$

where,

$$d_1 = \frac{x+\sigma^2 T}{\sigma\sqrt{T}}$$

and,

$$d_1 = \frac{x+\sigma^2 T}{\sigma\sqrt{T}}$$

Substituting for u, x, and τ, we obtain the value of a call option in terms of the Black-Scholes parametres:

$$C(S,t) = SN(d_1) - Ke^{-r(T-t)}N(d_2)$$

where,

$$d_1 = \frac{In(S/k)+(r+\sigma^2/2)(T-t)}{\sigma\sqrt{T-t}}$$

$$d_2 = d_1 - \sigma\sqrt{T-t}.$$

The price of a put option may be computed from this by put-call parity and simplifies to,

$$P(S,t) = Ke^{-r(T-t)}N(-d_2) - SN(-d_1).$$

FINITE DIFFERENCE METHODS FOR OPTION PRICING

Finite difference methods for option pricing are numerical methods used in mathematical finance for the valuation of options. Finite difference methods were first applied to option pricing by Eduardo Schwartz in 1977.

Finite difference methods can solve derivative pricing problems that have, in general, the same level of complexity as those problems solved by tree approaches, and are therefore usually employed only when other approaches are inappropriate. At the same time, like tree-based methods, this approach is limited in terms of the number of underlying variables, and for problems with multiple dimensions, Monte Carlo methods for option pricing are usually preferred. The approach is due to the fact that the evolution of the option value can be modelled via a partial differential equation (PDE), as a function of (at least) time and price of underlying. Once in this form, a finite difference model can be derived, and the valuation obtained.

Here, essentially, the PDE is expressed in a discretized form, using finite differences, and the evolution in the option price is then modelled using a lattice with corresponding dimensions; here, time runs from 0 to maturity and price runs from 0 to a"high" value, such that the option is deeply in or out of the money.

The option is valued as follows:

- Maturity values are simply the difference between the exercise price of the option and the value of the underlying at each point.
- Values at the boundary prices are set based on moneyness or arbitrage bounds on option prices.
- Values at other lattice points are calculated recursively, starting at the time step preceding maturity and ending at time = 0. Here, using a technique such as Crank-Nicolson or the explicit method:
  - The formula is discretized per the technique, such that the value at each lattice point is specified as a function of the value at later and adjacent points;
  - The value at each point is then found using the technique in question.
- The value of the option today, where the underlying is at its spot price is then found by interpolation.

These methods and tree-based methods are able to handle problems which are equivalent in complexity. In fact, when standard assumptions are applied it can be shown that the explicit technique encompasses the binomial and trinomial tree methods. Tree based methods, then, suitably parametreized, are a special case of the explicit finite difference method.

PUT-CALL PARITY

In financial mathematics, put-call parity defines a

relationship between the price of a call option and a put option-both with the identical strike price and expiry. To derive the put-call parity relationship, the assumption is that the options are not exercised before expiration day, which necessarily applies to European options. Put-call parity can be derived in a manner that is largely model independent.

7

Risk and Return

INTRODUCTION

Investors have many motives for investing. Some investors invest in order to gain a sense of power or prestige. The control of corporate empires, thus, is an important motive. For most investors, however, the prime interest in investments is largely to earn a return on their money. However, selecting stocks exclusively on the basis of maximization of return is not enough. The most investors do not place available funds into the one, two, or even three stocks promising the greatest returns suggests that other factors must be considered besides return in the selection process. Investors not only like return, they dislike risk.

To facilitate our job of analysing securities and portfolios within a return-risk context, we must begin with a clear understanding of what risk and return are, what creates them, and how these should be measured. In fact, we find the answer to the following two questions while taking investment decisions:

- What securities should be held, and
- How many rupees should be allocated to each.

These decisions are normally made in two steps. First, estimates are made of the return and risk associated with available securities over a forward holding period. This step is known as security analysis. Second, return-risk estimates must be compared in order to decide how to allocate available funds among these securities on a continuing basis. This step comprises portfolio analysis, selection, and management. In fact, security analysis provides the necessary inputs for analysing and selecting portfolios..

Returns on Financial Assets

People want to maximize expected returns subject to their tolerance for risk. Return is the principal reward in the investment process, and it provides the basis to investors in comparing alternative investments. Measuring historical returns allows investors to assess how well they have done, and it plays a part in the estimation of future, unknown returns.

We often use two terms regarding return from investments, realized return and expected return. Realized return is after the fact return- return that was earned (or could have been earned).

Realized return is history. For example, a deposit of Rs. 5,00,000 in the Punjab National Bank on January 1 in a certificate of deposit at a stated annual interest rate of 5 per cent will be worth Rs. 525000 one year later. The realized return for the year is Rs. 25000 or 5 per cent.

Expected return is the return from an asset that investors anticipate they will earn over some future period. It is a predicted return, and it may or may not occur.

Components of Return

Return on a financial asset, generally, consists of two components. The principal component of return is the periodic income on the investment, either in the form of interest or dividends. The second component is the change in the price of the asset- commonly called the capital gain or loss. This element of return is the difference between the purchase price and the price at which the asset can be or is sold.

The price change may bring a gain or a loss as it may be in any side. The income from an investment consists of one or more cash payments made at specified intervals of time. Interest payments on most bonds are paid either semi-annually or yearly, whereas dividends on common stocks are usually paid on yearly basis. The distinguishing feature of these payments is that they are paid in cash by the issuer to the holder of the asset.

We often use the term yield to express return. Yield refers to the income component in relation to some price for a security. For our purposes, the price that is relevant is the purchase price of the security. The yield on a Rs. 1,000 par value, 6 per cent coupon bond purchased for Rs. 950 is 6.31 per cent (Rs. 1,000 par value, 6 per cent coupon bond purchased for Rs. 950 is 6.31 per cent (Rs. 60/Rs. 950). However, we need to remember that yield is not, for most purposes, the proper measure of return from a security. The capital gain or loss must also be considered.

Equation is a conceptual statement for total return.

Total return = Income + Price change (+/-)

Note that either component of return can be zero for a given security over any given time period.

A bond purchased for Rs. 800 and held to maturity provides both type of income: interest payments and a price change.

The purchase of a non-dividend-paying stock that is sold four months later produces either a capital gain or a capital loss, but no income. Thus, a measure of return must consider both dividend/interest income and price change.

Returns over time or from different securities can be measured and compared using the total return concept. The total return for a given holding period relates all the cash flows received by an investor during any designated time period to the amount of money invested in the asset. Total return is defined as,

$$r = \frac{(P_{t-1} - P_{t-1}) + D}{P_{t-1}} \times 100$$

where, r = total return, Pt = price of an asset at time (t), P_{t-1} = price of an asset at time (t-1), D = dividend or interest income in simple terms.

Example: Tata Steels share's price on June29, 2004 is Rs. 900 (Pt-1) and the price on June 28, 2005 (Pt), is Rs. 950. Dividend received is Rs. 76 (D). Determine the rate of return.

$$r = \frac{(P_{t-1} - P_{t-1}) + D}{P_{t-1}} \times 100$$

$$= \frac{(950 - 900) + 76}{900} \times 100$$

$$= \frac{50 + 76}{900} \times 100$$

$$= 14\%$$

Calculation of Average Returns

The total return is an acceptable measure of return for a specified period of time. But we also need statistics to describe a series of returns. For example, investing in a particular stock for ten years or a different stock in each of ten years could result in 10 total returns, which must be described mathematically.

There are two generally used methods of calculating the average return, namely, the arithmetic average and geometric average. The statistics familiar to most people is the arithmetic average. The arithmetic average, customarily designated by the symbol X = X n, or the sum of each of the values being considered divided by the total number of values.

Example: The return of stock A for four quarters is as follows:

Quarter-I = 10%; Quarter-II= 8%; Quarter-III= -4%; and Quarter IV= 20%.

The average return is,

X = {10 + 8 + (-4)} + 20/ 4 = 8.5%

The arithmetic average return is appropriate as a measure of the central tendency of a number of returns calculated for a particular time, such as a year. However, when percentage changes in value over time are involved, the arithmetic mean of these changes can be misleading. For example, suppose an investor purchased a stock in Year 1 for Rs. 50 and it rose to Rs. 100 by year-end. This is a 100 per cent return [(100-50)/50]. Then the stock went from Rs. 100 at the start of Year 2 to Rs. 50 at the end of that year. The return for year 2 is -50 per cent [(50-100)/100)]. The arithmetic average return is 25 per cent

[(+100-50)/2)]. But, realistically, if an investor bought a stock for Rs. 50 and held it two years and it was still at Rs. 50, clearly there is no return at all.

From the it is obvious that an analyst should use a different average to describe accurately the true rate of return over multiple periods. The geometric average return measures compound, cumulative returns over time. It is used in investments to reflect the realized change in wealth over multiple periods.

The geometric average is defined as the nth root of the product resulting from multiplying a series of returns together, as in Equation,

$$G = [(1 + r_1)(1 + r_2) \ldots (1 + r_n)]^{1/n} - 1$$

where, r = total return, n = number of periods.

Return relative: On adding 1.0 to each return (r), we shall get a return relative. If the return for a period is 10 per cent (.10), then the return relative is 1.10. The investor has received Rs. 1.10 relative to each Rs. 1 invested. If the return for a period is -15 per cent (-.15) then the return relative is.85 (1-.15). Return relatives are used in calculating geometric average returns because negative total returns cannot be used in the math.

For our stock that started at Rs. 50, rose to Rs. 100, and then dropped to Rs. 50 over a two-year period, the geometric return would be calculated as follows:

Return relative, Year 1 = 1.00 + 1.00 = 2.00

Year 2 = –.50 + 1.00 =.50

$$\text{Geometric average, (G)} = [(2.0)^*(.5)]^{1/2} - 1$$

$$= [1.0]^{1/2} - 1$$

$$= 0.00$$

Here, we also need to note that the geometric average rate of return would be lower than the arithmetic average rate of return because it reflects compounding rather than simple averaging.

Risk in Holding Securities

Risk is generally associated with the possibility that realized returns of securities will be less than the returns that were expected. The source of such risk is the failure of dividends (interest) and/or the security's price to materialize as expected. There are numerous forces that contribute to variations in return- price or dividend (interest). These forces are termed as elements of risk. Some factors are external to the firm and cannot be controlled. These factors affect large numbers of securities. In investments, those forces that are uncontrollable, external, and broad in their effect are called sources of systematic risk. Other forces are internal to the firm and are controllable to a large degree. The controllable, internal factors somewhat peculiar to industries and/or firms are referred to as sources of unsystematic risk. That portion of total variability in return caused by factors affecting the prices of all securities is known as systematic risk. Economic, political, and sociological changes are sources of systematic risk.

Their effect is to cause prices of nearly all individual common stocks and/or all individual bonds to move together in the same manner. For example, if the economy is moving towards inflation and corporate profits shift upward, stock prices may rise across a broad front. Nearly all stocks listed on the National Stock Exchange (NSE) move in the same direction as the S and P Nifty index of NSE. that on the average, 50 per cent of the variation in a stock's price can be explained by variation in the market index. Conversely, the portion of total risk that is unique to a firm or industry is called unsystematic risk. Factors such as management capability, consumer preferences, and labour strikes cause unsystematic variability of returns in a firm. Unsystematic factors are largely independent of factors affecting securities markets in general. Because these factors affect one firm, they must be examined for each firm.

Sources of Systematic Risk

As discussed, the main constituents of systematic risk include- market risk, interest rate risk and purchasing power risk.

Market Risk

The price of a stock may fluctuate widely within a short

span of time even though earnings remain unchanged. The causes of this phenomenon are varied, but it is mainly due to a change in investors' attitudes towards equities in general, or towards certain types or groups of securities in particular. Variability in return on most common stocks that is due to basic sweeping changes in investor expectations is referred to as market risk.

Risk which is common to an entire class of assets or liabilities. The value of investments may decline over a given time period simply because of economic changes or other events that impact large portions of the market. Asset allocation and diversification can protect against market risk because different portions of the market tend to underperform at different times. also called systematic risk.

The reaction of investors to tangible as well as intangible events causes market risk. Expectations of lower corporate profits in general may cause the larger body of common stocks to fall in price. Investors are expressing their judgement that too much is being paid for earnings in the light of anticipated events. The basis for the reaction is a set of real, tangible events-political, social, or economic.

Intangible events are related to market psychology. Market risk is usually touched off by a reaction to real events, but the emotional unstability of investors acting collectively leads to a snowballing overreaction. The initial decline in the market can cause the fear of loss to grip investors, and a kind of herd instinct builds as all investors make for the exit. These reactions to reactions frequently culminate in excessive selling, pushing prices down far out of line with fundamental value. With a trigger mechanism such as the threat of war, or an oil shortage, virtually all stocks are adversely affected.

Interest-rate risk: The risk of variations in future market values and the size of income, caused by fluctuations in the general level of interest rates is referred to as interest-rate risk. The basic cause of interest-rate risk lies in the fact that, as the rate of interest paid on Indian government securities rises or falls, the rates of return demanded on alternative investment vehicles, such as stocks and bonds issued in the private sector, rise or fall. In other words, as the cost of money changes for risk-free securities, the cost of money to risk-prone issuers will also change.

People normally regard government securities like treasury bills risk- free. The interest rates demanded on these securities are thought to approximate the"pure" rate of interest, or the cost of hiring money at no risk. Interest rates on gilts shift with changes in the supply and demand for government securities. For example, a large operating deficit experienced by the Indian government will require financing. Issuance of added amounts of Indian government securities will increase the available supply. Potential buyers of this new supply may be induced to buy only if interest rates are somewhat higher than those currently prevailing on outstanding issues. If rates on gilts advance from, say, 8 per cent to 8¼ per cent, investors holding outstanding issues that yield 8 per cent will notice a decline in the price of their securities. Because the 8 per cent rate is fixed by contract on these"old" gilts, a potential buyer would be able to realise the competitive 8¼ per cent rate only if the current holder"marked down" the price. As the rate on guilts advances, they become relatively more attractive and other securities become less attractive. Consequently,bond purchasers will buy governments instead of corporates. This will cause the price of corporates to fall and the rate on corporates to rise. Rising corporate bond rates will eventually cause preferred and inturn common stock prices to adjust downward as the chain reaction is felt throughout the system of security yields. Thus the direct effect of increases in the level of interest rates is to cause security prices to fall across a wide span of investment vehicles.

Also there are indirect effects on common stocks. First, lower or higher interest rates make the purchase of stocks on margin (using borrowed funds) more or less attractive. Higher interest rates, for example, may lead to lower stock prices because of a diminished demand for equities by speculators who use margin. Second, many firms, such as public utilities finance their operations quite heavily with borrowed funds. Others, such as financial institutions, are principally in the business of lending money. Advancing interest rates can bring higher earnings to lending institutions whose principal revenue source is interest received on loans. For these firms, higher earnings could lead to increased dividends and stock prices.

Purchasing-power risk: Purchasing-power risk refers to the uncertainty of the purchasing power of the money to be received. In simple terms, purchasing-power risk is the impact of inflation or deflation on an investment. When we think of investment as the postponement of consumption, we can see that when a person purchases a stock, he has foregone the opportunity to buy some goods or service for as long as he owns the stock. If, during the holding period, prices on desired goods and services rise, the investor actually loses purchasing power. Rising prices on goods and services are normally associated with what is referred to as inflation. Falling prices on goods and services are termed deflation. Both inflation and deflation are covered in the all-encompassing term purchasing-power risk. Generally, purchasing-power risk has come to be identified with inflation (rising prices); the incidence of declining prices in most countries has been slight. The anticipated purchasing power changes manifest themselves on both bond and stocks.

Unsystematic Risk

Market, purchasing-power, and interest-rate risks are the principal sources of systematic risk in securities; but we should also consider another important category of security risks-unsystematic risks.

Specific risk is a risk that affects a very small number of assets. This is sometimes referred to as"unsystematic risk". In a balanced portfolio of assets there'd be a spread between general market risk and risks specific to individual components of that portfolio. Determination of the extent of exposure to individual risks is made using models such as Treynor-Black in which the optimal share of a security is inversely proportional to the square of its specific risk.

An example would be news that is specific to either one

stock or a group of companies, such as the loss of a patent or a major natural disaster affecting the company's operation. The portion of total risk that is unique or peculiar to a firm or an industry, and beyond that affecting securities markets in general is called unsystematic risk. Factors such as management capability, consumer preferences, and labour strikes can cause unsystematic variability of returns for a company's stock.

Examples of Unsystematic Risks

- *Business risk:* Business risk relates to the variability of the sales, income, profits etc., which in turn depend on the market conditions for the product mix, input supplies, strength of competitors, etc. The business risk is sometimes external to the company due to changes in government policy or strategies of competitors or unforeseen market conditions. They may be internal due to fall in production, labour problems, raw material problems or inadequate supply of electricity etc. The internal business risk leads to fall in revenues and in profit of the company, but can be corrected by certain changes in the company's policies.
- *Financial Risk:* This relates to the method of financing, adopted by the company; high leverage leading to larger debt servicing problems or short-term liquidity problems due to bad debts, delayed receivables and fall in current assets or rise in current liabilities. These problems could no doubt be solved, but they may lead to fluctuations in earnings, profits and dividends to share holders. Sometimes, if the company runs into losses or reduced profits, these may lead to fall in returns to investors or negative returns. Proper financial planning and other financial adjustments can be used to correct this risk and as such it is controllable.
- Default or insolvency risk: The borrower or issuer of securities may become insolvent or may default, or

delay the payments due, such as interest instalments or principal repayments. The borrower's credit rating might have fallen suddenly and he became default prone and in its extreme form it may lead to insolvency or bankruptcies. In such cases, the investor may get no return or negative returns. An investment in a healthy company's share might turn out to be a waste paper, if within a short span, by the deliberate mistakes of Management or acts of God, the company became sick and its share price tumbled its face value. Other Risks Besides the described risks, there are many more risks, which can be listed, but in actual practice, they may vary in form, size and effect.

Some of such identifiable risks are the Political Risks, Management Risks and Liquidity Risks etc. Political risk may occur due to the changes in the government, or its policy shown in fiscal or budgetary aspects, changes in tax rates, imposition of controls or administrative regulations etc.

Management risks arise due to errors or inefficiencies of management, causing losses to the company. Marketability liquidity risks involve loss of liquidity or loss of value in conversions from one asset to another say, from stocks to bonds, or vice versa. Such risks may arise due to some features of securities, such as callability; or lack of sinking fund or Debenture Redemption Reserve fund, for repayment of principal or due to conversion terms, attached to the security, which may go adverse to the investor. All the types of risks are of varying degrees, resulting in uncertainty or variability of return, loss of income, and capital losses, or erosion of real value of income and wealth of the investor. Normally the higher the risk taken, the higher is the return.

Risk Measurement

Understanding the nature and types of risk is not adequate unless the investor or analyst is capable of measuring it in some quantitative terms. The quantitative expression of the risk of a stock would make it comparable with other stocks.

However, the risk measurements cannot be considered fully accurate as it is caused by multiplicity of factors such as social, political, economic and managerial aspects.

Risk is measured by the variability of returns. The statistical tool often used to measure risk is the standard deviation. We know, standard deviation is a measure of the values of the variables around its mean or it is the square root of the sum of the squared deviations from the mean divided by the number of observations. This can be emphasised with an example.

The concepts of variance, standard deviation, covariance and beta coefficients etc., are also used to explain the measure of risk. In the context of portfolio of assets, or investment in any assets risk is inherent in all such dealings. This risk primarily arises first out of parting of your funds or loss of liquidity. Money lent or parted is always having an element of risk. This element is the same as the concept of total risk.

Capital Asset Pricing Model (CAPM)

CAPM uses the concept of Beta to link risk with return. Using CAPM, investors can assess the risk return trade off involved in any investment decision. Beta is a measure of non-diversifiable risk (Systematic Risk). It shows how the price of a security responds to changes in market prices. The equation for calculation of Beta is,

$R_i = \alpha_i + \beta_i R_m + e_i$

R_i = Estimated return on ith stock

α = Expected return when market return is zero (intercept)

β_i = Beta, a measure of stock's sensitivity to the market index

R_m = Return on market index

e_i = the error term

Using the Beta concept the Capital Asset Pricing Model will help to define the required return on a security. Normally the higher is the risk we take, the higher should be the return as otherwise we avoid risk. So, the higher the, the higher should be the return. The equation for CAPM is

$R_i = Rf + \beta\, i\, (R_m - Rf)$

Ri is the required return

Rf is the risk free return

R_m is the average market return

B_i is the measure of systematic risk which is non-diversifiable.

Presently, the risk free return is 6% as the Treasury Bill rate and market return is expected to vary with the chosen. Let us take as and expected market return is 18%, then the return on the stock i is as follows:

$R_i = 6\% + 1.2\ (18 - 6)$
$= 0.06 + 1.2\ (0.12)$
$= 0.06 + .144$
$= 20.4\%$

If the investor is risk taker and chooses a Beta of 1.8, then the expected return will be higher as shown.

$R_i = 6 + 18\ (18\text{-}12)$
$= .06 + 1.8\ (.12)$
$= .06 + .216 = .276 = 27.6\%$

Security Market Line (SML)

When the Capital Asset Pricing Model is drawn graphically, we get the S.M.L., which is shown in the chart. If the investor wants to decide on an investment with an expected return he would know the level of risk he has to take or alternatively given the level of risk, he has preferred to take, he would know the expected return from this chart. The investor has to assess whether it is worth taking a level of risk, if he has a target return which involves that risk, as he is assumed to be generally risk averse.

Thus, CAPM and SML help the investor in evaluating risk for a return, in making any investment decision. The principle of the higher the risk, the higher is the return is embodied in this Model.

Concept of portfolio Models: Risks in relation to portfolios are also to be understood in the present discussion. Therefore, the concept of Risk in two Major Models used in valuation is related to systematic, unsystematic and total risk. The two models are those of Markowitz and Sharpe which go by the name of Modern Portfolio Theory. The return on investments in financial assets takes the form of dividend and/or interest income and appreciation in the price of the asset held.

The risk associated with holding common stocks is really the likelihood that expected returns will not materialize. If dividends or price appreciation fall short of expectations, the investor is disappointed. The principal sources behind dividend and priceappreciation uncertainties are factors that are either controllable or not subject to control by the firm.

The sources of systematic risk, include market, interest-rate, and purchasing-power risks. Market risk reflects changes in investor attitudes towards equities in general that stem from tangible and intangible events.

Interest-rate risk and purchasing-power risk are associated with changes in the price of money and other goods and services. Increases in interest rates cause the prices of all types of securities to be marked down. Rising prices of goods and services (inflation or purchasing-power changes) have an adverse effect on security prices because the postponement of consumption through any form of investment means less'real' buying power in the future.

The major sources of unsystematic risk affecting the holding of common stocks are business risk and financial risk. Business risk refers to changes in the operating environment of the firm and how the firm adapts to them. Financial risk is related to the debt-andequity mix of financing in the firm. Operating profits can be magnified up or down, depending upon the extent to which debt financing is employed and under what terms.

The various sources of risk in holding common stocks must be quantified so that the analyst can examine risk in relationship to measures of return. A reasonable surrogate of risk is the variability of return. This proxy measure in statistics is commonly the variance or standard deviation of the returns on a stock around the expected return. Total risk of an investment consists of two components: diversifiable and non-diversifiable risk.

The former risk can be almost entirely by holding a large enough mix of carefully selected securities. The only risk an investor is compensated for taking is thus non-diversifiable risk. Beta measures this risk and can be used to determine the appropriate required return on a security. Conversely, the market risk is considered as non-diversifiable risk.

8

Capital Adequacy in Financial Conglomerates

INTRODUCTION

Is there something special, with respect to risk and capital, about a financial conglomerate that combines banking, insurance and potentially other financial and non-financial activities? To what degree is the risk of the whole less than the sum of its parts? This paper seeks to address these questions by evaluating the risk profile of a typical banking-insurance conglomerate and highlighting some of the key analytical issues relating to risk aggregation.

We provide a framework of analysis which builds up this risk profile and allows for coherent dissection of a financial conglomerate's diverse set of risks. We then use the analytical results to frame a policy debate for regulating the solvency of a multi-line financial conglomerate.

Increasing industry consolidation, financial deregulation, and globalization are fuelling rapid growth in the scope of large, multi-line financial conglomerates. The Joint Forum defines a financial conglomerate as "any group of companies under common control whose exclusive or predominant activities consists of providing significant services in at least two different financial sectors (banking, securities, insurance)." In fact, it is fair to say that virtually all of the large, multinational financial institutions operating around the world today are, to some degree, financialconglomerates by either the strict The merits and sins of specialization vs. conglomeration, small vs. big, have been debated at length, and most of that debate has been conducted using data and experience from the U.S. banking industry.4 There is some evidence suggesting that economies of scale exist in banking (Berger, Hancock and Humphrey, and Hughes and Mester. However, to achieve those gains from strict cost efficiency has proven to be difficult, Are bigger banks less risky? Demsetz and Strahan show that while large U.S. bank holding companies are better diversified than small ones, this diversification does not translate into lower risk. Effectively they 'spend' their diversification benefits through larger C&I portfolios.

For a review of the literature, Demsetz and Strahan. Economies of scope have also been used to explain the existence (or creation) of financial conglomerates. These economies of scope can take different forms: lower joint production costs, consumers desiring (and being willing to pay for) one-stopshopping, and more efficient internal capital markets. Putting these together firms might achieve economies of scale and scope to lower monitoring costs, or perhaps by using very large customer databases to cross sell retail financial products and services.

Using the U.S. insurance industry as their labouratory, Berger, Cummins, Weiss and Zi (2000), try to explain the coexistence of, in their terminology, the "conglomeration hypothesis" — diversified insurers — with the "strategic focus hypothesis" - pure life or P&C insurers. They do so using a concept of "profit scope economies, which measures the relative efficiency of joint vs. specialized production, taking both costs and revenues into account.".

They find that "the conglomeration hypothesis tends to apply more to insurers that are large, emphasize personal lines of business, [and] use vertically integrated distribution systems while the strategic focus hypothesis tends to apply more to insurers that are small, emphasize commercial lines, [and] use non-integrated distribution systems" But are conglomerates more or less risky? A stylized story promises reduction in earnings volatility as the business activities generating those earnings become more diverse. Stiroh (2002) debunks this story for the case of banking by showing that the U.S. banking industry did not achieve any obvious diversification benefits, in the form of stable profits or revenue, through an ongoing shift away from traditional interest income during the last twenty years. all argue that correlation will likely go up once business and product silos are placed under one roof. Moreover, risk may actually increase because monitoring goes down, either report that consolidation appears to have increased profit efficiency in banking. The idea of risk mitigation as a merger motivation is not new. There is a rich literature on co-insurance following the seminal paper, which discusses the impact of mergers on debt holders (and, indirectly, shareholders).through the bank monitoring its counterparties or the bank being monitored by others such as rating agencies argue that the risk of the whole may be greater than the sum of its parts, largely due to spillover effects from reputation risk. Moreover they point out that the practicalities of achieving integrated risk management are daunting and"appear to have discouraged firms from adopting consolidated risk management". Once those systems are in place, however, firms should expect to reap economies of scale in risk management

As suggested, examine the risk reduction, in terms of economic capital, that might be experienced by possible conglomerate profiles. Others have also considered different inter-sector marriages. Lown e, using pro-forma analysis of potential combinations of banks with either of securities firms, life or P&C insurers, find that the merger of bank with a life insurer resulted in the best risk-return benefit, largely because of enhanced revenue opportunities (economies of scope) and anticipated risk reduction, rather than anticipated cost savings or manufacturing scale (economies of scale). Estrella (2001), using a different approach based on options pricing and the arbitrage pricing theory (APT), finds potential diversification gains from virtually all combinations of banking and insurance (both life and P&C) arising from revenue gains and the already well diversified nature of an insurance portfolio. While these results are in harmony with ours, and as suggested, use some of Estrella's correlation estimates as a robustness check on our analysis later, we are less bullish about the degree of diversification that is actually realizable.

Finally, systemic risk concerns have been raised by several authors, either because the conglomerates are larger and might be considered too-big-to-fail —TBTF –, or that even if they are not "too big" they may become too-complex-to-fail – TCTF –. Moreover, one might be concerned that bank supervisors, in order to help prevent failure of a non-bank affiliate, might be tempted to extend the.

In his literature review, Stiroh points to eighteen studies collected in Saunders and Walter that examine safety net beyond just the bank. This would inhibit market discipline by reducing the incentive to monitor the financial institution and increase the risk of contagion across the pieces of the holding company.

Against this backdrop, we turn to a question that has not been examined previously in the literature: What does the risk structure of financial conglomerate imply for capital adequacy, particularly at the holding company level? In fact, where are the major sources of risk, and of equal importance, where are the diversification benefits within a financial conglomerate? As suggested, not speculate on possible revenue synergies or management span-of-control issues, but rather focus on the size and composition of the risk pie (e.g. how big is market risk in banking vs. insurance) and what that implies for different financial conglomerates (e.g. large universal bank merging with a small P&C insurer) from the perspective of capital adequacy.

Despite the increasing importance of financial conglomerates, the regulatory structure in most jurisdictions is still largely based around single business lines, on the notion that financial institutions, or their business lines, can be classified as banks or insurance companies or securities firms.9 This is particularly true of the regulatory approach to capital adequacy, which historically has treated different regulated businesses as independent 'silos' in setting capital requirements.

Analytically, the special problem of capital management

in a conglomerate stems from the need to aggregate risks across diverse business lines, such as banking and insurance. Our suggested approach for constructing a composite risk picture is to follow a 'building block' approach that aggregates risk at three successive levels in an organization (corresponding to the levels at which risk is typically managed):

Whether non-bank activities broadly are risk reducing; nine conclude yes, six no, and three have mixed results. Securities and asset management activities for third parties are deemed part of the bank or insurance group. These activities are, therefore, not explicitly and separately dealt with in this paper. Level I: The first level aggregates the standalone risks within a single risk factor (e.g. credit risk in a commercial loan portfolio)

Level II: The second level aggregates risk across different risk factors within a single businessline (e.g. combining the asset, liability, and operating risks in P&C or life insurance)

Level III: The third level aggregates risk across different business lines (e.g., banking and insurance).

Our analysis adopts this building block approach because it isolates the incremental effects of crossbusiness diversification that are unique to a conglomerate.

Empirically, diversification effects are greatest within a single risk factor (Level I), decrease at the business line level (Level II), and are smallest across business lines (Level III). Our estimates suggest that the *incremental* diversification benefits achievable at Level III by combining a bank with an insurance company are on the order of a 5-10% reduction in capital requirements, depending on business mix. In such a building block approach, the result of adding risks at the holding company level can be no more accurate than the standalone capital measures for individual risk factors (Level I) and business lines (Level II). The existing regulatory capital measures at these levels are inherently limited, and in particular, fail to reflect important diversification effects at Levels I and II. In our view, a well-constructed economic risk and capital management framework offers the best chance of overcoming the limitations of the silo approach to capital regulation. Specifically, such a framework can have the potential to address – in a flexible way that is sensitive to business mix–both the standalone distributions and correlation structures of different risk factors, leading to a composite 'aggregate' risk picture of the organization. Finally, by defining economic capital as a 'common currency' for risk, the framework has the potential to overcome inconsistent measurement of risks based on where a transaction is booked.

We suggest that supervisors respond to industry developments in risk measurement and management by supplementing existing supervision of regulated subsidiaries with oversight at the holding company level of a conglomerate's internal risk and capital management framework. This oversight should seek both to validate – and to leverage – internal capital models, harnessing their power to frame the right questions for each institution. Ultimately, rather than focusing just on the numbers, supervision of the holding company should focus on the effectiveness of the capital decision making process.

The limitations of a 'silo'-based approach to regulation and describe how these limitations give rise to the questions posed by the Project Sponsors. Section 3 describes an analytical framework for assessing the risk profile of a typical banking-insurance conglomerate and examines the scale and scope of aggregation effects. Section 4 highlights industry practices for measuring and managing risk and capital in a financial conglomerate. Section 5 concludes with a brief policy discussion.

CURRENT 'SILO'-BASED APPROACH TO REGULATION

Despite the increasing significance of financial conglomerates, the regulatory structure in most jurisdictions is still largely based around single business lines, on the notion that financial institutions, or their business lines, can be classified as banks or insurance companies or securities firms. This is particularly true in the regulatory approach to capital adequacy.

The current Basel Committee (BIS I) rules for the banking

industry, for example, limit capital requirements to the credit and trading activities of licensed banks. Life insurance capital regulation similarly focuses on reserve requirements for authorized underwriting activities. Capital requirements for securities firms, meanwhile, vary by jurisdiction. In countries with a universal banking heritage, such as the Netherlands and Germany, the requirements for securities firms fall under bank capital guidelines. In other countries, such as the U.S., the requirements for securities firms fall under different 10 Estrella was one of the first to highlight the importance of this issue.

The rules set by a separate authority The UK and Japan, through their respective Financial Services Authorities, have placed regulation of all three sectors underone roof.

LIMITATIONS OF THIS 'SILO' APPROACH

The approaches to capital regulation for banks, insurance companies, and securities firms have evolved from very different starting points, under different statutory regimes, accounting conventions, time horizons, intervention triggers, and policy objectives. This 'silo' approach to capital adequacy raises a number of issues:

First, the silo approach is inconsistent: it may lead to different treatment of similar risk types depending on where the risk is booked. As an example, consider a credit exposure to an 'A' rated counterparty. If the exposure were booked in a bank as a loan, it would, under current (BIS I) capital rules, require Tier I capital of 4% of outstandings. If it were booked as a credit insurance transaction in a P&C insurance company, the same economic exposure would, under EU regulation, require capital of only 0.16% of outstandings – or twenty-five times less capital than a bank loan. By comparison, if the credit exposure were held as a bond in a life insurance company investment portfolio, it would, under EU regulation, require an (implicit) asset risk charge of 3% of outstandings. Inconsis-tent treatment creates the potential for regulatory arbitrage: It may encourage institutions to book business in those subsidiaries or shell companies that face the lightest regula-tion, irrespective of their ability to manage or sustain the level of risk.

Gramm-Leach-Bliley, with the Financial Holding Company (FHC), makes this now possible in the U.S. as well.

An interesting recent proposal from the UK's FSA is in the form of CP136 which seeks to draft a framework for capital adequacy standards for each financial sector.

Banking Regulation/(BIS I)

EU Credit Insurance Regulations EU Life Insurance/ Regulations,

- Treat as commercial loan
- Tier 1 capital = 4% ofoutstandings
- Treat as credit insurance payingcredit insurance premium of 1%per annum
- Solvency capital = 16% of premiums Ò! 0.16% ofoutstandings
- Treat as an investment
- Implicit asset risk charge = 3% of outstandings

Second, the silo approach ignores aggregation because it fails to take account of risk concentrations or diversification across different operating subsidiaries. It is possible that an acceptable level of credit risk to a given counterparty in a firm's banking book may become a possibly unintended concentration if added to exposures to the same counterparty in the firm's trading book or insurance investment portfolios.16 For example, if a bank has extended a credit facility to the same business to which the insurance company has issued a catastrophic (CAT) risk insurance policy, the concentration of risks will be lost in the silo approach. More fundamentally, many of the major risk factors within an operating subsidiary will tend to be mitigated by offsetting and diversifying exposures in other businesses.

Third, the silo approach is incomplete because it ignores the capital requirements of unlicensed subsidiaries, including a top holding company. Unlicensed subsidiaries that are engaged in commercial activities impose incremental risk, even if limited to non-financial factors (such as business and operational risk), which suggests a need for additional capital. At the same time, it is at the holding company level that the benefits of diversification across business lines are ultimately realised. These diversification benefits, however, need to be evaluated in the context of a holding company's funding 16 In the EU, banking and trading book exposures within one firm (and group) are together subject to the large exposure rule practices and capital structure, taking into account such factors as the potential for double leverage. We summarize the problems of inconsistency, aggregation, and incompleteness

Inconsistent Treatment Aggregation Incompleteness

- Capital requirements dependent on where risk is booked
- Boundaries breaking down due to product innovation
- Increased demand/potential for regulatory arbitrage
- Concentration of risks across legal boundaries
- Diversification across risk classes within a legal entity
- Diversification of risks across business activities and operating companies
- Capital requirements of unlicensed operating companies
- Capital requirements/funding structure of holding company
- 'Strategic' investments in non-financial companies

The limitations of the current silo approach will continue to be exacerbated by industry consolidation and product innovation, which will further blur the boundaries between traditional business lines and risk classifications. If the regulatory structure fails to keep pace with these developments, the whole purpose of rule-based capital requirements may prove to be self-defeating. There is a danger that institutions will increasingly view risk and capital reporting as a game to be arbitraged, rather than as an opportunity to communicate their financial strength to the outside world. While there are no simple answers to these challenges, the development of integrated risk and capital frameworks for evaluating capital adequacy in a conglomerate context is progressing. These developments are being driven by a number of factors, including:

- The introduction of risk measurement methodologies and analytical tools for risk and capital management as well as performance measurement
- The evolution of enterprise risk management as a key corporate centre function
- The blurring of product boundaries through financial innovation, and the potential for regulatory capital arbitrage
- The increased reliance by rating agencies on enterprise-wide capital models for evaluating the ratings of financial conglomerates
- The pressure from some regulators for a consolidated view of risk and capital at the holding company level

As we conclude in Section 5, advances in internal risk and capital management practices offer the potential for innovative and more powerful regulatory approaches.

Recent Regulatory Debate

The debate in the regulatory arena around these issues has intensified in the last three to four

years. Notably, the New Basel Accord, sometimes called BIS (or Basel) II, proposes to "include, on a fully consolidated basis, holding companies that are parents of banking groups to ensure that it captures risks within the whole banking group" (Basel Committee on Banking Supervision. This includes especially securities and even insurance subsidiaries.18 More recently, in September 2002, the EU Council of Ministers approved an EU directive on the supervision of financial conglomerates.

This directive had four main objectives: 1) to ensure that the conglomerate be adequately capitalized, with particular attention focused on preventing 'multiple gearing;' 2) to introduce methods for calculating a financial conglomerate's overall solvency position; 3) to deal with issues of intra-group transactions, group-level risk exposure and internal risk management and control processes; and 4) to adopt a provision for lead supervisor by the member states for each financial conglomerate.

The Joint Forum at the BIS has also tackled the issue of risk measurement and management in a financial conglomerate head-on.20 This Joint Forum grew out of a "Tripartite Group" formed in 1993. The purpose of the Group was to identify and provide solutions for problems that financial conglomerates pose for supervisors. It was the first time three sets of supervisors worked.

A bank that owns an insurance subsidiary bears full entrepreneurial risks ofthe subsidiary and should recognise on a group-wide basis the risks included in the whole group."

Together. In 1995, the Group submitted the Tripartite Report, which, while not officially endorsed by the Basel Commission, the International Organization of Securities Commissions (IOSCO), and the International Association of Insurance Supervisors (IAIS), served as the launching point for the Joint Forum consisting of these three regulatory bodies. Fundamentally, the Tripartite Group agreed that supervision of financial conglomerates cannot be effective if individual components of a group are supervised on a purely solo basis. The solo supervision of individual subsidiaries continues to be of primary importance, but it needs to be complemented by an assessment from a groupwide perspective. The paper laid out simple policy alternatives and proposed some accounting and managerial guidelines but did not provide any answers to the questions of diversification or concentration.The 1999 Joint Forum Report, under the aegis of the Basel Committee on Banking Supervision(Basel Committee), IOSCO and IAIS, was meant to take forward the work completed by the 1995 report. The report is a set of five papers around capital adequacy, supervisory principles and information sharing and co-ordination. While the first paper on Capital Adequacy made significant progress on the 1995 effort, it focused less on diversification and concentration effects and more on issues such as double (or multiple) leverage, regulatory arbitrage (across distinct bodies), and provided a very simple, banking focused approach to risk aggregation.

The most recent report explicitly compares approaches to risk management and capital regulation across the three sectors of banking, securities and insurance. It not only gives the comparative regulatory view but also summarizes many of the different approaches employed by financial firms across the three sectors, including, of course, practices by financial conglomerates.

EU Directive on Supervision of Financial Conglomerates, Commission to the European Communities,SEC(2002) 995 Final. This report in turn builds on their earlier work.

Risk Profile of a Financial Conglomerate: Measurement and Management

The special problem of capital management in a conglomerate stems from the need to aggregate risks across a diverse set of businesses.22 This section seeks to size the magnitude of aggregation effects by examining the risk profile of a banking-insurance conglomerate. In effect, it asks just how big a problem risk aggregation actually is: are aggregation effects so severe that a typical conglomerate is over-capitalized to the point of inefficiency (in particular to shareholders), or under-capitalized to the point where it causes undue risk of insolvency to debtholders and policyholders? Very High Very Low/ None

A financial conglomerate is, by definition, a combination of diverse businesses operating under a common ownership structure. The organization can be broken down into major 21 The 2002 EU directive on the supervision of financial conglomerates adopted the 1999 Joint Forum recommendations.

Business lines, each of which has a distinct risk profile. For example, the universal banking activities – consisting of retail, corporate, and investment banking — are dominated by credit risk. Life insurance activities are dominated by market (investment) risk, and P&C activities by insurance (CAT) risk. In addition, non-licensed subsidiaries may be part of the conglomerate structure. While the common ownership structure is typically in the form of a holding company, it need not be. The analysis and results in this section are independent of the specific legal structure of the conglomerate.

The capital management problem for a conglomerate is to determine – both within and across businesses – how much capital is required to support the level of risk taking. The problem is of concern to different constituencies. On the one hand, debtholders, policyholders, regulators and rating agencies are primarily concerned with the *solvency* of the institution. For them, the key issue is whether the institution holds sufficient capital to absorb risk – or the potential for loss – under all but the most extreme loss scenarios. Put another way, they are seeking capital to backstop the organization's risk taking at a high degree of confidence.

On the other hand, shareholders, participating policyholders, and investment analysts are primarily concerned with the *profitability* of the institution. For them, the key issue is whether the institution is earning a sufficient return (at or above hurdle rate) on the capital invested to support risk taking. While capital is the common denominator that links the debtholders and shareholders, their interests pull in different directions. Lower capital for a given degree of risk taking will make an institution less solvent, but more profitable, and vice versa.

A conglomerate poses special challenges for capital management: internally, for managers charged with balancing the risk, capital, and return equation, and externally, for regulators concerned with the safety and soundness of the institution. The first challenge is to determine the standalone risk of an activity within a business line – such as the credit risk in a commercial loan portfolio or the 22 Given the myriad ways in which a financial conglomerate can be structured, the only valid method for aggregating risks is one that is based on underlying risk fundamentals and is independent of legal structure. catastrophe risk in a P&C insurer's homeowners portfolio. A number of techniques have been developed within banks and insurance companies to assess risk at this level.

The next challenge is to combine the different risk factors within a business line or licensed subsidiary. Because risks are less than perfectly correlated, they cannot be strictly added together. The licensed subsidiaries include banks, insurance companies, and securities firms that are subject to specific capital requirements. The potential for diversification suggests that the whole will be less than the sum of the parts.

A further challenge for a conglomerate results from the presence of unlicensed subsidiaries. They generally fall into two categories: financial subsidiaries that engage in financial businesses such as financing, insurance, and brokering outside of a licensed banking group, insurance company or securities firm; and commercial subsidiaries that are principally engaged in non-financial activities. In both cases, unlicensed subsidiaries impose an incremental need for capital, at a minimum to cover the incremental operating risks (including both business and event risk) inherent in the business. For a nonlicensed financial subsidiary – such as a consumer finance or leasing company – the need for capital will be similar to that for other regulated activities. For an unlicensed commercial subsidiary, the incremental capital will be analogous to that held by a non-financial firm, and will be needed to cover operating risks, including business and event risk.

At the same time, the top holding company within a conglomerate structure may also be an unlicensed entity. Because of the scope of activity, the holding company raises unique issues of aggregation.

Economic Capital as a Common Currency for Risk

In order to assess capital requirements in a diverse conglomerate, there needs to be a 'common currency' for risk that can equate risk taking in one activity or business line with another. Economic capital is often used as that common currency for risk measurement, irrespective of where the risk is incurred. Under the economic capital approach, the risks of a conglomerate – or of the individual businesses within it – can be classified into primary components of asset risk, liability risk, and operating risk. These risks can be further decomposed. Asset risk is typically broken down into credit risk and market/ALM (asset/liability mis-match or management) risk. Insurance liability risks can be separated into P&C catastrophe risk; P&C experience-based risks; and life risks. Operating risks can be split into business risk and event risks.

This framework does not explicitly address what is sometimes referred to as "reputation risk." Reputation risk has two separate connotations: the first is the spillover risk to one business resulting from the insolvency of an affiliated entity. This effect is not incorporated in an economic capital framework because it is not a result of risktaking per se. Rather, it is a result of the failure to hold sufficient capital to prevent the insolvency of the affiliate, and of the legal or market conventions that transfer some or all of the resulting loss to the surviving business.

This "risk" can be mitigated by setting high solvency standards for all entities within a conglomerate. Equally, if risks are correctly aggregated, then the total amount of economic capital at the top of the organization will determine the amount of financial resources (capital) necessary to support all of the organization's risk taking at the desired confidence level, inclusive of any spillover effects.

Another meaning of "reputation risk" refers to franchise risk associated with a major fiasco – such as the damage to a financial institution that could result from a large internal fraud or involvement in illegal money laundering. In principle, any direct losses stemming from such occurrences should be captured as an "event" risk within an economic capital framework. The more diffuse harm to franchise value is not something which capital resources are effective at alleviating.

Although each of these risks has distinct statistical properties – as reflected in the stylized risk distributions shown for them – economic capital sets a common standard for measuring the degree of risk taking. The standard is defined in terms of a confidence interval in the cumulative loss distribution, assessed over a common time horizon.25 By setting capital for different risks at the same confidence interval, the economic capital requirements for different risk factors and types of activities can be directly compared. Only by having such a common standard can one meaningfully assess the risk for a complex conglomerate with a diversity of business activities across the financial spectrum.

A typical approach is to tie the degree of capital protection to the target debt rating of the institution. One convention is to adopt a one-year time horizon. The economic capital requirement is set to protect against losses over one year at the 99.9% level – roughly equivalent to the default risk of an 'A' rated corporate bond. Put another way, a business that holds capital to protect against one-year losses at the 99.9% confidence interval would have a default risk consistent with a 'A' debt rating. Setting capital for the individual risks within a conglomerate at this confidence interval assures that each of them, on a standalone basis, is protected to a level consistent with the target rating.

Economic capital models are typically built up from the specific analytical approaches for individual risk factors. Lists common modeling approaches for the main risk types. While the specific tools for risk factors such as credit, CAT, P&C experience and market risks differ, the common denominator in an economic capital framework is the attempt to describe the risk distribution in probabilistic terms, and set capital at a common confidence interval.

The different risks have traditionally been measured at often rather different time horizons. The one-year horizon is indeed typical for banking. In insurance, longer time horizons are considered. Just as risks can be decomposed into individual factors, they can also be re-aggregated. The distribution drawn at the bottom of shows conceptually how the various risk distributions of a financial conglomerate can be combined to yield a single, cumulative loss distribution – and economic capital requirement — for the institution.

In practice, aggregating the various risk distributions in a complex financial organization is a challenging task and somewhat arbitrary. Ultimately, the total amount of economic risk at the top of an organization is independent of how risks are aggregated within it. One proposed method for constructing a composite risk picture is to follow a 'building block' approach that aggregates risk at successive levels in an organization. There are three key levels, corresponding to the levels at which risks are typically managed:

Level I: The first level aggregates the standalone risks within a single risk factor in an individual business line. Examples include aggregating the credit risk in a commercial loan portfolio; the equity risks in a life insurance investment portfolio; and the catastrophe risks in a P&C underwriting business.

Level II: The second level aggregates risk across different risk factors within a single business line. Examples include aggregating the credit, market/ALM, and operating risks in a bank; or combining the asset, liability, and operating risks in P&C or life insurance.

Level III: The third level aggregates risk across different business lines, such as banking and insurance subsidiaries. This leads to the composite picture – or cumulative loss distribution – at the top (holding company) level.

Our analysis adopts the building block approach because it allows the risk profiles of each of the businesses within a conglomerate to be considered separately, *before introducing the cross-business aggregation effects that are unique to a conglomerate.* Put another way, Level I and Level II aggregation effects are already present within regulated banks and insurance companies. The unique problems of a conglomerate are associated with Level III.

Differences in corporate structure, business line definitions, legal requirements, or risk management philosophy may lead some organizations to follow other hierarchies in aggregating risks than the three-level building block approach of overall risk at the top of the organization, alternative approaches to risk aggregation will yield different results at lower levels.

Estimating Aggregation Effects: General Principles

The starting point for risk aggregation is to begin with standalone estimates of the economic capital required for individual risk factors. The specific techniques for calculating risk at this level are beyond the scope of this paper. Given estimates of standalone economic capital, one can aggregate risks – to a first-order approximation — based on the relative amounts of economic capital, and then consider correlations between risk factors. The diversification benefits that accrue from aggregation are driven by three main factors:

- The number of risk positions (*N*)
- The concentration of those risk positions, or their relative weights in a portfolio
- The correlation between the positions

In general, the diversification benefit increases with the number of positions, decreases with greater concentration, and decreases with greater correlation. The diversification benefits for a portfolio of equally weighted assets or liabilities for two different levels of correlation.

Diversification within a Risk Factor

As the number of positions28 increases for a given level of correlation, the diversification ratio decreases – i.e., there is an increase in the diversification benefit. For a given number of positions, as the correlation decreases the diversification benefit increases. For a correlation level typically experienced in market risk – around 40% – the full diversification benefit amounts to about one-third; this is achieved fairly rapidly, after about 30 positions. For the much lower correlations typical of a credit portfolio – around 2% – the diversification benefit is significantly greater – around 75%. However, it takes longer to get there; this limit is achieved after around 100 positions.

Though the deals with equally weighted positions, as concentration increases thediversification benefit decreases. This is most easily seen at the extreme. The diversification benefit obtained by one risk factor that is nine times the size of another will be very small, even if the two risks The term 'positions' is used to highlight the fact that this holds universally for assets, liabilities, number of risk factors, etc.

It is important to note that some credit portfolios with considerably more than 100 loans do not converge on the systematic risk limit, because the loans are not equally weighted. Often, a few individual loans can each account for as much as 2-3% of the portfolio, which limits diversification because of concentration effects. are completely uncorrelated (independent). At zero correlation, the largest diversification benefit possible cannot exceed 10%.30.

The Capital Asset Pricing Model (CAPM) breaks total risk into specific (or idiosyncratic) and systematic risk. While the two curves represented in the graph show the systematic risk associated with average correlations of 40% and 2%, respectively, it is possible to conceive of different systematic risk curves for a given risk factor, reflecting different average levels of correlation. For example, a systematic risk curve for a domestic equities portfolio will have a higher level of average correlation – and lower diversification benefit – than a systematic risk curve for a globally diversified equities portfolio. Similarly, the systematic risk curve for a regionally concentrated credit portfolio will have a higher level of average correlation than a systematic risk curve for a globally diversified credit portfolio. Thus, the diversification benefit obtainable within a given risk factor will vary with the scope of activity.

With these principles in mind, the general characteristics of the three levels of aggregation can be stated as follows:

- Level I has many risk factors (individual assets or liabilities) that are neither strongly concentrated nor highly correlated. As a result, there should be a high diversification benefit at Level I. The achievable diversification benefit will be driven by the scope of activity.
- Level II has fewer risk factors, and they are likely to be more concentrated and more correlated. Consequently, there should be a lower diversification benefit at Level II than at Level I.
- At Level III, there are only a few risk factors; some are likely to be much more highly concentrated than others, and correlations will tend to be high. Level III should therefore This result follows from Equations: if *EC*1 = 9 and *EC*2 = 1, and ñ = 0, then

ECT= 92+12>9 and the diversification benefit *DB* < 10%. yield the smallest diversification effects of the three levels.

Level I Diversification

Level I diversification benefits reflect the degree of diversification achievable for a single risk factor within a given business line. At this level, the number of positions in a portfolio is quite large – typically well over 1,000 policies or loans in an insurance or loan portfolio, and over a hundred positions in an investment portfolio. As a result, diversification benefits will converge fairly rapidly to the systematic risk limit. That for an equity portfolio, a one-third reduction is achievable due to diversification of idiosyncratic risk alone, while for credit risk the lower correlations allow for a fourfifths reduction.

Beyond the number of positions, differences in the scope of activity can have a dramatic impact on the level of systematic risk, and hence the achievable diversification benefits. The increasing benefit from diversifying the credit risk of an equally weighted commercial loan portfolio internationally across geographies, essentially diversifying the portfolio with respect to the most fundamental of systematic risks, the (national) business cycle.31 We present results using correlation based on GDP changes from 1991 to 2000.32 31 A discussion of the methodology. Global is represented here by the EU, Japan, Australia, Indonesia, Brazil and South Africa. Source: IMF: In this example, the economic capital requirement for a U.S. only portfolio is indexed to 1.0 If that portfolio were combined with an equivalent sized portfolio of U.K. commercial loans of similar ratings, the capital requirement (as a percentage of exposure) would be reduced by about one-fifth. Adding a German portfolio of equal size would increase the diversification benefit to 30%, while a fully diversified global credit portfolio would require slightly less than half as much capital, per unit of exposure, as the regionally concentrated U.S. portfolio.

Not surprisingly, diversification is a major rationale for

financial institutions to internationalize portfolios. For a given amount of expected loss, the same notional exposure leads to less loss volatility and lower capital requirements. Note that this result is not unique to credit risk, rather it can be generalized beyond just banking to insurance as well as non-financial activities.

The same principles apply to equity portfolios – where international diversification is the only means of lowering the systematic risk in any one market. And equally, in P&C insurance, diversifying CAT risk across product lines and geographies produces a similar effect. Since CAT risk for hurricanes and earthquakes is uncorrelated, a U.S. insurer exposed to Florida hurricanes can lower systematic CAT risk by underwriting Tokyo earthquake policies. This explains one of the key benefits of internationalization for insurance companies, particularly P&C and reinsurance. As in the credit example, single risk factor diversification benefits can be on the order of 50% or more.

Significantly, existing capital requirements typically ignore differences in Level I diversification by assuming some 'average' level of correlation and hence systematic risk. As an example, current (BIS I) rules for bank credit risk set a 4% Tier I capital requirement for all commercial lending – irrespective of the degree of diversification in the portfolio. This would continue to be true under the internal ratings based capital reforms proposed in BIS II.33.

Level II Diversification: Level II diversification depends on the correlation of risks within a business line. The magnitude of Level II effects will differ systematically for banks, life insurers, and P&C insurers. For banks, the dominant risk, as reflected in BIS capital rules, is credit risk. This is corroborated by two benchmarking studies conducted in 2000. One was conducted by Oliver, Wyman & Company, which surveyed the internal economic capital allocations of ten large international banks in Europe and North America. Capital Market Risk Advisors conducted its own survey of 38 banks, six of which were classified as "large, global". The results presented are quite similar. The standalone economic capital requirements for the banks – as determined by their internal models – was broken down into three major risk factors: credit risk, market/ALM risk, and operating and other risks. On average, credit risk accounted for about half of the total economic capital requirement, market/ALM risk accounted for one fifth and operating and other risks accounted for one quarter to one third of the total economic capital. 33 The same applies to insurance, both under EU and NAIC guidelines.

Economic Risk Capital Breakdowns: Given the relative weights of the standalone economic capital for the risk factors, the Level II diversification benefits can be estimated from the risk factor correlations. In practice, there are a number of approaches for calculating correlations and diversification benefits. We discuss some in the focus on the results here. Taking the OWC economic capital breakdown as an example, we compute the diversification benefits under three different correlation assumptions, presented. The first set is taken from Dimakos and Aas who estimate correlations for a Norwegian bank which also owns a life insurance subsidiary. The second set comes from Ward and Lee who present risk aggregation results for a diversified insurer with the risk types broken out. Ward and Lee have separate correlations for market and ALM risk. 34 As we aggregate those risks here, we took the higher of the two correlations. Finally we present results based on the correlations used in Kuritzkes, Schuermann and Weiner,35 which are based on interview findings and reflect the values used by Dutch and other financial conglomerates in their internal capital models. 34 We group market and ALM risk together as the interest rate risk associated with ALM is typically the dominant risk factor in market risk.

Supports the proposition that as the level increases, the magnitude of the diversification benefit decreases. The explanation is straightforward: at the bank level, there are only three risk factors; they are concentrated (credit risk alone accounts for over half of total capital); and have relatively high correlations (for the more conservative KSW case, 40% or greater).36 This provides a possible justification for why existing bank capital regulations ignore Level II benefits: both the present and proposed BIS guidelines treat credit and market risks on a standalone basis, and simply add together the combined requirement without any deduction for cross-risk factor diversification. Many banks do the same in their internal economic capital frameworks. This underscores the importance of Level I diversification relative to Level II for the banks.

The same analysis can be repeated for insurance companies. Three risk profiles: a life insurer, a P&C insurer and a diversified insurer. Note that the risk profile of the insurers differs significantly from that of a bank and also from each other. Credit risk, for example, accounts for only about 5% and 10% of the total economic capital of a typical P&C and life insurer respectively, although the Ward and Lee estimate is closer to 20% for the diversified insurer, compared to 50% for a bank. At the same time, market/ALM risk accounts for 50% of the capital requirement of a life insurer, 44% of the diversified insurer, 37% of the P&C insurer while only 21% of the total risk of a bank. They may, in fact, not be all that conservative. It is well known that in times of stress, correlations oftenincrease

While grouping ALM and Market Risk is generically useful, life insurance has potentially distinctive ALM features stemming from the unique obligations to its policy holders. Specifically, the policyholders (i.e. liabilitiesto the insurer) often bear some of the market risk from the asset side of the balance sheet.

Studies reporting inter-risk correlations for insurers are harder to come by than for banks. We are aware of only one,, who do so for a diversified insurer. Thus we present diversification benefit results for a life, P&C and diversified insurer using their correlations as well as the correlations used in KSW. With only one exception (the correlation between operating and life risk), our correlations are higher (often much higher) than those of Ward and Lee. Level II diversification benefits for a life and P&C insurer using two different correlation assumptions. The lower correlations of Ward and Lee result in larger diversification benefits than do our more conservative estimates. This benefit is 46% for a P&C and 38% for a life insurer, while the higher correlation version results in 27% and 19% respectively.

Diversification at Level II (Insurance): In both cases, the larger diversification benefit for the P&C insurer result from P&C risk being relatively uncorrelated with other risk types. This lower level of correlation overcomes the high concentration that P&C risk represents in the risk profile of a P&C insurer.

Despite the larger diversification benefits at Level II for the insurers relative to a bank, the main hypothesis holds, namely, in moving from Level I to Level II, the diversification benefit decreases.

The results for the diversified insurer are very similar to those of the P&C insurer. While the incremental diversification benefits encountered at Level II are less than at Level I, they can nevertheless be economically important and often are not accounted for by regulatory capital rules. For example, the bank capital regulation (under both BIS I and BIS II) simply adds together the standalone requirements for credit, market, and prospectively, operational risk without any offset for diversification. Similarly, existing European insurance capital requirements assume some "average" level of correlation within one licensed insurance entity. If several such entities form part of an insurance group, as is typically the case, any diversification effects (e.g., geographic diversification) are ignored.

Considering an example from insurance, in the U.S. the P&C risk based capital (RBC) formula for underwriting risk capital has two components: reserve risk and premium risk. The reserve risk charge is calculated by multiplying net premiums written with a set of RBC factors. The factors are different for each line, thereby introducing some diversification benefit.

This is called the Loss Concentration Factor (LCF), which is linearly related to the ratio of the volume of the reserves for the largest line to the total reserves. Suppose that for two companies A and B, the largest line comprises one-fourth of total reserves – but the two lines are different. Then each line will have a different standalone risk and different correlations with the rest of their respective business lines. Nevertheless the capital requirements will be the same.

Level III Diversification: Having addressed the diversification benefits at Level II, the incremental diversification benefits at Level III can be estimated by combining banking and insurance activities in varying proportions. As discussed earlier, the three key factors in quantifying diversification benefits are the number of assets or liabilities, the concentration of risk factors, and the cross-risk factor correlations.

Note, however, that in Existing European insurance capital requirements assume some 'average' level of correlation within one licensed entity. In case several of such entities form part of an insurance group, any additional diversification effects (e.g., geographic diversification) are ignored, combining an insurance company with a bank, there are only two business lines, and they share many of the same risk factors (e.g. exposure to a common business cycle). In addition, one of the subsidiaries may well be larger than the other one. These factors will tend to limit the possible diversification benefits.

To aid in understanding the potential diversification benefits at Level III, we consider five different conglomerate profiles reflecting possible different mixes of a universal bank (bank plus securities firm), life and P&C insurers, plus in one scenario, the addition of a small non-financial, commercial subsidiary. The proportions represent the unit's level of standalone economic capital. These risk profiles are meant to capture a wide range of possible structures, from banking-dominated conglomerates to insurance-dominated conglomerates. For each profile, the diversification benefits were calculated by breaking down the bank, life, and P&C businesses into their Level II risk factors. The Level II risks were then re-aggregated based on the cross-risk factor correlations.

Sub Units
Universal
Bank

P&C Life Non-financial
Profile 1 "Bank/P&C-lite" 70% 30% 0% 0%
Profile 2 "Bank/Life-lite" 70% 0% 30% 0%
Profile 3 "Bank/P&C" 50% 50% 0% 0%
Profile 4 "Life/Bank-lite" 25% 0% 75% 0%
Profile 5 "Mixed" 35% 30% 30% 5%
Conglomerate Profiles
The LCF formula is LCF=0.7+0.3*ratio. This adjustment reduces the capital required for reserve risk.

Obviously, LCF is a rough approximation for the true diversification benefit.

We then estimate diversification benefits for these profiles given the standalone levels of economic capital by risk type and their correlations as described We do so using several different sets of inter-risk correlations taken from different studies, including the correlations used in our original study. These correlations are presented as well as a brief synopsis of each study. we present the results, including an average across all four correlation specifications.

Conglomerate Diversification Benefits

Several observations come to light. First, the overall results confirm our initial hypothesis: the benefits at Level III are smaller than at Level I and Level II. For three of the four correlation specifications, the benefits only range from 0% to 12%.44 For the specification which combines correlation estimates from Dimakos and Aas for banking and from Ward and Lee for insurance, the implied diversification is larger: 5% to 16%.

Indeed, under any of the correlation assumptions from this broad range, diversification benefits are modest. Expected benefits likely fall in the 5% to 10% range Second, across the range of estimates, the largest diversification benefits stem from combining a bank with a P&C insurer. This follows because credit risk (the dominant risk in banking) is uncorrelated with catastrophe risk (the dominant risk in P&C). Third, relative size matters. The biggest bang for the diversification buck comes from combining risks of equal size.

Moving from an equally weighted Bank-P&C group, for example, to a 70% bank – 30% P&C combination reduces the diversification effects by about five percentage points on average.

The Fallacy of Composition

The diversification effects estimated through the building block approach reflect an *economic* view of risk aggregation, in which risks are first aggregated within a single risk factor; then within a business line; and then across business lines at the level of the conglomerate. This approach to risk aggregation isolates the *incremental* effect of diversification across business lines. It also corresponds to the way risk and capital is managed at the group level in leading banking-insurance groups.Ultimately, the total amount of economic risk at the top of an organization is independent of how risks are aggregated within it. However, to the extent that risks are added differently at each of the three levels, then the magnitude of the diversification effects at those levels will also differ. Insurance companies tend to be broken down If a bar is missing, the diversification benefits are near zero. The results differ somewhat from KSW due to slight differences in standalone risk specification.

There is an effect that may tend to reduce capital requirements at Level III beyond the potential for diversification. Certain risks could actually be offsetting in different subsidiaries, e.g., if one subsidiary is "long"the risk and the other subsidiary is "short" the risk. This could lead to a net reduction in the particular risk factor.

Although theoretically possible, the only major risk for which an offset is likely to occur is interest rate risk between banks and insurance companies. The magnitude of this effect will depend on a number of factors, including the size of the bank asset/liability mismatch gap and the insurance investment portfolio mix. For other major risk factors, banks and insurance subsidiaries are each likely to be long the risk. by geography and product line into a number of operating subsidiaries, each of which is separately capitalized under local law (Chart A). In many cases, the operating subsidiaries carry their own ratings in terms of default and policyholder protection. Historically, this has made centralized risk and capital management less of a pressing issue for insurance companies than for banks. However, the trend currently is increasingly towards centralization, especially for large, globally active insurers and more particularly for financial conglomerates, which require this centralized view of risk and capital.

Fallacy of Composition

They differ in the way the insurance subsidiaries are aggregated at Level II. If the insurance subsidiaries are *not* aggregated into one business line at Level II, then the *perceived* aggregation benefits from Level II to III could be greater than the 0-12% range, simply because there are a greater number of small businesses at Level II. 46 But this is an artifact of organizational structure; the amount of risk and the cross-business line diversification effects do not differ by moving to Chart B, where the insurance subsidiaries are first aggregated into one insurance line. To be sure, there is nothing to prevent management from also splitting up the banking line into many individual subsidiaries at Level II.47 Obviously this would not change the amount of risk or cross-business diversification effects either. It is not uncommon for large insurers to have well over 50 separate subsidiaries. An extreme case would be if each bank branch were a distinct subsidiary and separately capitalized.

In practice, the diversification potential for insurance subsidiaries located in different geographies and hence capitalized (and regulated) separately is often not exhausted prior to Level III aggregation. But the problem here is that the standalone insurance capital requirements fail to take account of the level of diversification already present within the insurance "silo." It is not a feature of cross-business line diversification associated with a conglomerate. The "fallacy of composition " – or the sensitivity of perceived diversification benefits to how risk units are added within an organization –

drives home a central point: Given the myriad ways in which a financial conglomerate can be structured, the only valid method for aggregating risks is one that is based on underlying risk fundamentals, such as the economic capital approach, and is independent of legal structure.

Compounding Risk and Model Mis-Specification

The diversification effects estimated also underscore a basic tenet of portfolio theory: the risk of the whole cannot be greater than the sum of the parts. *Provided standalone risks are correctly measured,* this means that the economic capital for a conglomerate cannot exceed the total standalone economic capital of the individual business units. Concern that combining businesses within a single entity can somehow increase, rather than reduce, total capital is really a concern about mis-specification of risks at lower levels. For example, in the case of Long Term Capital Management, there was a compounding exposure to credit spread risk, as positions in different trading books were aggregated, Lowenstein (2000)). But the fundamental problem was that the underlying risk estimates for individual positions were mis-specified since they failed to account of the potential for extreme credit spread movement.

Ultimately, no method of risk aggregation can overcome mis- Legal requirements will, however, imply restrictions on the use of capital and assets within a conglomerate. Cumming and Hirtle argue that the spillover effects resulting from reputational risks may result in this inequality not necessarily holding. 50 Some have argued that the whole may actually be riskier than the sum of the parts (Santomero and Eckles due to reputation and spillover effects. for sound arguments why it is very difficult to cleanly separate market and credit risk. specification of underlying risks. The best antidote to mis-specification is to stress the model parametres and supplement traditional analysis with scenario testing across a wide range of market movements.

Indeed the industry is placing greater importance on stress testing and scenario analysis to explore the edges of the risk space for the very reason that the models are almost always estimated with data dominated by "normal" times. Yet risk managers care disproportionately about the "non-normal" times, i.e., the tails and not the middle of the distributions. This is the risk manager's dilemma: she understands the unimportant part of the loss (or value change) distribution quite well but not the part which really matters to her, namely the tails. With the current state of the art this can only be characterized through stress testing and scenario analysis.

Time Horizon

Another challenge of evaluating risk within a conglomerate is specifying a uniform time horizon. At one end of the spectrum, market risk is typicallymeasured on a daily basis and scaled up to ten days for capital requirements under Basel. Credit risk istypically calibrated to a one year horizon, as is operational risk. In banks, the convention for modelingrisks and assessing capital is to adopt a one-year horizon. The logic to a one-year horizon is that it typically ties to reported business line P&Ls, corresponds to the internal capital allocation and budgeting cycle, and is a period in which an institution can access the markets for additional capital. It is also the horizon used in the New Basel Accord (BCBS. Alternatively, insurance companiesare often capitalized for longer decision horizons. This is particularly true for life insurers, where the obligation to policyholders is unique and often extends to 30+ years. In our approach, in order for economic capital to serve as a 'common currency' for risk, a common time horizon needs to be specified. We adopt a one-year perspective rather than a longer-term Industry

Practices

A foundation for evaluating the risk profile and aggregation effects of a financial conglomerate, this section highlights industry practices for risk modeling and capital management within conglomerates. These trends are important for defining the "world of the possible" for policy reform.

Perhaps the most important trend, as noted by the Joint Forum, is that internationally active financial institutions are adopting economic capital as the fundamental measure of risk. This is true of major banking-insurance groups, which have either implemented, or are in the process of implementing, economic capital frameworks across both banking and insurance business lines.

Our earlier study (KSW) confirmed that all of the major banking-insurance groups in the Netherlands are adopting economic capital as the cornerstone of an integrated risk and capital management framework. The economic capital framework allows for consistent measurement of risk factors across both banking and insurance lines. It also addresses risk aggregation at successive levels in an organization, through internal models that are sensitive to differences in risk profile and business mix. Yet risk modeling and measurement is only relevant to the extent that it drives management decision making. The corollary is that the structure of risk modeling and measurement needs to reflect both management processes and organization structure.

Financial conglomerates are building up group risk and capital management functions to oversee capital planning and decision making at the holding company level. This trend overcomes significant differences in the evolution of capital management for banks and insurance companies.

Banks historically expanded through branching. Branching, in turn, depends on a single balance sheet with centralized capital resources. When a bank entered a new market it typically did so on the strength of the capital resources at the head office.

This created a natural need for centralized risk and capital management in banking organizations.Insurance companies, by contrast, typically expanded either by starting up or acquiring new subsidiaries – whether in adjacent product lines, or in new geographic markets. Each of the subsidiaries, in turn, was subject to separate, standalone capital or reserving requirements, independent of the parent. As a result, insurance companies tended to be locally capitalized – in many cases, with operating subsidiaries rated separately in terms of debt and policyholder protection.

Historically, this made centralized risk and capital management less of a pressing issue for insurance companies than for banks. Notwithstanding these differences, internationally active financial conglomerates – including banking-insurance groups – are putting in place centralized risk and capital management units. The dominant approach is to adopt a 'hub and spoke' organizational model that corresponds to the three levels of risk modeling and measurement identified. At Levels I and II are the spokes, which are responsible for risk management within business lines.

Examples of activities at the spoke include the credit function within a bank, or the actuarial function within an insurance subsidiary or group, each of which serves as the front-line managers for most transaction decision making. Level II risk management – across risk factors within a business line – also typically takes place in the spokes, often in a finance unit that is responsible for funding and business reporting for the subsidiary. At Level III is the hub, which provides centralized oversight of risk and capital at the Group level. While the hub is dependent on risk reporting from Levels I and II, in many cases it is also responsible for overseeing the methodology development of an integrated economic capital framework that is then implemented within the spokes. The specific roles of the hub vary, but tend to include assuming responsibility for Group-level risk reporting; participating in decisions about Group capital structure, funding practices, and target debt rating; liaising with regulators and rating agencies; advising on major risk transfer transactions, such as CLOs (collateralized loan obligations) and securitizations; and, in some institutions, actively managing the balance sheet.

The 'hub and spoke' system is both a reflection of – and a reinforcement of – the importance of economic capital modeling. Risk measures, as manifested by internal economic capital models, increasingly drive management decisions, not just for loss prevention but for business optimization through efficient capital management. The group capital structure considers disparities in the different kinds of capital: Accounting capital vs. economic capital vs. regulatory capital vs. rating agency capital. As there is no single view on the relevant measure of capital, the group's task is to balance the requirements of different constituencies (regulators, shareholders, debtholders, rating agencies) with efficient yet prudent capital management.

The net effect is increasingly proactive management of risk, capital and value in conglomerate companies, both within business lines and at the group level. It strongly suggests a need for regulation to keep pace with internal developments and market structure.

Policy Discussion

So how should one interpret our analytical results? A naive interpretation would be that since Level III diversification effects are small, silo regulation is adequate and capital at the holding company level should simply be the sum of the parts. This would suggest that the de-consolidation approach taken in the New Basel Capital Accord (BIS II) is essentially correct – that insurance company capital should be subtracted, dollar for dollar, from holding company capital for a predominantly banking group. This is the equivalent of saying that holding company capital must equal banking capital plus insurance company capital.

A more nuanced interpretation of our results, however, would be that the naive interpretation is only correct if diversification effects are already fully captured at Levels I and II. But we know that is not the case with existing regulatory measures: Rules-based capital measures at both levels are based on a "lowest common denominator" approach that assumes an average level of correlation within a single risk factor and ignore cross-risk factor diversification at the business line level. As an example, consider the proposed credit risk capital rules under BIS II. The Level I capital requirements for credit risk under the internal ratings-based approaches assume just a single correlation factor for all commercial and industrial loan portfolios. Similarly, for the bank, the Level II requirements for credit, market, and operational risk will simply be added together, with no offset for cross-risk factor diversification. A key point is that capital regulation at Level III can be no more accurate than the standalone measures on which it is based.

Given the inherent limitations of existing regulatory measures at Levels I and II, a better approach to capital regulation for conglomerates would be to adopt a more supervision-intensive approach such as that contemplated by BIS II's second pillar. Such an approach would require conglomerates to put in place their own economic capital models for assessing risk and capital at successive levels. These customised models are the only real hope of being able to capture the complexity of diversification at all levels within a conglomerate.

In advocating new policy, we are not starting with a clean slate. The reality is that the regulation of financial conglomerates is rooted firmly in the silo approach. Any new policy proposal focused on addressing some of the unique problems of a multi-line financial conglomerate will have to reflect the very different starting points and traditions of banking, insurance, and securities capital regulation. In short, the silo approach is here to stay, at least for the foreseeable future.

Estrella (2000) provides a thoughtful discussion of the difficulties and trade-offs encountered in design of regulation for financial institutions. They include the different goals and objective functions of the different constituencies (for instance); the desire for simplicity (emphasis on rules) and flexibility (emphasis on supervision); at the same time we want to allow for market forces to provide a powerful monitoring and correction mechanism.

The framework of the New Basel Accord is partly motivated to strike a balance among these apparently competing forces. We think the main issues surrounding risk measurement and management in a financial conglomerate can fit within that framework of the New Basel Accord, perhaps with renewed emphasis on legal firewalls as a possible structural response to contagion of risks across distinct entities.

I: Rules *II: Supervision*

III: Market Mechanisms *IV: Legal Firewalls*

- Specific minimum capital requirements
- Lowest common denominator
- Imposed by regulator
- Non-discretionary, non-judgmental
- Review of internal capital approach
- Institutionspecific
- Internally driven
- Flexible
- Market evaluation of capital adequacy
- Aggregate judgment of multiple views
- Externally driven
- Limited to publicly disclosed information
- Legal mechanism for separating risks
- Jurisdiction & institution specific
- Recognized under law
- Both statutory and contractual

Proposed '3+1' Pillar Framework

The pillars would combine rules-based, supervisory-based and market-based approaches to capital regulation with legal mechanisms. Importantly, the pillars are designed to be mutually reinforcing; no one pillar by itself is sufficient.

The first pillar would incorporate specific, rules-based minimum capital requirements for a conglomerate at the holding company level. Given the findings on the magnitude of Level III aggregation effects, a simple rule-based approach to capital adequacy would be to add up the individual capital requirements for regulated subsidiaries at the parent holding company level, without any offset Estrella and Santos stress that risk and capital are hard to determine in the presence of safety net such as deposit insurance, and that the two design problems (capital adequacy, deposit insurance) should be addressed simultaneously for diversification. While this would tend to overcapitalize the conglomerate to some extent, the degree of overcapitalization attributable to cross-business line diversification is likely to be small – on the order of 5-10%.56 The incremental capital might be justified as compensating for the increased complexity of a multi-line financial conglomerate, for measurement and modeling error at Levels I and II, or alternatively, as imposing a somewhat higher solvency standard for a conglomerate.

The second pillar, however, should be the main load-bearing column of the regulatory framework. In the words of Estrella, this pillar would allow regulators to reap "the benefits of informed supervision. Mechanical formulas may play a role in regulation, but they are in general incapable of providing a solution to the question of how much capital a bank should have. At the margin, scarce public resources are better employed to enhance supervision than to develop new formulas whose payoff may be largely illusory."

Especially for a large, complex conglomerate, the supervisory review is likely to be far more important than the rule-based approach. It would enable the supervisor to evaluate the adequacy of an institution's internal risk management and capital decision processes along a number of dimensions. Importantly, this pillar should be a flexible approach that allows for differences across institutions. Such differentiation is necessary to accommodate variations in business mix, risk profile, legal structure, and level of sophistication.

The third pillar would leverage market judgements on capital adequacy. In the end, the market's judgement of capital for the holding company (and potentially individual subsidiaries) will be decisive, through its influence on pricing and access to funding. While it is attractive from a theoretical standpoint to place great weight on the market's consensus, in practical terms there are too many limitations in current accounting conventions and disclosure standards for this pillar to be sufficient on its own. Similar to the sentiment expressed by the Basel Committee in BIS II, our recommendation is A 5-10% difference in capital is likely within the tolerance range for capital planning, and is unlikely to prompt specific management action. This is especially true since regulatory capital for major financial conglomerates is a floor – and often non-binding. The capital ratios for banks in G10 countries, for example, currently average11.2%, or 40% above the 8% (Tier I plus Tier II) regulatory requirements. that regulators encourage improved accounting rules and better disclosure of the risk and financial structure of a conglomerate, to enable the market to do its job better.

The fourth pillar – legal firewalls – is a possible structural response to contagion of risks. Legal firewalls might be appropriate for a 'mixed conglomerate' that combines both financial and unlicensed commercial subsidiaries. In practice, there is a very broad range of non-financial subsidiaries that are owned by or affiliated with financial conglomerates. Given the difficulty of evaluating the capital requirements for such a broad array of businesses, an alternative might be to segregate the risks of these activities from the financial activities in a conglomerate. They could be erected by requiring that nonfinancial subsidiaries be separately capitalized, and by preventing inter-company funding of the subsidiary and cross-company guarantees. Such barriers might not fully mitigate against reputation risk, but they should go a long way towards limiting financial contagion. The specifics around legal firewalls – what exactly are they? how will they be enforced? – are very important and complex. We simply want to propose for discussion a possible solution to an obviously complex problem, namely that of assessing capital for unlicensed commercial (i.e. non-financial) subsidiaries.

Our proposed '3+1' framework will inevitably require more detailing – and debate – both within the regulatory community and among other constituencies. We look forward to the exchange. firms from 1.2 to 1.3 times the warning level and insurance companies more than 5 times required capital. 57 To be sure, financial institutions are particularly opaque, making assessments by delegated monitors such as rating agencies and equity analysts more difficult. Indeed Morgan (2002) measures this opacity by showing that bond raters disagree more about banks and insurance companies than about any other kind of firm.

19.Global Management and Asset Allocation

For the past 20 years, students of stock-market investing have worshipped at the twin altars of modern-portfolio theory and efficient-market theory. The first holds that the more diversified a portfolio, the less the risk from each of its components. The latter posits that active money managers have no more stockpicking prowess than a bunch of randomly tossed darts. Marry these theories, and what do you get? An index such as the S&P 500, which has vanquished all but a few extremely gifted — or is it merely lucky? — active managers, especially in recent years.

No surprise, you won't find too many portfolio jockeys at the wedding, throwing rice. Instead, the S&P's compelling example to the contrary, a small but growing cadre of investment pros is turning its back on both revered theories. These particular managers seek to beat the mighty index — and some have done so resoundingly — by concentrating their bets on no more than 25 stocks. And they're in arguably excellent company: Warren Buffett, the king of concentrators, confines his stock holdings to fewer than 10 anointed names.

Though it flies in the face of business-school doctrine, portfolio concentration has intuitive appeal. "If one manager holds 40 stocks, you might get his 10 best ideas, while the other 30 are filler," says Greg Horne, president of Ashbridge Investment Management, a Philadelphia-based investment adviser. "I would just as soon get the filet."

Others see no hope for glory without commensurate guts. "No hospital wings or college dormitories have ever been named by an indexer," declares James Oelschlager, founder of Akron, Ohio-based Oak Associates, which manages almost $5 billion in mutual funds and institutional accounts. "They've been named by people who invested in one or two stocks and rode them for a period of time."

By fund-manager standards, Oelschlager too might qualify for his own wing or dorm. Screening Morningstar's Principia Plus database turned up only three mutual funds with 25 or fewer stocks that beat the S&P 500 over three- and five-year periods: Oelschlager's White Oak Growth Stock, Oak

Value and Sequoia, a 15-stock fund run by Buffett confreres William Ruane and Richard Cunniff, that long has been closed to new investors. A few other relatively concentrated funds, including Clipper, Longleaf Partners and Ken Heebner's CGM Capital Development, also have amassed outstanding long-term records, but the slim ranks of tenured superstars hasn't deterred a batch of newcomers in the past year or two.

"Although some concentrated funds have been around for quite a while, it's just in the last 18 months that we've seen funds launched specifically to play on a concentrated theme," says Ken Gregory, a San Francisco investment adviser and newsletter writer. Some upstarts, such as Yacktman Focused, CGM Focus and PBHG Large Cap 20, were spawned by successful, more diversified parents. The infant Marsico Focus (along with a more diversified offering) is manager Tom Marsico's new act; the popular fund manager departed Janus Funds last fall. Lately, $1.2 billion Oakmark Select has had industry jaws dropping: the 19-stock fund, managed by William Nygren, returned 55% in '97, its first full year, and another 13.4% in the quarter ended March 31. Nygren's top holdings include U.S. Industries, USG, Tele-Communications Liberty Media Class A and PartnerRe.

Concentration seemingly is more popular, or at least has met with more widespread success, among institutional money managers. Screening Invest-Works Pro, a database maintained by Barra RogersCasey, for similar composition and performance characteristics yielded 14 products, ranging from $25 million in institutional tax-exempt accounts run by Sorema Asset Management to $4.3 billion in accounts managed by the aforementioned Oak Associates. And that list doesn't include firms that lack five-year track records or have trailed the S&P by so much as a whisker.

Wilson/Bennett Capital Management, of McLean, Virginia, is in the latter camp. In the last 10 years value investor John W. Fisher, the firm's founder and CEO, has managed to keep pace with and frequently beat the market by holding just 12-15 stocks. "I didn't make a conscious decision in 1987 to run concentrated portfolios," he says. "The analytical process

— valuing businesses and pieces of businesses — lends itself to a concentrated approach. We get to know the companies well, and if you're following 12 or 13 stocks, it's much easier to know what's going on in the underlying businesses."

Fisher is on intimate financial terms with, among others, Bankers Trust, Texaco, Mobil and Philip Morris. In Big Mo's case, he charges, the market currently is placing "almost $2 negative value" on the tobacco business.

In the past year, Fisher claims, he's received as many phone calls inquiring about concentration as he did in the previous nine. "The Buffett effect has had a lot to do with it," he surmises. "Also, some people finally have come to the cease that there is no way to follow 100 different companies, particularly large-cap multinationals. The guys buying 90-100 stocks really are closet indexers. They're simply trying to keep up with a benchmark."

Brett Robertson, president of Dallas-based Richmont Investment Management, seconds that rather inflammatory notion. Academic and industry studies, he notes, have shown that the inclusion of as few as 16 stocks in a portfolio eliminates as much as 93% of stock-specific risk, provided, that is, the stocks aren't closely correlated. "Yet in spite of the statistical facts, many managers hold more than 100 stocks," he marvels. "A lot of traditional shops don't concentrate because it means taking a lot of risk to the mother ship, and major blowups can mean the end of marketing. If they don't do anything wrong, money is going to pile into their funds, even if they're just mediocre. We think diversification is a recipe for mediocrity, especially if you measure the fees of a diversified portfolio against an S&P index fund."

Those are fighting words to proponents of diversification — namely, the vast majority of active managers, some of whom have racked up sterling returns with 100 stocks, and more. But they get to the heart of the increasingly raucous debate about whether less is more. And they lend credence to Bill Nygren's assertion that the current interest in concentration "stems directly" from the success of indexing.

How so? Investors who allocate their assets to a variety

of managers or funds, each with a diversified portfolio, in short order find, says Nygren, that they have replicated the S&P or another index, albeit at greater cost. Yet, the two investment approaches need not be opposed. "We believe concentration works hand in hand with indexing," he adds, suggesting that concentrated and diversified funds together can make better music than a collection of diversified funds alone.

It's easy to see the drawbacks to pure concentration, which Morningstar highlighted in several studies in the past two years. Sharply limiting the number of holdings in a portfolio does not, in itself, provide any performance edge. It's the manager who makes all the difference. In the hands of a great stockpicker, a tightly focused portfolio has an excellent chance of outperforming the market, as each winning issue packs much more of a wallop. But the exaggerated impact of a rotten egg or two, conversely, can spell disaster.

Some concentrated funds also are more volatile than their diversified brethren, although not necessarily more risky. Investors who take their financial temperature daily should steer clear, as White Oak Growth Stock's recent adventures emphasise. The fund "got slaughtered," in manager Oelschlager's words, in last year's tumultuous fourth quarter, only to snap back with a handsome first-quarter gain of 17%.

If concentration isn't for cardiac patients, neither is it for most short-term investors. In fact, Dennis Bertrum, founder and president of New York's Bank Street Advisors, believes that concentrated-fund holders must be willing to hang on for five years, at least, in order to reap maximum reward.

Nor should these investors confuse volatility with risk. "As soon as some people see higher volatility numbers in their portfolios, their minds shut down and they see risk," says Richmont's Robertson. "To me, if 20 years from now you haven't met your investment goal, that is the real risk."

Proponents of concentration, on the other hand, see ponderous problems with diversification. Chiefly, they cite diminished opportunities to beat the market as one's holdings collectively grow to resemble it.

To Ronald Surz, a managing director of Roxbury Capital

Management, in Santa Monica, California, the effort to diversify is a "distraction." Risk, he observed in a recent paper, increases as "a manager populates a portfolio with the unfamiliar for the sake of matching index characteristics. Once committed, the manager becomes dependent on others for both buy and sell signals, thus following the herd and incurring unnecessary turnover." That's particular problematic in today's market, with the leaders of the S&P 500 achieving the status of momentum stocks.

Indeed, minimal turnover sometimes is a happy byproduct of a more focused approach, as a manager who falls deeply in love with a few good, exhaustively researched ideas presumably will be less likely to fall out of love on a regular basis. Charlotte Beyer, director of the Manhattan-based Institute for Private Investors, concentration is particularly appealing to tax-sensitive investors, including the heirs to numerous family fortunes — especially considering that most of those fortunes were built on one or two great ideas.

How can individuals best utilize concentration? The answer lies less in the concept than the recipe. Oakmark's Nygren puts most of his own eggs in the basket he manages, although the idea probably won't appeal to more timid souls. For these nail-biters, a touch of Tabasco, achieved by blending concentrated with indexed assets, might be just enough.

Yet, such an admixture would seem to subvert the whole point of concentration — namely, the possibility of scoring a grand slam with a crackerjack stockpicker's very best ideas. Greg Horne, of Ashbridge, suggests a better way. "When you combine several concentrated portfolios using noncorrelated strategies, you have the best chance of beating a benchmark," he says.

Ken Gregory certainly hopes so; he and partner Craig Litman have designed the 15-month-old Masters Select Equity fund around the concept of an all-star team of concentrators. They've parceled out assets to six distinguished managers with distinct investment styles, and have charged each — Shelby Davis, Spiros Segalas, O. Mason Hawkins, Richard Weiss, Foster Friess and Jean-Marie Eveillard — with buying no fewer than five, and no more than 15, favourite stocks.

And the envelope, please? Last year, the fund returned a total 29.1% — easily beating the Dow Industrials and the average equity fund, though not the turbocharged S&P 500.

Still, proponents of few-stock portfolios think they can best the S&P, and some boast dazzling returns to prove it. Never mind fancy theories; all it takes, they say, are a few great ideas, a bit of time — and a lot of concentration.

9

Fixed-income Security Analysis

Theories of fixed-income security analysis are explained, and examples of theory applications are provided in exhibits. First, theories of default-free securities are described that incorporate valuation analysis, risk concepts (including interest rate and reinvestment risk), term structure (including yield curve theories), and maturity measurement (or duration).

Next, contractual risks are described that cause variation in bond payments, such as prepayment risk, conversion risk, put risk, and variable-rate risks. Subsequently, the risk of default is discussed within the context of protective debt covenants and bankruptcy laws. Finally, a comprehensive theory of fixed-income security valuation is explained, from the perspective of both a required expected return and a required promised return.

ANALYSIS OF DEFAULT-FREE FIXED-INCOME SECURITIES

The payments on a fixed-income security are specified in a contract between the debtor and the investor(s). Although the payments on most debt contracts are uncertain (because of contractual and/or default risks), some fixed-income securities have payments that are virtually 100% certain.

Debt obligations with risk-free payments are important in determining the required return on other securities through the R_f.

These types of securities merit special analysis. Obligations of the U.S. government are generally considered to be risk-free, as the government has unlimited power to pay off its obligations through taxation or the printing of money. Although the U.S. government's will to do so has occasionally been subject to question due to voter pressure to reduce taxes and inflation, and although there have also been some national governments in other countries that have refused to pay off their debts in their own currencies, such as after a communist revolution (or even in Russia in 1998 due to an economic crisis), national government debt in the domestic currency is widely considered to be as close to risk-free as an asset can be.

However, U.S. government debt is actually only risk-free with respect to default, insofar as the promised payments are certain to be made, and insofar as the promised payments fixed by the debt contract cannot legally be changed (with the exception of a very few U.S. government bonds whose payments can effectively be changed because they are repayable 5 years before maturity). Default-free securities without contractual risks can have substantial amounts of other types of risk for investors who do want or need cash flows at times that are different from those promised by the debts.

Valuation of Default-Free Securities

Default-free securities can be valued by simply discounting the promised cash flow by the yield available on similar default-free securities. Cash flows on debt can include not only principal repayments but also interest on the borrowed money, and the maturity of debt is specified to be the date of the last promised payment. *Yields on debt obligations are generally quoted as annualized returns with a compounding period equal to the frequency of the interest payments.* Such a computed return is called a yield to maturity.

Cash flows on U.S. government securities generally consist of periodic interest payments plus the return of principal at maturity (one exception are Treasury bills which have an initial maturity of one year or less and only one promised payment, The principal value is often called par value. Interest payments, which are frequently called coupon payments, are generally made semiannually but are quoted as an annual percentage of par value.

Because payments are semiannual, yields to maturity on T-bonds are quoted using semiannual compounding. The yield to maturity is computed as the discount rate that sets the sum of the present values of the promised cash flows from a debt equal to the market price (i.e., it is essentially an IRR using promised as opposed to expected cash flows). The yield to maturity differs from the current yield insofar as the current yield is merely the annual coupon divided by the market price, while yield to maturity includes the promised capital appreciation or depreciation on the security as it approaches par value. An example is provided

The maturity of a bond is the date upon which the final contractual payment of the bond is due. For most bonds, the principal is paid back on the maturity date. As with bond coupons, bond prices are generally quoted as a per cent of par value.

For brevity, bonds are often referred to by their coupon rate and the last two digits of their maturity year. In this quotation, the coupon is often separated from the maturity by an "s" (but typically only when there is no fraction quoted in the coupon). Thus, the name of the bond is 5.50s28 Treasury bond. Treasury bonds are also often referred to as T-bonds.

Bond Yields: General At the price of 108 1/32% of par, the bond had a yield to maturity of 4.98% quoted in Investor's Business Daily, which can be computed as a promised IRR with semiannual compoundthe final section of this for the exact pricing and yield formula).

In particular, 4.98% is the discount rate that equates the sum of the present values of the promised cash flows (interest and principal) from the bond to the price of 108 1/32% of par. This yield can be computed with a calculator, a computer, trial-and-error, or special bond tables.

The current yield of the bond is the coupon divided by the price. In particular, current yield = 5.50/108.03125 = 5.09%. The implied annual capital appreciation of the bond would be the difference between the yield to maturity and the coupon. In particular, yield to maturity 4.98- current yield -5.09%

implied appreciation -0.11%, The yield to maturity represents the total return on the bond, which consists of 4.98% in current yield and a negative 0.11% in capital appreciation.

Let's take two other examples: the 7.5s99 T-bond (price=103 11/32, with a maturity in October 1999), and the 6s02 T-bond (price=106 7/32, with a maturity in July 2002). 7.5s99 6s02 yield to maturity 4.14% 4.20% - current yield 7.26% 5.65% implied appreciation -3.12% -1.45% Bonds selling above par value (over 100) have an implied negative appreciation as maturity nears (i.e., depreciation).

Bonds selling below par value have an implied positive appreciation in their value as maturity nears. As a result, because accrued interest is taken out of the quoted price (except for bonds in or near default whose prices are quoted flat). Bond prices are normally quoted as where C is the promised periodic cash flow from the bond, T is the total number of future payments on the bond, Y is the yield to maturity on the bond, I is the number of coupon payments per year on the bond, and n is essentially the number of days since the last periodic payment date on the bond divided by the number of days between periodic bond payments.

The term C1n is called accrued interest, which represents a computed amount of interest that has been accrued since the most recent regular payment date for the bond. This accrued interest has been earned by the previous owner of the bond (the seller) and is accounted for separately in the total price paid for the bond.

In fact, the actual total price of the bond equals the above Bond Price Quote plus accrued interest. The actual price paid for a bond, therefore, is actually higher than the Bond Price Quote by the amount of C1n .

- For example, the 5.50s28 bond had a price quotation of 108.03125% of par on October 19, 1998. Given that there have been 2 months and 4 days between August 15 (the most recent scheduled payment date) and October 19, the bond now sells with. Accrued interest = ({2/6} + {[1/6][4/30]})(5.50/2) = 0.97778% of par. This fact implies that the true price that must be paid for the bond (which equals the quoted price plus accrued interest) would be

- True Price of Bond = 108.03125 + 0.97778 = 109.0090% of par, which equals $1090.09 per $1000 par value bond.
- On the other hand, a simple approximation of the clean price quote of the bond (without accrued interest) is
- Approximate Bond Price = 2.75(1 {1/1.0249}60)/.0249 + 100/(1.0249)60 = 108.055% of par.

The Risks of Default-Free Securities

Default-free securities have two types of risk: interest-rate risk and reinvestment risk. Both types of risk are related to changes in interest rates.

Interest-rate Risk

Interest-rate risk is the risk that the present value of an asset will change because of a change in interest rates. When interest rates fall, the present value of fixed future cash flows rises. When interest rates rise, the present value of fixed future cash flows falls.

Generally (all else being equal), the prices of fixed-income securities with longer maturities change more for a given change in interest rates than the price of short-term securities. Thus, longer-term securities generally have more interest-rate risk than short-term securities.

If interest rates rise, and investors need to sell a fixed-income security prior to maturity, they may have to sell the asset at a loss.

Many investors cannot afford the risk of selling their fixed-income security investments at large losses.

These investors, who are very averse to interest-rate risk, may prefer to invest in short-term fixed-income securities. Investors with near-term liabilities or cash needs (such as banks or other depository institutions) are often especially averse to interest-rate risk. An illustration of the concept of interest-rate risk is provided

Examples of Interest-Rate Risk

- Interest rate risk is the risk of price movement of a bond caused by a change in interest rates. A change in interest rates occurs when investors require a different rate of return on a bond (often because the yield or return on similar bonds has changed).
- The required return on bonds frequently changes because of a general change in investor demand for bonds, because of a general change in the supply of bonds, or both Aggregate changes in the supply and demand for bonds are often attributed to changes in inflationary expectations, since investors typically require higher nominal returns on bond investments when purchasing power losses from inflation are expected to be high.

  However, changes in the supply and demand for bonds can also occur even without a change in inflationary expectations when the supply of and demand for credit changes (implying "tighter" or "looser" credit conditions and changes in the difference between nominal interest rates and inflationary expectations). Regardless of the cause, aggregate changes in bond supply and demand result in a general change in the required yield to maturity on virtually all bonds.
- Irrespective of the cause of a change in interest rates, bond prices will rise when the required yield on them falls, and prices will fall when required returns rise. However, because interest rates and interest rate changes vary on different bonds (such as for bonds with different maturities), changes in required returns may vary for different bonds.
- In addition, for the same change in required yields on all bonds, bond price changes will vary depending, at least in part, on the maturity of the bonds. For instance, for all three bonds described, a 2% change in interest rates (or yield to maturity) for each bond will result in new prices as follows:

	Price for		
-Change in interest rates	7.5s99	-6s02	5.5s28
-0%	103.3438	106.2188	108.0313
-up 2%	101.3345	99.3239	81.5259
down 2%	105.4309	113.7064	149.5991

Clearly, the price of the bond with the longest time to maturity (5.5s28) moves the most for each change in interest rates, while the price of the bond with the shortest time to maturity (7.5s99) moves the least for each change in interest rates. Thus, the bond with the longest time to maturity has the most interest rate risk, while the bond with the shortest time to maturity has the least interest rate risk. The difference in interest rate risk can be seen more clearly by measuring the percentage change in price for each change in interest rates:

	Percentage Price Change for		
Change in interest rates	7.5s99	6s02	5.5s28
0%	0.00%	0.00%	0.00%
up 2%	1.94%	6.49%	24.53%
down2%	2.02%	7.05%	38.48%

- Mathematically, the reason for longer-term bonds having more interest-rate risk is that the effect of a change in the discount rate is compounded over more periods in the calculation of present value. Intuitively, this fact can be seen from the perspective of an investor. For instance, the near-term repayment of principal on a short-term bond permits quick reinvestment in higher-yielding bonds when interest rates rise. However, when interest rates rise for a long-term bond, investors are locked into a lower yield for a long time before maturity arrives and before the principal can be reinvested at the higher rates (so that it is worth less).
- The concept of interest-rate risk can potentially be more clearly shown with zero-coupon bonds.

  For example, the 0-coupon T-bond maturing in one

has a $\{1+.0417/2\}^2$-1=4.21% return using annual compounding. Discounting the par value of 100 at 4.21% for one year gives us a present value of 100/$\{1.0421\}^1$=95.96). If annual interest rates rise 2% to 6.21%, the bond price will fall to 100/$\{1.0621\}^1$=94.15 for a loss of 1.89%. On the other hand, if annual interest rates fall 2% to 2.21%, the bond price will rise to 100/{1.0221}1=97.84 for a gain of 1.96%.

- A 0-coupon T-bond maturing in 15.5 years with a yield to maturity of 5.44% (5.51% discount rate using annual compounding) has a present value of 100/$\{1.0551\}^{15.5}$=43.54. If annual interest rates rise 2% to 7.51%, the bond price will fall to 100/$\{1.0751\}^{15.5}$ = 32.55, for a loss of 25.25%. If annual interest rates fall 2% to 3.51%, the bond price will rise to 100/$\{1.0351\}^{15.5}$=58.58 for a gain of 34.55%. The absolute value of the gains and losses are much larger on the longer-term bonds because the change in interest rates is compounded over more periods. Note, however, that the 15.5-year 0-coupon bond has approximately the same interest-rate risk as the 5.5s28 bond that has a substantially longer maturity of 30 years (this fact will be explained subsequently with a concept called duration or weighted-average maturity of all cash flows from the bond).

Reinvestment Risk

Reinvestment risk is the risk that the future value of an investment will change because of a change in reinvestment rates. A rise in interest rates will permit investors to reinvest cash received from investments (either interest or principal) at a higher rate, whereas a decline in interest rates will force investors to reinvest money at a lower rate. As a result, a rise in interest rates results in a higher future value than would otherwise exist, while a fall in interest rates results in a lower future value than would otherwise exist. Generally (all else being equal), the future value to which an investment will grow will vary more with a change in reinvestment rates if it is a short-term bond than if it is a long-term bond. Thus, shorter-term fixed-income securities have more reinvestment risk than long-term securities.

When investors have fixed future liabilities that must be met, they may not be able to afford large fluctuations in the future value of their investments. Because such investors (like pension funds and life insurance companies) are averse to reinvestment risk, they typically prefer long-term fixed-income securities to short-term securities.

Examples of Reinvestment Risk

- Reinvestment risk represents the risk of being forced to reinvest funds at a lower interest rate. Like interest-rate risk, reinvestment risk arises when interest rates change. However, the lower levels of future wealth that can result from reinvestment risk are caused by interest-rate changes in a direction opposite that which causes losses in present value related to interest-rate risk.
- For instance, assume that you buy one of the three bonds mentioned in at the existing market price given for October 19, 1998, and assume that reinvestment rates remain constant at about 5%.

  Then reinvestment of all cash flows received will result in having the following increases in wealth by the year 2028:

Assuming 5% Reinvestment Rate	Terminal Value in 2028 for		
Measurement Criteria	7.5s99	6s02	5.5s28
Amount per dollar of par value held	450.6	455.8	474.0
Percentage Increase Over Beginning Investment	336.0%	329.1%	338.7%

Assume now that interest rates fall to 0%, so that all cash flows received from the bond (the coupon and principal payments) must be reinvested at a 0% interest rate.

In this case, by the year 2028, you would have accumulated the following different amounts of money, depending on which bond you bought:

Assuming 0% Reinvestment Rate	Terminal Value in 2028 for		
Measurement Criteria	7.5s99	6s02	5.5s28
Amount per dollar of par value held	107.5	124	265
Percentage Increase Over Beginning Investment	4.0%	16.7%	245.3%

[Example using the 5.5s28 bond: receive 60×2.75 payments plus 100 at maturity for a total of 265, which divided by the market price of 108.03125 indicates an increase in value of {265-108.03125}/108.03125=245.3%].

The bond with shortest time to maturity (7.5s99) offers the lowest percentage -increase in wealth, while the bond with the longest time to maturity (5.5s28) offers the largest increase in wealth under this scenario.

The reason is that the shorter-term bond pays off its entire cash flow earlier, which forces an investor to reinvest at the lower rates sooner when interest rates fall. The longer-term bond locks an investor into a higher rate of return for a longer period of time, when interest rates fall.

- On the other hand, when interest rates rise, the future value of an investment in each of the bonds would be higher if the investor had invested into short-term bonds (and not locked the investment into a long-term rate). For instance, if interest rates were to rise after the purchase of any of the foregoing bonds, and investors could reinvest all cash flows at a 10% annual reinvestment rate (using semiannual compounding), the future value of an investment in the bonds would, in 30 years, be:

Assuming 10% Reinvestment Rate	Terminal Value in 2028 for		
Measurement Criteria	7.5s99	6s02	5.5s28
Amount per dollar of par value held	1824.5	1626.4	1072.4
Percentage Increase Over Beginning Investment	1766%	1531%	993%

[Example using the 6s02 bond: the future value of an annuity of 6/2=3 every 6 months for 4 years is $3\{1.05^8-1\}/.05=28.65$, which is the amount plus 100 par value that is received in 4 years assuming reinvestment of the coupons at 5% every 6 months. This amount of 128.65 would then grow to $128.65(1.05)^{26\times2}$=1626.4% of original principal after 26 more years of investment at 5% every 6 months. This amount divided by the initial price of 106.21875 indicates a percentage increase over the initial investment of {1626.4-106.2}/ 106.2=1531%].

- Thus, an increase in interest rates subsequent to an investment into a bond can increase the future value to which the investment can grow. The increase is higher for initial investments into short-term bonds because the principal is paid off more quickly for such bonds, which can then be reinvested at the higher rates sooner.
- Reinvestment risk, therefore, can work both ways. When interest rates fall, future values fall, with the future value of investments in short-term bonds falling the most. When interest rates rise, future values rise, with the future value of investments in short-term bonds rising the most. Thus, short-term bonds can be said to have the most reinvestment risk, since the future values of investments into such bonds are more sensitive to interest rate changes (whereas short-term bonds have the least interest rate risk, since the present values of such bonds are less sensitive to interest rate changes.
- This concept can be more simply demonstrated with zero-coupon bonds. For instance, a 1-year zero-coupon bond with a yield to maturity of 4.17% has a present value of 95.96% of par. If interest rates fall to 0% (as they did for a long period during the Great Depression in the 1930s in the U.S., and as they were in Japan in 1998), an investor holding this bond will receive 100% of par in one year, which then must be invested at 0%. The investor will, therefore, have 100% of par in 30 years also, for a total increase in wealth of 4.2%.
- On the other hand, a 15.5-year 0-coupon bond with a yield to maturity of 5.44% has a present value of

43.52. If interest rates fall to 0%, an investor holding this bond will receive 100% of par in 15.5 years, for a total increase in wealth of 229.8%.

- Thus, the longer-term bond allows the investor to lock in the yield to maturity over a longer period of time (for zero-coupon bonds, over the maturity of the bond). Locking in a yield over a long period of time can be vital for individuals and institutions with long-term liabilities. For instance, if a pension fund has a pension

Different Definitions of Interest-Rate Risk

Because changes in both the present and future values of a fixed-income investment are related to changes in interest rates, both types of risk are often labeled under a more general definition of interest-rate risk. Under such a definition, the interest-rate risk of changes in bond present values is defined as price risk, while the risk of changes in future value is defined as reinvestment risk. However, interest-rate risk has historically been used in a more narrow sense to define fluctuations in bond prices, and this more traditional definition is preserved in this book. -

In any event, it is now possible to define the concept of a risk-free investment as being a relative term. In particular, a bond is risk-free only for investors who want and need cash flows exactly when the bond promises them. For investors who prefer or need cash flows earlier, a longer-term bond has interest-rate risk (or price risk). For investors who prefer or need cash flows later, a shorter-term bond has reinvestment risk. While bonds with interest-rate or reinvestment risk to an investor are not risk-free, investors may still choose to invest into them as part of their diversified portfolio of risky assets.

There, also exist investors who prefer or need cash flows that grow with inflation (such as those saving for retirement consumption needs). For these investors, bonds that make payments which are indexed with inflation are risk-free. In particular, there are numerous Treasury bonds in existence that pay a real coupon rate on a principal value that grows with the inflation rate

For example, on October 19, 1998, the 3.625s28 bond had a price of 100.4375% of par value and a yield to maturity quoted of 3.60%, although the true return on the bond will actually equal the quoted yield to maturity of 3.60% plus the inflation rate (because the bond's principal is contracted to grow with consumer prices). Those who find such inflation-indexed bonds riskfree may still invest into other Treasury bonds as part of their risky portfolio.

Yield Curve Theories: When investors in the aggregate have no systematic aversion to either interest-rate risk or reinvestment risk, the same expected return will be required on both short-term and long-term bonds over a long time horizon. In other words, investors will expect the same return from investing in long-term bonds as from rolling over investments in short-term bonds. The expectations theory of interest rates hypothesizes this situation.

When investors are systematically more averse to interest-rate risk than to reinvestment risk, investors will require a higher return on assets with longer maturities. This situation is hypothesized by the liquidity premium theory of interest rates. This theory assumes that investors are willing to pay a premium for the liquidity of securities near maturity in order to reduce interest-rate risk. As a result, if the liquidity premium theory of interest rates holds, investors will expect a higher return from investing in long-term bonds than from rolling over investments in short-term bonds.

On the other hand, when investors are more averse to reinvestment risk, higher returns may be required on assets with shorter maturities. This possibility can exist under the market segmentation theory of interest rates, which hypothesizes that lower returns will be required on bonds for which there is a systematic preference. The market segmentation theory of interest rates is consistent with the liquidity premium theory of interest rates when there is a systematic preference for short-term securities. The theory is consistent with the expectations theory of interest rates when there is no systematic preference for short-term or long-term bonds.

Empirical evidence from tests on past data indicates a liquidity premium of about 0.5% for securities with maturities of 1 year or more. Some evidence implies that this higher required real return is relatively lower (perhaps 0.25%) for securities maturing very far in the future (over 25 years). This situation may result from high pension fund and life insurance company demand for securities with maturities over 25 years and even higher depository institution demand for securities with maturities under 1 year.

Graphs of different yield curves at different points in time are provided. Within the context of these actual yield curves, the implications of the various term structure theories are emphasised.

Duration and Interest-Rate Risk: In particular, using calculus, an equation for the approximate change in price (as a per cent of market price) for a given change in interest rates can be derived

Equation (5-6) holds for extremely small changes in interest rates and holds approximately for larger changes in interest rates. For instance, for a bond with a 25-year maturity, semi-annual coupon payments, a 10-year duration, and an 8% yield to maturity, a 1% rise in interest rates would cause a bond price change.

Since equation (5-6) is only an approximation for large changes in interest rates, an even simpler approximation is frequently employed by merely multiplying the interest rate change by the duration, i.e.,% Change in Bond Price = -Duration(Change in interest rate), which, for the prior example of a 1% rise in interest rates on 10-year duration bonds, would approximate% Change in Bond Price = -10(1%) = -10%. (5-9).

In order to increase the accuracy of equation (5-8) in estimating price changes, many analysts insert what is called modified duration into the equation, where modified duration equals duration as computed by equation (5-6) divided by I plus the periodic coupon yield on the investment (i.e., divided by 1+{Y/I}). For instance, in the prior example, modified duration would equal 10/11.04)=9.62 years, so that a 1% rise in interest rates would be estimated to cause the bond price to fall by -9.62×1%=-9.62%.

Thus, for a given change in interest rates across all maturities, the relative interest-rate risk of debt is proportional to the duration of the debt. While interest rates do not change by the same amount for each maturity, the correlation between short-term and long-term interest rates is fairly high (especially for reasonably long-term holding periods such as a quarter, where the correlation coefficient is about.80). In addition, although short-term interest rates are usually more volatile than long-term rates (about 1.5 times as volatile), interest-rate risk is generally an increasing function of duration.

As a result, if investors with specific future liabilities construct portfolios of assets with the same duration as a matching amount of liabilities, the present value of the assets will move by approximately the same amount for a given change in interest rates as the present value of the portfolio of liabilities.

Investors can thereby immunize their positions from being affected by changes in interest rates (i.e., assets with the same present value and duration as a group of liabilities will have a zero present value regardless of changes in interest rates).

Determinants of Duration

The duration of a fixed-income security is a function of three major factors: the coupon of the security, the amount of principal amortization prior to maturity, and the maturity of the final payment. Of these three factors, the positive relationship between maturity and duration is the clearest. For fixed-income securities with the same coupon and principal amortization schedule, duration is lower for securities with shorter maturities than for securities with longer maturities.

For debts with the same maturity and principal amortization schedule, duration is lower for high-coupon securities than for low-coupon securities. The reason is that securities with higher coupons have more of the present value of their cash flows concentrated in nearer-term cash flows, in comparison to securities with lower coupons. Thus, the maturity of the nearer-term cash flows are weighted more heavily in the duration calculation, and the weighted average maturity of all the cash flows is shorter.

Fixed-income securities which make payments of principal prior to maturity have lower durations for the same coupon and maturity than debts which pay principal only at maturity. Once again, the reason is that the earlier principal payments are weighted more heavily in the duration calculation..

One special relationship exists between maturity and duration for zero-coupon bonds that make no payments prior to maturity. In particular, the duration of a zero-coupon bond equals its maturity, as the weighted-average maturity of the single cash flow from a zero-coupon bond is its maturity. For all other bonds which make interest and/or principal payments prior to maturity, duration will be less than maturity, as the maturity of the payments prior to maturity will have some positive weight in the duration calculation.

Duration and Reinvestment Risk

The relationship of duration to reinvestment risk can sometimes more easily be explained with zero-coupon bonds. In particular, for zero-coupon bonds that make no payments prior to maturity, an investor is locked into a single yield until maturity. Regardless of whether interest rates rise or fall, the investor is assured of receiving a specified amount at maturity.

On the other hand, for debts that make payments prior to maturity, an investor must reinvest cash flows prior to maturity at whatever the market interest rate is at the time. If interest rates fall, the investor must reinvest cash flows received prior to maturity at the lower rate and will therefore have less wealth accumulated from the reinvested cash flow than if interest rates had stayed the same (or had risen). Thus, the amount of wealth accumulated by maturity is a function of how much in cash flows is received prior to maturity and at what interest rate those cash flows must be reinvested. The more cash flows that are received before maturity, the greater is the variation in the future value to which the investment will grow, so that bonds with higher coupons have higher reinvestment risk than for bonds with lower coupons and the same maturity. Thus, these bonds with shorter durations have higher reinvestment risk (while bonds with longer durations have less reinvestment risk).

To some extent, bonds that make payments prior to maturity do lock investors into a fixed yield if the bond is held for a number of years equal to its duration. For instance, an investor may buy a bond with a 25-year maturity, a 10-duration, and an 8% yield to maturity, and the investor would be reasonably assured of earning an 8% return if the bond was held exactly 10 years regardless of what happened to interest rates immediately after the purchase of the bond.

In particular, if interest rose, the investor would be able to reinvest the coupon income at the higher rates for the next 10 years (which would result in greater wealth accumulation after 10 years from this source), but this gain would be exactly offset by the fall in the present value of the bond (which would lead to a loss when the bond is sold in 10 years). On the other hand, if interest rates fell, the investor's lower wealth accumulated from reinvested coupons would be offset by a higher price that would be received for the bond when it is sold in 10 years. Thus, the reinvestment risk of the 10-year duration bond is similar to that of a 10-year zero-coupon bond despite the fact that its maturity is over twice as long.

Duration is an important tool that is used by investors for purposes of controlling, reinvestment risk..

Duration and Immunization

Duration for the T-bonds listed are as follows:

	7.5s99	6s02	0s14	0s25	5.5s28
-Duration (in years)	1.0	3.4	15.5	27	15.5

- As shown in the reinvestment risk is highest on the 7.5s99 bond, which has the shortest duration. As can be seen from the positive coupon bond with the most interest-rate risk is the 5.5s28 bond, which has the longest duration of these bonds.

- However, in comparison to a 27-year zero-coupon bond, the 5.5s28 bond has a lower duration. The 27-year zero-coupon bond, therefore, has more interest-rate risk and less reinvestment risk than the 5.5s28 bond. For instance, when interest rates rise 2%, the loss on an investment in the 5.5s28 bond is 24.53% (as shown in, compared to a loss of 39.75% for an investment in the 27-year 0-coupon bond (note that estimates based on equation (5-6) and (5-8) only approximate this true return because they are only accurate for very tiny changes in interest rates]. On the other hand, when interest rates fall to 0%, the future value to which an investment in the 5.5s28 bond will grow in 30 years is 245.30%, which is less than the 319.29% to which an investment in the 0s25 bond will grow.
- In fact, the 5.5s28 bond has interest rate and reinvestment risk more similar to that of a zero-coupon bond with a maturity of 15.5 years, because the cash flows of both bonds have a weighted average maturity of 15.5 years. As a result, the change in price for a small change in interest rates will be approximately the same for the 5.5s28 bond as for a 15.5-year 0-coupon bond. Similarly, the future value of an investment in the 5.5s28 bond will grow to an amount that is approximately the same as for an investment in a 15.5-year 0-coupon bond for any small change in reinvestment rates. For similar reasons, the 6s02 bond has interest rate and reinvestment risk equivalent to a zero-coupon bond with a maturity of 3.4 years, and the 7.5s99 bond has interest rate and reinvestment risk equivalent to a zero-coupon bond with a maturity of 1.0 year.
- The similar interest rate and reinvestment risk characteristics of bonds with the same duration can be emphasised with an example. If interest rates fall by 0.1%, the price of the 5.5s28 bond would rise by 1.5%, just as would the price of a 15.5-year 0-coupon

bond. In addition, if interest rates rise by 0.1%, the price of the 5.5s28 bond would fall by 1.5%, just as the price of a 15.5-year 0-coupon bond would. The latter price fall is much smaller than the 2.6% fall in price that would result on a 27-year 0-coupon bond if interest rates rose 0.1%. All these price changes are consistent can be verified with a bond calculator or simplepresent value calculations.

Classical Immunization

- As shown in zero-coupon bonds can be used to ensure that some fixed liability in the future can be met with one single fixed investment. Such an investment strategy is called immunizing the liability.
- More generally, a bond immunization strategy involves an investment into a bond (or bonds) which will grow to a future value that is independent of fluctuations in interest rates (and that can be used to pay off a fixed liability or liabilities without risk). Bonds with positive coupons, as well as zero-coupon bonds, can be used as part of a strategy to immunize the future value of a portfolio against the effects of interest rate changes. In particular, because coupon bonds have the same reinvestment risk as zero-coupon bonds with the same duration, such bonds can be used to ensure the same future value that a zero-coupon bond can.
- For instance, assume on October 19, 1998 a life insurance company has a specified $1,000,000 contractual payment to a policyholder due in 15.5 years. As 15.5-year zero-coupon T-bonds (0s14) had a yield to maturity of 5.44% on that date, the life insurance company could immunize this liability by investing $1,000,000/(1.0272)15.5×2=$435,205.79 into the 15.5-year zero-coupon bond. Then, in 15.5 years of 2.72% semiannual yields, it would have the full $435,205.79(1.0272)15.5×2=$1,000,000.
- Alternatively, the life insurance company could

invest some amount into the 5.5s28 bond, and it would still be able to immunize the $1,000,000 liability in 15.5 years.The reason is that this bond also has a 15.5-year duration and therefore similar reinvestment risk to the 15.5-year 0-coupon bond.

- However, because the yield to maturity on the 5.5s28 bond is lower than for the 0s14 bond, it would take more money to immunize the liability. In particular, dividing the liability by 1 plus the bond's yield raised to a power equal to the duration indicates that $1,000,000/(1.0249) 31=$466,523.70 would be needed to immunize with the 5.5s28 bond because its yield to maturity is only 4.98%. A change in interest rates would not change the future value to which the $466,523.70 would grow in 15.5 years, as a decline in interest rates would increase the value of the bond but would reduce the reinvestment rate for the coupons as they are received, while a rise in interest rates would lower the value of the bond while increasing the rate at which the coupons could be reinvested. For instance, if interest rates rose so that the reinvested coupons from the 5.5s28 bond grew to a value of $600,000 in 15.5 years, the calculus of duration mathematics would indicate that the 5.5s28 bond could be sold for $400,000 in 15.5 years, so that a $466,523.70 investment in the 5.5s28 bond would grow to $1,000,000. Alternatively, if interest rates fell so that the value of the bond could be sold for $550,000 in 15.5 years, the reinvested coupons would only be worth $450,000 at that time because of the lower reinvestment rate. In any case, the effect of the change in the value of the bond exactly offsets the effect of the change in the reinvestment rate at the duration point, so that the bond plus the reinvested coupons have a value of $1,000,000 in 15.5 years
- In addition, duration is additive, so that a portfolio of bonds with a weighted-average duration of 15.5 years could be used to immunize the liability (to

measure the weighted-average duration of a portfolio, the weights are set equal to the amount of the portfolio invested in each bond). The optimal portfolio chosen would be that combination of bonds with a weighted-average 15.5-year duration and the highest weighted average yield to maturity (where the weights would again be determined by the per cent invested into each bond).

- All such use of duration to immunize liabilities is called classical immunization. Classical immunization that uses coupon bonds does entail some monitoring. In particular, as time and interest rates change, the duration of a coupon bond changes. For instance, for the 5.5s28 bond, the duration would change to the following number of years for the following changes in the time to maturity (assuming time lapses with no change in the yield to maturity) and for the following changes in the yield to maturity (assuming the change in interest rates is immediate and the 30-year maturity of the bond stays the same):

	Yield to Maturity=4.98%				*Maturity=30 years*			
	Maturity				*Yield to Maturity*			
	29 yrs	28 yrs	20 yrs	10 yrs	4%	5%	6%	10%
Duration	15.3	15.1	12.6	7.9	18.8	15.5	14.5	10.8

- As time passes, the bond's duration falls but not as fast as time. Thus, after 1 year, although a 15.5-year liability might have a duration of 15.5-1.0=14.5 years left, the 5.5s28 bond has a duration of 15.3 years. Thus, the duration of the bond is too long to match that of the liability, and so another bond (or portfolio of bonds) must be chosen. Similarly, if long-term interest rates suddenly fell to 4%, the duration of the 5.5s28 bond would change to 18.8 years, which is too long for a liability with a duration of 15.5 years. As a result, another bond (or portfolio of bonds) must be chosen if such a scenario occurs.
- Such changes in a bond's duration relative to the

changes in the duration of the liability being immunized can require frequent monitoring and occasional rebalancing of the portfolio to maintain an immunized position. Because any necessary rebalancing can entail transaction costs, investment reserves in addition to the funds invested to exactly immunize the liability may be needed by the investor to pay such costs. On the other hand, if immunization is conducted with 0-coupon bonds, no monitoring or rebalancing costs are required.

Contingent Immunization

- In addition to classical immunization, investors may also use a form of immunizing a liability called contingent immunization. In contingent immunization, investors freely invest their funds into risky portfolios that they determine are optimal with the intention of possibly generating higher returns than a classical immunization strategy. These portfolios may be diversified into stocks, bonds, and other assets in order to maximize expected return at the lowest possible risk level
- The values of these portfolios are constantly monitored in order to ensure that they do not fall below the level that would be required to classically immunize the liability. If the value of an investor's funds drops to the level required for classical immunization, the investor must commit those funds to the immunizing bonds. Otherwise, the investor can continue to hold the more risky portfolio with higher expected returns. If the investor's portfolio earns returns that average or exceed the return on the immunizing bond, it is not necessary to invest in bonds in order to classically immunize the liability.
- For instance, in the foregoing immunization example with $435,205.79 needed for classical immunization, assume the investor actually had $500,000 at her or his disposal. Instead of investing $435,205.79 into the

immunizing bonds and $64,794.21 into other assets, the investor could decide to invest the entire $500,000 into a diversified portfolio of stocks and other assets. The investor could keep the funds so invested as long as the market value of the portfolio stayed above the classical immunization level. Because of changes in both the market value of the portfolio and because of changes in the classical immunization level (due to changes in interest rates), fairly frequent monitoring is necessary. For instance, if on the first day of this strategy, interest rates stayed the same (so that approximately $435,205.79 would still be necessary to immunize the liability), but the market value of the diversified portfolio crashed to $435,205.79, the investor would have to sell all securities and buy the classical immunization portfolio (actually, in order to cushion the transaction costs of the switch, a value somewhat above the classical immunization level would have to be used as a threshold for triggering a switch).

Immunization with a Portfolio of Bonds

- It is also possible to use a portfolio of bonds to immunize any liability by matching the bond portfolio duration with the liability duration, where portfolio duration is measured. When the portfolio duration needs to be changed (because it no longer matches the liability duration), it is generally necessary to replace only a few of the bonds in the bond portfolio. For instance, if the portfolio duration needs to be increased, the shortest-term bonds can be replaced with bonds with very long durations (and vice- versus when the portfolio duration needs to be reduced).
- Some investors attempt to maintain a constant duration for their bond portfolio either because the duration of their liabilities is constant or because they wish to maintain a constant level of interest-rate and

reinvestment risk. Portfolios with constant durations are called evergreen portfolios.

Immunizing a Portfolio of Liabilities

- In addition, it is also possible to use a portfolio of bonds to immunize a group of liabilities with different maturities and durations. It is only necessary to match the portfolio duration with the weighted-average duration of the liabilities. The weighted-average duration of the liabilities is computed as the duration of each liability multiplied by the value of each liability divided by the value of all the liabilities being immunized (i.e., the weights are determined by the ratio of the value of the liability to the value of all the liabilities) as in equation (5-10).
- A bond portfolio constructed to match the duration of a group of liabilities can be used to classically immunize the liabilities. For instance, assume a pension fund has projected liabilities each year for the next 50 years. Assume the weighted average duration of these liabilities is 9 years. In this situation, the pension fund would need to invest into a portfolio of T-bonds with a weighted-average duration of 9 years. The immunizing portfolio could include T-bonds with many different durations, as long as the portfolio duration was 9 years. A set of T-bonds with a portfolio duration of 9 years would be chosen that has the highest weighted-average yield to maturity. This portfolio could be selected using linear programming if inputs on yields and durations for the many different T-bonds in existence are collected. Once selected, it is possible to invest into this portfolio and classically immunize the liabilities.
- A portfolio of liabilities may move differently with interest rates and time than a simple liability with the same duration but due in a single time period, just as the duration of a portfolio of assets may move

differently with changes in interest rates and time than a 0-coupon bond. As a result, classically immunizing an entire portfolio of assets and liabilities may require less monitoring than attempting to immunize a single liability with a coupon bond (or bonds).

- A classical immunization portfolio of assets can also be constructed on paper in order to calculate the trigger point at which a strategy to contingently immunize a portfolio of liabilities would have to trade a risky investment portfolio for the risk- free classical immunization portfolio. In particular, an investor can invest all funds into a diversified portfolio of risky assets but use the value of the classical immunization portfolio as the minimum level to which the risky portfolio could fall before the investor would have to switch to the classical immunization strategy. Major Immunization Problems and Solutions.
- It should be noted, however, that in all cases where the timing of the cash flows from a set of liabilities is different from the timing of the cash flows from a portfolio of assets constructed to immunize them, the present and future values of the asset portfolio may not always move one-to-one with the present and future values of the liability portfolio. In particular duration changes differently with changes in time and interest rates for securities with different cash flows, and it is generally prohibitively expensive in terms of transaction costs to make the continuous adjustments to a portfolio that would be necessary to keep the duration of a portfolio exactly matched with the duration of a set of liabilities.
- As a result, many investors try to match asset and liability portfolios not only on duration but also on a parametre called convexity. Convexity is defined as the change in the change in a portfolio or asset value for a given change in interest rates (i e., the

second derivative of price relative to interest rates). In order to more accurately measure a bond price change for larger changes in interest rates, it is possible to add the squared change in interest rates times the bond's convexity to the product of the interest rate change and the bond's duration. By matching asset and liability portfolios on convexity as well as duration, the asset portfolio duration tends to change more closely with the liability duration when interest rates change, thereby reducing the need for portfolio rebalancing.

- Nevertheless, even matching asset and liability portfolios on both duration and convexity does not ensure that their present and future values will move exactly one-to-one. In particular, duration measures interest rate and reinvestment risk accurately only for a very small change in interest rates, and convexity measures changes in bond price changes for only small changes in interest rates, so that even the combined parametres do not completely characterize a bond's price change relative to larger interest rate changes. In addition, duration and convexity computations are valid only if interest rates change by the same amount across the entire term structure (and only if there is no change in time to maturity).

  In actual fact, short-term interest rates often change by a different amount than long-term interest rates (and sometimes even in opposite directions), and maturities (and durations) do change, thereby causing the present and future values of portfolios matched on duration and convexity to move differently if the cash flows are received at different times (since the different changes in the discount rate across the term structure changes the present and future values of cash flows received at different times). To avoid this problem, the cash flows of the asset portfolio can be exactly matched with those of the liability portfolio, such as with exact zero-coupon bond matching.

- On the other hand, some investors try to match the asset portfolio's value sensitivity to that of the liability portfolio for various simulated interest rate changes that may differ across the term structure. In particular, they estimate the value of assets under different possible future interest rate environments (such as a scenario with rising short-term interest rates and falling long-term interest rates) and construct portfolios of assets whose values tend to move as closely as possible with those of the liabilities in all environments.

Immunizing Liabilities That Grow with Inflation

- Although many liabilities are fixed and independent of inflation rates, some such as inflation-indexed pension payments vary in value with future inflation rates. Liabilities whose values grow with inflation can only be immunized by investing into inflation-indexed security investments whose duration of real cash flows equals that of the liabilities. In particular, the duration of the promised cash flows before considering the future inflation adjustments to the cash flows must be equal to the duration of the liabilities estimated in a zero inflation environment (and the inflation adjustment for both the assets and liabilities must be the same). Immunization with Bonds That Are Subject to Contractual or Default Risk 3
- The foregoing analysis applies to bonds that are not subject to default risk or contractual risk, i.e., to most debt of the U.S. government. However, many institutions also compute duration for other types of investments using equation (5-4) and then use these duration calculations and bonds in various immunization strategies.

  Immunization portfolios constructed using bonds subject to default and/or contractual risks are not true classical to default and/or contractual risks are not true classical immunization portfolios, as the default and contractual risks make the returns on such portfolios behave differently than the returns on risk-free portfolios.

Instead, any portfolio that is constructed with risky assets represents a contingent immunization portfolio that would have to be monitored in order to ensure that its value does not fall below the value of a true classical immunization portfolio.

- The advantage of matching the duration of a contingent immunization portfolio of risky assets with the duration of the investors liabilities is that such duration matching makes the risky portfolio value move more closely with that of the classical immunization portfolio. In particular, given that assets or portfolios with the same duration tend to move together for a given change in interest rates, it may be less likely that the value of such a contingent immunization portfolio will fall below the classical immunization portfolio value than for a risky portfolio that is not so matched with the liabilities on duration. As a result, it is less likely that a switch to the classical immunization strategy would be necessary.
- Nevertheless, even when the duration of the contingent immunization portfolio is matched to equal that of the duration of the liabilities, the existence of default and contractual risks can still cause the value of a duration-matched risky portfolio to fall below the classical immunization level. For instance, duration and its implications for interest-rate and reinvestment risk are irrelevant for any asset that fails to make promised fixed payments. Assets can fail to make fixed promised payments not only because of the default or bankruptcy of the issuing organization, but also because many assets have special contractual risks. The most common type of contractual risk is that of call or prepayment that is

permitted in many debt contracts (where no further payments are made on assets that are paid off prior to maturity by an issuing organization).

- In order to better match the values of different asset and liability portfolios, some investors utilize simulations, where the values of the assets and liabilities are estimated under various different interest-rate and economic environments (using software like the SIA software). An attempt is made to find a portfolio of assets whose values will change by approximately the same amount as that of the liabilities under all those simulated environments.

Present Value Immunization

- Although the foregoing analysis has focused on immunizing the future value of a specified set of liabilities, a similar framework can also be used to immunize the present value of a portfolio of assets and liabilities from the effect of interest-rate changes In particular, by matching the duration of a portfolio of assets with that of a portfolio of liabilities, the values of the asset and liability portfolios will both move according to equation (5-6) by the same amount for any change in interest rates, and so their matched present values will be unaffected by changes in interest rates (and are therefore immune to them).
- However, when immunizing the present value of liabilities, the same caveats with respect to immunizing future values must be considered. For instance, if the assets are subject to default risk or have call risk different from that of the liabilities, then there will be some changes in net present value as a result of such different risks.

Examples of the Effects of a Failure to Properly Immunize

- Thete are numerous examples of companies going bankrupt because of a failure to immunize properly. In fact, almost an entire industry went bankrupt recently as a result of a failure to immunize. In particular, savings and loan institutions had historically financed long-term fixed-rate mortgage investments with short-term deposit liabilities. When interest rates went up greatly in the late 1970s and early 1980s, the present value of the savings institutions' long-term assets fell below that of their short-term liabilities. Many savings institutions became insolvent at this point, although many tried to cover the rising interest cost of their liabilities by investing in assets with higher yields but greater default risk. Some of the still solvent institutions even attempted to immunize their asset portfolios of long-term callable mortgages by increasing the maturities of their liabilities which were not prepayable. However, when default losses soared in the late 1980s and early 1990s, many of the saving institutions that had increased the default risk of their asset portfolios went bankrupt. In addition, many of the savings institutions that had tried to immunize their prepayable mortgage portfolios with long-term liabilities that were not prepayable also went bankrupt when interest rates dropped, as the mortgages were prepaid, forcing the savings institutions to reinvest the money at lower interest rates, while the institutions continued to have to pay high interest rates on the long-term liabilities that could not be contractually prepaid.

- There are many other examples of the hazards of failing to immunize properly. For instance, numerous life insurance companies went bankrupt in the early 1990s as a result of a failure to immunize their liabilities properly. In particular, in the late 1970s, when higher interest rates and deregulation of financial services in the U.S. resulted in increased investment opportunities and enhanced sophistication for investors, especially individuals, life insurance companies had to transform themselves from simply "selling" life insurance policies to marketing an array of complex products, including some that promised high rates of returns (like 13%) to investors for a long period of time. Unfortunately, many life insurance companies invested these funds in callable bonds, mortgages, and other earlier redeemable assets (earning about 17%). When interest rates fell later in the 1980s, these high- yielding assets were redeemed early and the life insurance companies had to reinvest their money at then lower market interest rates (of around 10%) while they continued to have to pay the higher interest rates (13%) on their liabilities. In an attempt to gamble their way out of this desperate situation, many life insurance companies invested heavily in very risky bonds and real estate assets. Although some of these promised high yields (of more than 13%), many had very high risks, both of default and of being retired before their original stated maturity. As the recession of the early 1990s began taking hold, rising bankruptcies resulted in a suspension of cash flow payments from many of the insurance companies' bond and real estate investments, while many other assets were paid off early as interest rates continued to fall.

CONTRACTUAL RISKS

The terms of a fixed-income security are specified in a legal contract between the borrower and the investor(s). For publicly recorded debts called bonds, the debt contract is labeled an indenture. For widely held bonds, performance on the clauses of the contract is often monitored by a third-party trustee (usually a bank) specified in the indenture. Debt contracts issued by organizations other than the U.S. government are typically more complex than for U.S. Treasury securities.

A debt contract normally provides for payment of coupon and principal on set dates. Bond coupon, principal, names, and pricing quotes are typically stated as a per cent of par value in the same manner as explained for Treasury securities. For instance, the Mercury 7.75s06 bond has a coupon equal to 7.75% of par and matures in the year 2006. Most bonds specify the coupon to be the same every year, but some debt has coupons set to change over the bond's life (such as deferred-interest and step-up bonds, whose coupons rise over the life of the bond).

Although par value for both Treasury and corporate bonds is usually set in units of $1000 per lot in the bond indenture, some bonds have other unit values (such as $5000 for bonds typically issued by state and local governments). In addition, while principal payments may be concentrated at maturity for some debt contracts (as for U.S. Treasury bonds), many debt contracts specify that principal must be paid back in installments over time called principal amortization.

If there is to be any principal amortization, it can be specified in the contract to be either pro rata (where each investor receives a pro rata share of each principal payment in relation to his or her par value holdings of the debt), serial (where each holder of a portion of a debt has a serial number that indicates in the contract when the total principal is to paid for that particular serial number), or sinking fund (where the debtholders to whom scheduled principal payments are to be made are determined by a lottery just before payment).

Pro rata amortization, which is most often required for loans to individuals and businesses, mandates that a proportional amount of each amortizing principal payment must be paid to each investor (often there is only one investor for smaller loans).

Many pro rata amortization schedules are set up so that a constant payment, which includes interest and principal, is made each period through maturity. Such constant payments (where the payments include more principal payments than interest as maturity approaches) are called regular amortization of principal. Other methods of principal amortization (called irregular amortization) frequently require a constant payment until maturity, at which time a much larger principal payment called a balloon must be made.

Serial amortization, which is most often required for the

debt of state and local governments, mandates that bonds specified by serial number in the indenture are paid off in full at specified dates. With serial amortization, some bonds are retired before others are (and so represent separate bonds, often with different coupons, although they are covered by the same indenture).

Sinking funds, which are the most frequent method of principal amortization required in the indentures of publicly traded corporate bonds, mandate the retirement of a specified number of bonds either via purchase from investors at a mutually agreeable price or via full payment of principal by the issuer. Sinking funds allow issuers to choose the cheapest of these two methods of bond retirement. As a result, if interest rates have risen and the price of the bonds has fallen, the issuer can generally find a bondholder willing to sell at a price less than par value. On the other hand, if interest rates have fallen and the price of the bonds has risen, the issuer will optimally retire the number of bonds specified in the sinking fund at par value. If the issuer chooses to purchase the bonds for the sinking fund at par value, the bondholders who receive payment in full for their bonds ate determined by the indenture trustee through a lottery that allows the winning bond serial numbers the full principal payment (naturally, winning this lottery when interest rates have fallen implies that the winning bondholders lose, as they must reinvest their money at lower interest rates).

In addition to mandatory sinking fund payments, many indentures have sinking fund clauses that permit the issuer to retire more bonds than the minimum number specified. Typically, these optional inking fund payments allow an issuer to make additional redemptions equal to the minimum number that must be made. As a result, bond retirements at par value often equal twice the mandatory minimum when interest rates fall.

Debt contracts may also contain clauses that permit the basic promised payment of interest and principal to be altered. Clauses permitting such alterations can be of three type: those providing for changes at the discretion of the borrower or issuer, those providing for changes at the discretion of the investor, and those providing for changes to be determined by independent events.

The most important debt contract clauses permitting alterations at the discretion of the borrower are call features. Call features permit the borrower to repay the loan at a prespecified price, which is often par value, or par plus some premium of 10% or so, with any premium contractually declining towards par as maturity approaches. Typically, calls must provide for 30-60 days' notice to the investor.

Calls are sometimes restricted to certain time intervals. For instance, many calls are permitted beginning only at least 5 years after issue. Such prepayment rights that can not be exercised immediately after issue are termed deferred call features. Most call features allow the borrower to prepay the entire issue at any time after a specified date. However, some call features may be restricted to the early repayment of only a portion of the principal due. In addition, some bonds (such as extendible bonds) may only allow an issue to be effectively prepaid on a specified date (the date upon which the issuer must determine whether to extend the maturity of the bond or not).

Some debt contracts permit prepayment only under certain circumstances. A common example is a bond that cannot be refunded with a new issue at a lower interest rate. The exact wording of such call clauses prohibits the issue of a new bond at a lower interest rate within a specified time period (like 6 months) of the bond call.

Such call restrictions, which may only exist for a portion of the bond life (like the first 5 years), constrain the ability of the borrower to replace high coupon debt with lower-cost debt when interest rates fall (and therefore represent a form of limited call protection, although companies can still prepay such bonds by financing the call price with cash from operations or from an equity issue).

A few debt contracts also provide the borrower with some discretion in making coupon payments. For instance, some bonds permit a corporation to make coupon payments in stock (with the market value of the stock paid specified to equal the coupon on the payment date) instead of in cash. Some bonds also permit the issuing corporation to change the coupon payment at some point in time (but the latter bonds typically also permit the investors to sell the bonds back at par if they are not satisfied with the changed coupon).

Some debt contracts also permit alterations at the discretion of the investor. One example is a putable bond. Putable bonds allow the investor to sell or put the loan back to the borrower at a prespecified redemption price (usually par value). For some putable bonds, the company (or an auction process) periodically determines the coupon to be paid on the bond, and the investor can put the bond back to the debtor at par if the offered coupon is not sufficient. Other types of bonds permitting alterations at the discretion of the investor include convertibles. Convertibles have contract clauses that allow the investor to convert the loan into a fixed number of units of some asset like the common stock of the borrowing corporation.

The number of fixed units is called the conversion ratio (which is generally adjusted for stock splits and other noncash distributions for bonds convertible into equity). While not typical, some convertible bonds contain rights to convert into a fixed number of shares of subsidiary stock, into another bond (such as a bond with a different coupon or maturity), or even into real assets (such as silver for some bonds issued by silver mining companies). Although convertibles are typically also callable at the discretion of the issuer, a mandatory call notice period of 30-60 days is generally required, during which time convertible holders can convert if they so choose.

The most important debt contract clauses with payment alterations determined by independent events are variable-rate features. Variable-rate features generally set the coupon rate as a function of some market interest rate like a specified U.S. Treasury bond yield to maturity on a specified date.

Often, there is some adjustment in the formula that determines the coupon rate, with many debt contracts providing for a ceiling (called a cap) on how high the coupon rate can go (some contracts also stipulate a floor rate below which the coupon cannot fall). Some debt contracts provide for a mix of fixed and variable rates over different periods of the loan. For instance, teaser loans offer an initial low fixed rate for some period (like one year) that is then followed by a rate that floats with some market rate.

A few variable-rate features are more unorthodox and set interest payments as a function of some other market price or value. For instance, certain equity-linked bank deposits pay additional interest above a minimum based on the performance of some stock market index. Commodity-linked bonds have the coupon rate or the principal payments tied to the market price of some real asset like oil or silver. Catastrophe bonds have interest and principal payments reduced if policy claims against the casualty insurance company issuer exceed a specified amount.

In addition, some bonds called income bonds provide for payment of the coupon only if it is earned from the corporation's income. For such bonds, the interest generally cumulates from year to year if it is not earned (unless otherwise stated in the indenture).

RISK OF DEFAULT

Fixed-income securities not only have risks related to contractual clauses and changes in interest rates, but there also exists the risk of default on the contractual terms. I lie risk of losses resulting from the failure to pay promised interest and principal payments is often reduced by protective clauses placed into the fixed-income security contracts. The clauses protect not only against the risk of default, but they also affect the ability of the fixed-income securityholder to receive a return of invested capital in case of default.

Protective Clauses

Protective clauses are placed into many fixed-income security contracts to prevent the debtor from taking some action that might impair the ability of the debtor to make contractual payments. If a debtor defaults on its contractual obligations, the debt contract itself typically provides for immediate payment of all principal and interest.

Many protective clauses prevent owners or equityholders with a residual claim on the organization from distributing large amounts of the organization's wealth to themselves. Such distributions could leave the fixed-income securityholders with little or nothing from which interest and principal could be paid. Examples of clauses that protect against distributions to equityholders include constraints on the amount of cash dividends that can be paid to the equityholders. Such constraints often forbid payment of future dividends except to the extent of some fixed dollar amount (like $10,000,000) plus the summed profits that have been earned since the issue of the fixed-income security. Protection is also sometimes provided against noncash distributions to equityholders, like the spinoff of stock of subsidiaries.

Some debt contracts are also protected from greater risk of nonpayment arising from inctreased leverage of the organization. Increased leverage, or debt, can make it more difficult for the organization to pay off both the new and old fixed-income securityholders. An example of a leverage restriction placed into contracts is a prohibition against new debt issues if the total book value of interest-bearing debt plus financial leases exceeds the book value of equity by some amount (such as 225%). Some indentures allow new fixed-income securities to be issued by the organization that would violate such ratio constraints as long as they are made legally subordinated in claim to the prior issue with the constraining clause. Legal subordination of claims is often achieved by putting into a security contract a clause stating that the new bond is subordinated in claim to all other interest-bearing debt not contractually defined to be subordinated in their own respective contracts.

In addition, it is also possible to obtain a prior claim on specific assets of the organization in case of default by placing clauses into the contract providing for a security or collateral claim on the asset. *Collateral* represents a prior claim on an asset (such as a building or inventory or receivables) above that of any other securityholder if promised payments are not paid. Collateralized debt obligations are termed secured debt. If the collateral is real estate, the claim is called a mortgage. A claim on other collateral is typically referred to as a lien.

More than one collateral claim may exist on the same asset, but typically the claims are rank ordered, with the first claim having a prior claim over a second collateral claim, which in turn represents a prior claim on the asset over all other claims. For instance, a holder of a first mortgage on real estate collateral has a prior claim on the real estate over that of a second mortgage, while the holder of the second mortgage has a prior claim on the asset (once the first mortgageholder has been satisfied) over all other claims.

Some debt is collateralized by assets that are legally owned by a special third-party trustee. This ownership structure provides the creditors with better control of the assets if their claim is not paid off. Typical examples of such structures are trust certificates, which represent claims on lease payments made by a borrower for the use of certain fixed assets. The assets are legally owned by a trustee until the final lease payment has been made.

Claims that rank above other claims in priority are defined as *senior* claims. Claims that are subordinated to other claims are defined as *junior* claims. For instance, a second mortgage on real estate ranks junior to a first mortgage, but it is senior to all unsecured claims on the real estate. On the other hand, some unsecured debt are specified in their contracts to be subordinated to specified other debts (including senior unsecured debts), indicating that the subordianted debts' claims on all the firm's assets are junior to those of the specified senior debts (typically, subordinated debt specifies all interest-bearing nonsubordinated debt to be senior). Whether senior or junior, unsecured bonds are often labelled *debentures*.

A few bond indentures permit the seniority status of a bond to change over its life as soon as it is possible without violating other debt covenants. Such bonds are called springing bonds. Protective clauses from other debt may have necessitated the issuance of the springing bonds with a junior claim, but the springing bonds have an indenture clause that permits their claim to become senior as soon as the other debts with the restrictive protective clauses are paid off.

Legal Consequences of Default

In case of default on any contractual provision in a debt contract, debtholders may sue to obtain a court order requiring debtor action consistent with the violated provision. For instance, after a typical grace period of 30 days or so, a court order can be obtained to force the debtor to pay delinquent interest and principal, or face the prospect of legal seizure of assets by the creditor. All such suits and court orders may be frozen by a declaration of bankruptcy. Bankruptcy may be declared by either the borrower (to protect against law suits) or any material creditors of the borrower (to protect against arbitrary preferential treatment being given to other creditors) if the borrower defaults.

Bankruptcy Rules

In bankruptcy, all prebankruptcy suits are frozen, and all prebankruptcy claims are handled as a group instead of individually. While in bankruptcy, the bankruptcy judge may allow existing managers to continue to run the organization, or may appoint new management if it is felt to be in the best interests of the creditors. Creditor committees are usually formed that petition the court to issue orders in their best interests (such as restricting certain management actions, replacing management with a court-appointed trustee, etc.).

During bankruptcy proceedings, interest is accrued only to the extent that it is secured (i.e., interest accrues only on secured debt and only on the estimated market value of the collateral at that time). In addition, lease and other contracts entered into prior to bankruptcy can be broken during bankruptcy, and all penalty payments resulting from breach of contract are frozen. However, even in bankruptcy, the property underlying a lease or other contract can be legally repossessed by the lessor or owner upon breach of contract.

In bankruptcy, an organization can either be liquidated

or reorganized. The reorganization alternative is generally chosen only if the company is worth more as a going concern than it would be if all the assets were liquidated or sold individually. It generally takes a great deal of time and effort for a bankruptcy plan of reorganization to be prepared and approved, and an average of over two years typically lapses before a company can emerge from bankruptcy. The large fixed legal and administrative costs of reorganization make it fairly difficult for a small company to reorganize, and so over 80% of the bankruptcies of small companies (with assets less than $50 million) result in liquidation compared to fewer than 10% for larger corporations. A summary of the rules under each type of bankruptcy are provided.

Bankruptcy Liquidation

- If the liquidation alternative is chosen, all assets are sold, and the cash from the liquidation is divided according to the following order of preference as stated in the debt contracts:
- *First,* secured debt holders receive cash from the sale of the collateralized assets (up to the amount of the secured debt claim). If the secured debtholders' claims are not fully satisfied by the sale of the collateralized assets, the remaining claim becomes unsecured ranking equal to other unsecured interest-bearing debt claims.
- In the *second* step, all liabilities incurred after bankruptcy are paid in full from the remaining cash. Prebankruptcy employee and customer claims (including policy claims from insurance companies) are subsequently paid up to a limit. Next, tax claims (such as state sales taxes and federal excise taxes due) are paid off in full.
- In the *third* step, all remaining claims, including any remaining secured debt claims not satisfied in full by the collateral and including all penalty claims resulting from contracts broken in bankruptcy, are then pooled into a pot of unsecured claims. Any

remaining cash is distributed pro rata to this pool of unsecured claims on paper. However, cash can be paid to debtholders only up to the amount of the claims. If all debt claims are satisfied, anything left over is distributed to preferred stockholders up to their par value or liquidation claim as stated in the Substances of Incorporation, and any final residual cash is paid to the common stockholders.

- In the *fourth* step, the subordinated creditors' pro rata share of the unsecured pot is given to claims that are senior, until all senior claims are satisfied. If the subordinated creditors transfer enough to pay off the senior claims in full, they are allowed to keep the remaining portion of their payoff from the third step, but otherwise they receive nothing (note that the transfer in the fourth step is only from the subordinated to the senior creditors and does not affect other creditors, such as trade creditors, in any way).
- An example of the liquidation claim ordering follows. Assume the ABX company is being liquidated accordingof the bankruptcy code. All the assets have been sold for cash, which yields the following amounts after deducting the administrative costs of bankruptcy:
  - Cash from sale of Factory -$40
  - Cash from sale of Other Assets -$700
  - Total cash -$740 Creditor claims are as follows: -
  - Post-bankruptcy claims -$70
  - Wages -$5
  - Excise taxes -$3
  - Mortgage Debt -$100 (secured by the factory)
  - Unsecured Bank debt -$150 (not subordinated)
  - Debentures -$50 (not subordinated)
  - Subordinated debentures -$800
  - Other unsecured claims -$572 (non-interest bearing)
  - Total claims -$1750 First, the secured creditors

would receive $40 of their $100 claim from the cash - received upon the sale of their collateral (the factory). Then, the $70 in postbankruptcy claims would be paid, back wages of $5 would be paid, and the excise taxes of $3 would be paid.

REQUIRED YIELD TO MATURITY MODEL

As an alternative to computing the present value of future expected cash flows, the present value of promised cash flows can be computed if the required yield to maturity used as the discount rate takes into consideration all the relevant factors and risks. The analysis in the parts indicates that the required yield to maturity on a fixed-income security may be written

Required Yield to Maturity

Once the required yield is computed, the investment decision is straightforward. In particular, if the required yield is less than the actual yield to maturity, present value analysis would indicate the bond is a good buy. If the required yield is greater than the actual yield to maturity, the present value will be less than the price, and the bond should not be purchased. While the investment criterion is simple, estimation of each of the premiums is a complex task. The premium yield for default risk represents the additional promised return that is required in order to offset the losses expected on debts of that risk. Adding this premium to the risk-free rate ensures that the average return from investing in a large number of independent bonds of such risk equals the risk-free rate.

The premium for call risk should be a function of the same variables as for any call option. Just as with call options on other assets, the higher the call price (i.e., the exercise price of the prepayment option) relative to the present value of the promised bond cash flows (i.e., the value of the underlying asset), the less valuable is the call feature (and therefore the lower the call premium required). In addition, the call premium should be a positive function of the general volatility of bond prices, as the call option (like all options) has a higher value when the volatility of the underlying asset is higher.

This phenomenon implies high call premiums when interest rate volatility is high, since high interest rate volatility means high bond price volatility. In addition, call premiums should be higher on debt with longer durations, as debts with longer durations are more volatile. Finally, the call premium should be a negative function of the number of years to next call, as restrictions on the right to early exercise of an option reduce its value.

Another way to look at call option premiums is that they represent compensation to investors for giving the borrower the right to prepay the debt at a lower interest rate if and when interest rates fall.

The exercise of such a right forces investors to reinvest their funds at a lower rate. Thus, the existence of such prepayment rights creates substantial reinvestment risk for investors (and lowers their future expected returns). On the other hand, although lower interest rates do not permit a very large rise in value because of the call price ceiling, higher interest rates cause such bonds to fall in value just like for noncallable bonds. Because long-term callable bonds have both interest rate and reinvestment risk, investors require a higher yield on such bonds.

The unfavourable dichotomy in sensitivity to interest-rate changes in different directions is sometimes called negative convexity, which characterizes the fact that a callable bond's price moves down more for a rise in interest rates than it moves up for a fall in interest rates of the same magnitude. Convexity (which represents the second derivative of a bond's price change for a change in interest rates) can be estimating for callable debts by using a computer model, such as in, to calculate the value of the bond both for a small rise in risk-free rates and for a decline in risk-free rates of the same magnitude. Solving algebraically for convexity (i.e., the change in the change in bond prices for small interest rate changes), two times the current price is subtracted from the sum of the prices estimated for the rise and fall in interest rates.

A bond's price change for a change in interest rates can theoretically be estimated by adding the price change estimated using equation to the product of 1/2 of the bond's convexity parametre and the square of the interest rate change (e.g., if the bond with the-106.42 convexity had a modified duration of 11.64, it would be computed to rise by {.02x-11.64}+{$.02^2$x-106.42}=19.02% for a 2% fall in interest rates). However, this methodology is extremely imprecise for callable debt. A much more accurate procedure for estimating price changes (and risk) is to use equation to simply simulate the value of the debt over different possible interest rate environments (e.g., in the prior example, the simulation results from the SIA software indicated a price rise of only 11.17% for a 2% fall in interest rates).

The premium for transaction costs should be a negative function of the size of the debt issue. In addition, the trading volume and costs for the debt can affect the transaction cost premium. Because transaction costs reduce the net yield received, investors require higher yields on bonds with higher transaction costs. One approximate estimate of the additional premium yield required for this factor (based on prior studies) can be obtained by dividing $.01 million into the market value of the security outstanding (e.g., a $10 million issue would have a premium extra return required of $.010/$10=0.1%).

The absolute value of the premium sacrificed for put rights should be a negative function of the ratio of the present value of the promised cash flows to the next put price, the number of years until the debt can be first put back to the issuer, and the risk-free rate of interest. As with the call risk premium, the absolute value of this premium should be a positive function of interest rate volatility and debt duration. Because putable bonds provide investors with some protection against interest rate risk, investors therefore require lower yields on such bonds.

The premium sacrificed for conversion rights should be a function of many of the same factors as a call option on the assets into which the debt can be converted. In particular, because the conversion right is an option to use the debt to purchase a specific number of units of other assets (like shares of stock), the value of the conversion a right (and the premium sacrificed for conversion rights) is a positive function of that number of units (called the conversion ratio) into which the debt is convertible. In addition, the premium sacrificed for conversion rights will be a function of the market value of the asset into which the debt is convertible. Incorporating each of these factors into a single variable, the premium sacrificed for conversion rights can be stated to be a positive function of the conversion value of the debt, where conversion value = (conversion ratio)(underlying asset market value).

The higher the conversion value relative to the principal or par value of the debt (where par value is essentially the exercise price of the convertible option), the higher is the yield premium sacrificed for the conversion rights. This relationship can be examined in a similar fashion by comparing the market value of the underlying asset to the effective exercise price of the convertible per unit of the underlying asset. The effective exercise price can be computed by the conversion price conversion price = par value/conversion ratio.

In addition, as with other options, the value of the conversion rights is higher for options on assets with higher volatility. Thus, the premium sacrificed for conversion rights should also be a function of the annual price standard deviation of the asset into which the debt can be converted and the time to expiration of the option (with the time to expiration normally represented by the maturity of the debt). Moreover, as with other calls, the value of (and premium sacrificed for) the conversion rights should be a positive function of the risk-free rate, as a higher risk-free rate makes the option to delay paying the exercise price more valuable. The value of (and premium sacrificed for) the conversion rights should also be a negative function of the payout (dividend or interest) on the underlying asset (which the convertible holder does not receive).

Because some of these required return premiums cannot be easily estimated without a computer model, many fixed-income investors use a form of comparative analysis to evaluate the required yield on any particular debt security. In particular, an analyst can usually find bonds trading in the marketplace with risk characteristics similar to the debt being analysed. The yield to maturity on these other bonds can be used as the required yield on the particular debt being investigated.

Often, however, some differences exist in the risk characteristics of the trading bonds and the investigated debt, and minor adjustments to the required yield to maturity have to be made. For instance, if the security under investigation has slightly higher call and default risk than some other comparable bonds, the required return on the investigated debt would have to be slightly higher than the yield to maturity on the comparable bonds.

To estimate the required yield to maturity is to determine the value of a debt investment. Discounting the promised cash flows at the required yield to maturity indicates the value of the debt. If the value exceeds the price of the debt, it is a good addition to a diversified portfolio (otherwise it is not). This procedure is similar to the rule of buying bonds whose required yield to maturity is less than the promised yield to maturity.

This framework can also be used to value new fixed-income securities for which there is no market price. The promised payments can be discounted at the required yield to maturity to determine the value. Usually in practice, the borrower and lender negotiate the promised coupon in the debt contract to be approximately equal to the required yield to maturity. Setting the coupon in the debt contract to approximate the required yield to maturity results in the value (and offering price) approximating par value.

Index